THE HISTORY OF
THE SALVATION ARMY

Volume V

1904—1914

by

Arch R. Wiggins

THE SALVATION ARMY
NEW YORK

THE HISTORY OF THE SALVATION ARMY

Volume V

First Published 1968
Reprinted 1979

The Salvation Army Supplies and Purchasing Department, 145 W. 15th Street, New York, N.Y. 10011 by special arrangement with Thomas Nelson and Sons, Ltd.

ISBN 0-89216-034-9

FOREWORD

I HAVE awaited with interest the appearance of Volume V of *The History of The Salvation Army*, if only for the reason that I had some share in the publication of Volumes I and II some twenty years ago.

By the turn of the century the sixty persons mentioned on page 46 of Volume I as constituting The Christian Revival Union had become a host whose presence could be seen and whose message could be heard in all five continents.

To write about the exploits of a few in a single geographical setting presents far fewer difficulties than to describe the witness of the many whose advances during the decade under consideration reached from Korea to Chile and from the Celebes to Costa Rica. Yet the author, whose pen has continuously been used in Salvation Army service for the whole of his life, has wisely refused to weigh himself down with a mass of detail so that he might recapture on paper the sense of an Army still marching along.

This decade saw the death of the Army's Founder. Some wondered whether this would not prove a mortal blow. The narrative testifies to the fact that He who buries His workmen carries on His work—for which truth may His name be praised !

FREDERICK COUTTS
General

London
September 1967

CONTENTS

CONTENTS

III William Booth's Unflagging Zeal

IV Making the Message Clear and Plain

V The Business Side of Soul-Saving

CONTENTS

CONTENTS

XII THE BRITISH TERRITORY

XIII AFTER-WORDS

EPILOGUE

APPENDICES

LIST OF ILLUSTRATIONS

LIST OF ILLUSTRATIONS

INTRODUCTION

ANY historian writing an account of The Salvation Army is faced with at least four major considerations : (1) He is expected to write interestingly for the average general reader ; (2) He must give due thought to the student on a variety of aspects of the work of an organization that is both spiritual and social ; (3) He has to provide for the demand of the Salvationist regarding matters of little interest to those outside the Army's ranks, for certain information that he may require is to be found in no other work ; and (4) He is, of necessity, bound to use terms familiar to Salvationists but enigmatic to the general reading public. Matters, therefore, that may appear to some to read as drily as a company chairman's minutes or a statistician's tables must inevitably be interspersed with the romance of the Army's history.

In its single decade of history Volume V not only records the passing of the Army's Founder, but marks the end of the Army's first era and the beginning of its second, on the threshold of which the world stood apprehensively, for so often had it been stated and believed that William Booth's huge edifice would automatically crumble after his demise. The spectacular International Congress of 1914, however, violently shook the pessimists and stabilized Salvationists, who rallied closely and firmly around the banner of their new Commander-in-Chief. General Bramwell Booth took up the sword his father had laid down and leapt into the fray amid the full glare of public life with an ease surprising to the uninformed.

William Booth left an Army which had completely

matured at forty-seven years of age, and was continuing to widen its horizons, although the opportunities for so doing between the years 1904 and 1914 were not so many or so good as they had been during those between 1886 and 1904, as recorded in Volume IV. Experiments were unceasingly tried out during the last eight years of his restless command, and the first two of his successor. Some succeeded, others perished, almost at birth. Changes were frequent, as they had to be if stagnation was to be avoided.

As pointed out in the Introduction to Volume IV, little mention can be made of the Army's social work, as Volume III carries its history to the year 1953 ; but here and there, where something of interest was inadvertently overlooked by Volume III, or has been freshly discovered, it is included in this volume.

The period at present under observation is notable for the falling, symbolically, of some of the noble oaks that flourished and towered in the forest of the early-day workers and supporters of the Organization : the great, but humble, George Scott Railton, the first Commissioner among its officers, and R. C. Morgan, T. A. Denny and John Cory among its substantially financial friends. There were heavy losses, too, in the higher officer ranks, through both resignation and dismissal, that caused the supreme leadership deep anguish of heart and mind ; but the storm was weathered in each unfortunate instance.

The " fight for the streets " had lost its severity, but occasionally, and in different parts of the world, some sudden burst of antagonism or overbearing authority was to be encountered and subdued by always-victorious Salvationists, who were more certain than ever that the Organization to which they belonged, to which they had given their lives— indeed, their all, in officer circles—was God-ordained and God-sustained.

The Churches might still have their qualms about rites and ceremonies, about Holy Communion and Baptism, as essential to Christian fellowship and acceptance into the Kingdom on earth, but the remarkable stirrings of the Spirit of God throughout Great Britain and over-spilling into Europe and the other hemispheres only confirmed Salvationists in their belief of a God-given ministry. Perhaps in no other period of the Army's history was the news of great spiritual awakenings more encouraging. Soul-saving results in some places were phenomenal, hence the lengthy account.

Little John Wesley encompassed the remote districts of his homeland on horseback, carrying with him his fiery cross of salvation ; the septuagenarian William Booth seized the magnificent opportunity that the comparatively new " horseless carriage " offered him, and the cities, towns, villages, and even lanes, of the United Kingdom, heard with almost bated breath his compelling and arresting messages. If anyone thought that his eightieth birthday would curb the General's enthusiasm for this modern method of contacting sinners, and warning them to flee from the wrath that was to come, they were mistaken. Although blinded in the fight, William Booth went forth wielding his double-edged sword with amazing octogenarian vigour. Not until Death finally laid him low was that rasping, unforgettable voice silenced.

I NEW WORLDS TO CONQUER

CHAPTER ONE

INVADED AND ANNEXED

AS the first International Congress had unquestionably fired the imagination of those who attended it to a greater endeavour to take Christ to the world and bring the world to Christ, so the Second and Third International Congresses, of 1894 and 1904 respectively, gave fresh impetus to those who sought still more new worlds to conquer. Invasions were organized, a footing firmly established and annexation completed in some countries ; but in others the pioneers were repulsed, to try again at a later date, or to accept temporary defeat as inevitable and to await the day in some far-distant time when a miracle would reverse the religious embargo of centuries. Pioneering assaults were made on no fewer than twenty-two countries between the ten years beginning with 1 July 1904 and ending with the outbreak of the First World War on 4 August 1914, within which dates this period of Salvationist history is concerned. Today sixteen of these countries are flying the Army flag.

That restless adventurer, George Scott Railton, was, as usual, here, there and everywhere ; even the General himself was at a loss on occasion to know just where to contact his first Commissioner. But Railton was all the time blazing the trail, although some of the countries in which he prospected on his lonely expeditions have even yet to see another Salvationist.

While the expansion of the Army's battlefront was not as wide or as rapid as the previous volume records, there was no lack of initiative, enthusiasm or courage. Rather was the lack of money the prime cause of frustration, for the work already established was a considerable and continual drain upon the exchequer at International Headquarters.

The non-Christian millions of China lay heavily upon William Booth's heart and mind, but he did not live to see it welcome his Army, although visits to the country were made from time to time and in 1909 a Territorial Commander was actually appointed and cadets commissioned to commence the work there. Korea, China's next-door neighbour, however, cheered the old man when, four years before his passing, its doors were flung open to the Army's advance forces.

Russia was another mighty country that caused him deep disappointment, for, when it was almost taken for granted that permission would be given the Army to begin operations, that permission was at the last moment withheld by the government.

The chapters which follow in this first section are as weighty with romance as those which describe the golden deeds of pioneering in Volumes II and IV.

CHAPTER TWO

KOREA

Commissioner George Scott Railton, the first Salvationist to set foot in so many countries, visited Korea, " The Land of the Morning Calm " or " The Hermit Kingdom," with

Colonel (later Commissioner) John Lawley, following the General's campaign in 1907. During the following year the pioneers, Colonel (later Commissioner) and Mrs Robert Hoggard, were dedicated to Korea by William Booth at the Crystal Palace demonstration which celebrated the Army's forty-third anniversary. They arrived in Seoul, the capital, in August.

The story of the Army's beginnings in Korea reads like a page from the Acts of the Apostles. The first converts sought Christ in a meeting conducted in the Hoggards' parlour on Pyeng Dong Compound before even a hall could be secured ; one was a clerk in the government Treasury offices and another was a doctor. Within six weeks 100 converts had been registered, including a number of students. Nearly all were dressed in the national costume : long white cotton robes and black, varnished, cone-shaped hats similar to those worn by women when attired in the national costume of Wales. The first hall was a " go down " or storeroom situated at the back of a second-hand shop. The new converts had previously erected a large tent to accommodate 300 persons, but torrential rains and fierce winds blew it down before it could be used. The proceedings at the opening of Seoul 1 hall commenced with a Sunday-morning march, a thing unprecedented in Korea. The first Corps Sergeant-Major was a former military man. Later, nine members of the Imperial Household Band, considered to be the finest in the Eastern world, became converted. Within nine months the first Korean corps officer, Lymn Moon Sang, a former police inspector, had been commissioned and appointed to Kang Kyeng Yi. The first Korean cadet to complete a training session was commissioned in the autumn of 1910. One of the " translators " employed during the early days later confessed that he did not know what was being said in English ! He became a convert and eventually

3

interpreter in the training college, also translating the major part of the *War Cry* articles.

In those days the nation was divided into three main divisions : the coolies, the gentlemen and the nobility. As a whole the Koreans were poor. For centuries the country had been drained by heavy taxation, and most people were careful not to produce more than a bare living in order to avoid becoming targets for further taxation. There was a strong family tradition and any who were fortunate to have an income were expected to keep the rest of the family. No Korean who had any family connections need go without food or shelter. This was a social problem that seriously affected salaried Salvation Army officers ; in fact, it still does. There were no important manufacturers or sources of money-making.

Appeals reached the Colonel from many parts of the country where it was hoped the work would be started. " We are living in darkness," wrote the leader of a deputation, " without the light of God ; we don't know how to love one another, so we are in much difficulty." Having accepted Christianity in Army meetings converts would return to their own districts and immediately establish a Salvationist community. When Colonel Hoggard, travelling by pony, visited some of these districts, he was met by contingents of embryo Salvationist-soldiers carrying perfectly designed home-made flags and singing Army songs and choruses. Sometimes whole villages became Salvationist centres.

Commissioner (later General) Edward J. Higgins visited Korea during the latter part of 1909,[1] which by this time could report that more than fifty villages were proud to have the Army flag flying in their midst. A headquarters and

[1] p. 69

training college had been erected upon the Army's own land and a band had been formed. The publication of a *War Cry* (*Koo Sei Sin Moon*), an eight-page monthly, in July 1909, became an essential, for Buddhism had fallen into disfavour, the teaching of Confucius did not satisfy the mind of the upper classes, Shamanism, the worship of primitive ancestors, was ardently practised by the unenlightened multitudes, and Koo Sei Kun (The Save-the-World Army), with its uniforms and banners, was something quite new as a religion. Considerable misapprehension and confusion was created, however, by bad interpreters and by the use of the " Save-the-World " title, which was interpreted politically. It was thought that an army of liberation had come to overthrow the occupying power then dominating the country. The miracle is that many who were thus deluded found spiritual salvation. Many other perplexing problems faced the pioneers, among whom were Major and Mrs Bonwick, Staff-Captain (later Colonel) and Mrs Wilfred E. W. Twilley, Staff-Captain and Mrs John F. Crispin, Adjutant Edith Ward, Captain (later Lieutenant-Colonel) Charles S. Sylvester and his wife-to-be, Captain Nellie Harling, and Captain (later Commissioner, C.B.E.) Herbert Lord and his wife-to-be, Captain Margaret Newnham, who was a member of the original Hoggard party.

Practically the only means of travel for the officers and their wives was by pack ponies, which carried bed and bedding, food, cooking utensils ; in fact, everything necessary for a journey, for the pioneers never knew when or where they might be called upon to stay for the night. Colonel and Mrs Hoggard were intrepid and daring travellers, experiencing all manner of dangers, difficulties and disabilities, and often visiting inland districts where white people had never before been seen. The indomitable Mrs Hoggard frequently journeyed alone. She performed exploits with the Korean women and her name was revered from end to end of the territory.

On the occasion of the laying of the foundation stones of the Seoul 1 building, the first central hall to be erected by the Army in Korea, the Japanese Resident-General and the Lord Chief Justice were present. The former, Prince Ito, had previously granted an interview to Colonel Hoggard and Major Bonwick, during which he promised his personal support to the work of the Army. He was assassinated by Koreans at Harbin, Manchuria, in 1909. His successor, Viscount Sone, sent a message of appreciation to be read at the International Congress in 1914, when a contingent of eight converts represented Korea. At that time there were 2,500 Salvationists in the country, 1,000 of them women, a very high percentage in a land where women were shut off from all communication with any but their own sex and husband. In the meetings a wall or a curtain divided the men from the women. Girls were of small account ; boys were the pride of the home. At Seoul 1 corps some boys formed what they called the " Earnest Brigade," drawing up a set of ten rules " for the sake of the future," which they submitted for approval to Mrs Crispin, who was in charge of the young people's work in the capital. Girls had to be separately catered for, they being much more backward.

A Salvation Army band marched along the main street of Seoul for the first time on Sunday morning, 13 February 1910. The band consisted of Colonel Hoggard, his only son, Robert (now Commissioner, retired), Captains Lord and Sylvester and a Korean cadet.

On 29 August 1910 Korea lost its identity as a separate state. It became absorbed in the Japanese Empire and was renamed Chosen. This led to the emancipation of women in the country. A former Vice-Governor of Korea and his brother, a military officer, became Salvationists, as also did an ex-colonel, two captains, an ensign, a lieutenant of the recently disbanded Korean army, and the grandson of a former Prime Minister, following the takeover by Japan.

The first officer to be promoted to Glory from the Korean battlefield was Lieutenant Jenny Sofia Frick, a Swedish girl, in the summer of 1912.

CHAPTER THREE

TURKEY

Commissioner Railton addressed several public meetings in Constantinople during his visit to Turkey in the latter part of 1908. In a vivid impressionistic sketch of the Army at work in that country of hitherto religious intolerance, Frederick Moore wrote in the *Daily Chronicle* :

When a priest of the Koran listens to the preaching of a Salvation Army man, and stoops to kiss his hand, a state of humility has indeed come over Turkey. That injunction which Mohammed gave vent to in his wrath—" When ye meet those who misbelieve, then strike off their heads until ye have massacred them "—has given place, under the Young Turks, to one, quoted on every occasion now, which prescribes counsel with neighbours. . . . In the company of a young Englishman, I went from European Pera one evening over into Koom Kapoo, a quarter of Stamboul where many Armenians and some poorer classes of Turks have their homes. It was in the month of Ramazan, now past, a period when Moslems fast by day and pray much, and when fanaticism has in former times run high. We crossed the Golden Horn in a caique, because the rickety old Galata Bridge, called the " new " bridge, is unsafe footing in the dark. It was about one o'clock, Turkish time, that is to say an hour after sunset, and all good Moslems were coming out of their homes, after breaking the long fast, and hurrying to the various mosques. A score of men were washing hands and feet at the fountain of the mosque opposite the Quaker Mission when we arrived there. This was where the Salvation Army man was to speak.

The writer was anxious to see how the Turks would receive " this scout of The Salvation Army," as he described the Commissioner, and was curious to know how he would address them.

The Armenians—men on one side, women on the other—filled the meeting room, with the exception of half a dozen benches left at the front for the Turks. They had sung several hymns before the prayers in the mosque ended, and the Turks came over the road. In all there were about thirty, and they appeared but little out of place, though it was a new experience for many to be in a room where men and women associated. There was a green-cloaked Mullah, with a green cloth round his red fez ; another with a brown cloak and white turban ; two or three Softas, or religious scholars, also cloaked ; several officers of the army, intelligent-looking young men ; one policeman, a veritable fanatic in appearance, with beady eyes and a terrible hook of a nose ; of the others, dressed mostly *à la franca*, one or two wore white fezzes, a feature of the boycott against Austria, whence the red fezzes come.

The following little cameo shows the Commissioner in action :

He stood in his military uniform, the Turkey-red shirt conspicuous, at one side of the reading-desk, whereon lay the Bible, and an Armenian, a portly, dark man in a frock coat, stood on the other side, translating the sermon, sentence by sentence, into Turkish—which is understood of Armenians as well as Turks. I do not remember the text, but it might well have been that of the new régime, " Love one another."

A youthful Turk expressed appreciation of the Commissioner's address.

As every one is attached to his faiths and beliefs [he said], we could not thank too much the honourable person who, at the cost of a thousand troubles, has come from England to remind us of this holy duty [prayer]. . . . England assures material tranquillity to all creatures living under man's name ; and, not content with that, she organizes the great Salvation Army, and sends the chiefs of that Army to the ends of the universe to work for the eternal salvation of humanity.

It was at the conclusion of this meeting

that the long-cloaked Muezzin stooped to kiss the hand of The Salvation Army man, a sign of respect which a Christian rarely receives. . . . We understand [continued Moore] that the Commissioner has discussed with some Young Turks the project of taking over one of the old battleships that lies perpetually moored in the Golden Horn, in order that they may make of it an Elevator, a lifter of humanity.

This was typically Railtonian, but nothing happened !

During the latter part of 1912, however, Commissioner Ulysse Cosandey was sent to Constantinople to supervise the Army's ambulance work, and to help relieve the distress caused as the result of the terrible conflict then raging in the Balkans. The war in Turkey, and the reference in the *War Cry* to the presence of Salvationist blue-jackets, prompted a Liverpool comrade, W. Shepstone, to inform the editor that

in the last week in September 1894 the British Fleet [having been cruising around the Turkish Islands at the mouth of the Dardanelles] anchored at Thaso Island, and it was here that the first Salvation Army meeting [in Turkey] was held. . . . Those comrades never met again as they did that Sunday afternoon.

CHAPTER FOUR

AUSTRIA

As far back as 1895 friends in Vienna, " one of the gayest, wickedest, and most beautiful cities of the world," offered liberal assistance to the Army if work were opened up there ; and an article in *All the World* for November 1906 tells of an Austrian officer serving in another Continental country who courageously wore his uniform while furloughing in his homeland, was well received by his friends and neighbours, conducted meetings at their request and led a number of them to Christ. This may very well have been Captain Pankratz, of Switzerland, who later, in 1905, was transferred at his own request to Argentina to work among the Gauchos.

The work in Austria was officially commenced in Gablonz on 23 November 1906 through the instrumentality of Robert Feix, who had been converted in an Army meeting in Cape Town. After fighting in the South African War, in which he was badly wounded, he returned to his native city, where his father was a well-known businessman, and laboured for the establishment of the Army there. Not only did he win a number of converts, but friends were made and misunderstanding removed, thus opening the way for Commissioner W. Elwin Oliphant, the Territorial Commander in Germany, to send Captain Paul Hühner and Lieutenant Zochler to take command of the nucleus of a corps. Unfortunately the pioneer himself died the day before. Within a year or two Gablonz was able to send a cadet to the German training home. A children's and a men's home were later established and in 1911 the authorities asked that the officer in charge of the former should become responsible for the administration or relief to the city's poor. Gablonz is situated in Bohemia, which, until the war of 1914, was part of Austria-Hungary. Operations closed down toward the end of the war and were not opened again until 1927.

The German Staff Band crossed the Austrian border during its 1913 tour to visit the town of Reichenberg, where it contacted some 200 Turkish soldiers who were interned there during hostilities between the two countries. Later it became the first Salvation Army band to play in Austria, when it presented a festival in Goblenz market square. Austria was Roman Catholic in the main, uniform-wearing was forbidden, public meetings without Government authority were not allowed, and *War Cry* selling was discountenanced. Yet all these infringements took place in the presence of the burgermeister!

CHAPTER FIVE

MANCHURIA

In 1906 the Army flag was planted in Dalny, Manchuria, one of the chief cities of the Liao Tung Peninsula, made famous during the siege of Port Arthur in the Russo-Japanese War. Dalny, originally part of the Chinese Empire, was occupied first by Japan and then by Russia, but was then once again placed under the control of Japan. Captain and Mrs Kono were the pioneer officers, taking over immediately a rescue home which had been established by the Y.M.C.A.

Dalny was visited in the early part of 1909 by Acting-Commissioner Hodder, who then went on to Port Arthur, where he conducted public meetings and had an interview with General Oshima, Governor-General of the Peninsula and first representative of the Emperor of Japan in Manchuria. The first corps was opened later in the year.

BRAZIL

Although the Army's flag was not planted officially on Brazilian soil until 1922, an outpost had been established in the country many years before from the border corps at San Eugenio in Uruquay.[1] Brigadier Frank Smith prospected in Brazil during his 1905 visit to South America.

Brazil was visited again in 1910 by Colonel Hammond, a travelling representative of International Headquarters, who returned with glowing accounts of the prospects which awaited the Army there, the sympathy of the government being toward religious liberty. The Colonel was granted an interview by the President and the Governors of many of the states, all of whom were interested in the object of his visit ; some had seen the Army at work in England and been great impressed.

SOUTH SEA ISLANDS

The islands of the Pacific, including Fiji, Samoa and Tonga were prospected in 1904 by Lieutenant-Colonel (later Commissioner) Isaac Unsworth, who was then stationed in Australia. While taking a river trip in Fiji the Colonel met a young white woman who was wearing an Army shield and reading *The Soldier's Guide*. She was a soldier from Auckland, New Zealand, and a nurse with a family living on the island. On Sundays she donned full uniform and went through her duties as a Salvationist, holding a company

[1] p. 53

meeting for young people. In Samoa the Colonel was received by the paramount chief, King Mataafa, but the Army has never had its flag flying in these islands.

PALESTINE

Following the General's visit to Palestine, from 8 to 11 March 1905, Lieutenant-Colonel Roussel, a member of his party, remained in Jerusalem to encourage and instruct the converts of the spiritual awakening which had broken out, and sent to London for supplies of Articles of War, *Soldiers' Regulations* and S's. A Dutch officer, Ensign Anna Knuttel, had worked for eighteen months in Jerusalem when her photograph and an account of her ministrations, particularly among the poor, were published in the 28 July 1906 issue of the *War Cry*.

GERMAN SOUTH-WEST AFRICA

Major (later Lieutenant-Colonel) Gustav Schade, a native of Germany, together with his wife, was appointed in June 1913 to pioneer the Army's work in German South-West Africa, which was to have been commenced at Windhoek on the occasion of the twenty-fifth anniversary of the reign of Kaiser Wilhelm II. However, Mrs Schade suddenly became seriously ill, remaining so for several months. Marching orders were therefore cancelled, and the outbreak of the First World War put an end to all further plans. While serving in the German Navy the Major was made a personal attendant to the Kaiser on the Royal Yacht *Hohenzollern*.

PORT SAID

Colonel Hammond, of International Headquarters, was sent by the General to Port Said in November 1909 on a prospecting expedition, but apparently nothing came of the venture.

LATVIA

During the period under review, some of the Christian inhabitants of Riga, the Baltic seaport, having heard of The Salvation Army and its methods, but seeing no prospect of its visiting their city, resolved to form a mission of their own. This was called " The Street Mission," a title which seems to show that they had acquired a correct idea of the purposes of the Army. The authorities welcomed the mission and told its members that they could hold as many meetings as they wished.

II "WIDER STILL AND WIDER"

CHAPTER ONE

MAINTENANCE AND GROWTH

WHILE the tricolour flag was unfurled in but few new countries during the ten years from 1904, it fluttered bravely at the top of the mast in most of those in which the Army had gained a footing, and, as the years have proved, became very firmly established. Authorities on the Continent, particularly the police, had by this time made certain that it had no political significance, as they had thought, and although its methods were " strange and much misunderstood," it was having a sobering effect upon the people, and its members were gradually being accepted in religious circles, with the exception of the Roman Catholic countries, where opposition and persecution remained expectedly rife. But even in some of the tolerant countries open-air meetings were prohibited, and this proved a great disadvantage to the spread of the work, although, as will be seen, enterprising officers occasionally found a way out of their frustration. The Press, too, began to moderate its criticism and to see good in the flamboyancy of the Salvationist image, this change of view being largely assisted by the patronage bestowed upon the Army by royalty. The Man in the Street joined with the Man in the Mansion in giving his financial support to maintain the Army in their midst.

Missionary lands were, on the whole, fruitful in proselytizing, but were a tremendous drain upon International

15

Headquarters funds; indeed, they always have been, as usually the masses of indigenous people live precariously near the poverty-line, and more often than not actually overstep it. Nevertheless, social amelioration and spiritual endeavour continually moved forward, supported by governments.

Commander Eva Booth's appointment to the command of the work in the United States of America was undoubtedly one of the wisest of her General-father's decisions, for Salvation Army activities in that vast expanse of country raced ahead in an almost alarming fashion, and have never ceased to be the admiration of its millions. Operations in the white countries of the British Empire also made a steady and important advance, and opposition ceased for good, governments beaming with approval on hitherto persecuted Salvationists and collaborating with them in good works.

CHAPTER TWO

GERMANY

The advance of the work in Germany, it was reported in September 1905, was one of the most striking and encouraging facts in Salvation Army history. During the summer councils of that year the Police " President " gave permission for some 1,000 Salvationists to march through the streets of Berlin, they being accompanied by an escort of police, to the Tempelhofer Feld, the Kaiser's parade-ground,[1] where a huge open-air meeting was held. Commissioner Oliphant, the Territorial Commander, stated that, apart from international demonstrations, it was the most brilliant spectacle he had

[1] This is now the airport

ever witnessed. A new training home was opened soon after and fifty-nine cadets installed therein.

In 1906 the favourable change in public opinion was demonstrated in a remarkable manner. In connection with the annual congress the Commissioner secured a large " *biergarten* " within a stone's throw of the Column of Victory in Berlin, and provided the city with a series of spectacular object-lessons on the ramifications of the Army. The experiment proved a great public attraction, and it was estimated that 20,000, including members of the Royal Family, attended to see and hear the Salvationists at work. At the end of that year the soldiers of Witten corps, and especially the stretcher-bearers of the " Drunkards' Brigade," were highly commended by the Lord Mayor for their heroic work in connection with the terrible explosion at the Roburit works in Westphalen, where many people were killed and injured and nearly all the buildings in Annen, a town of 10,000 inhabitants, destroyed.

A commercial travellers' hotel opened in Cologne in 1907 was the first of its kind established by the Army. By this time the social work was attracting the influential people of the country, and among those who assisted financially were the Crown Prince of Germany and the Queen of Hanover. Following attendance at Salvation Army meetings, Hedwig Wangel, a famous actress, left the stage in 1909. Toward the end of that year the Territorial Headquarters, situated at No. 1 Blücherplatz, Berlin, being sold over the Army's head, Commissioner Oliphant secured an imposing building named " Handelstaette " at the corner of the Breitestrasse, near to the Cologne Fish Market, in the German capital. Shortly afterward Commissioner McAlonan was appointed to succeed Commissioner Oliphant in the command of Germany.

A curious story of a laugh and its consequences came from

Saxony in 1910. A factory hand was charged in court with laughing in a Salvation Army meeting. His defence, that he was amused at the accent of a Dutchwoman trying to speak German, availed him nothing and he was sentenced to a week's imprisonment !

The saloon-keepers of Dresden brought an action against the General and the Territorial Commander for an alleged libel contained in an article in all the other editions of the *War Cry* throughout the world in 1900, and reprinted in Germany in its issue of 6 January 1912. In this characteristically trenchant article the General attacked the brothels and drinking dens that were such an ugly blot upon civilization in every country, but the Dresden saloon-keepers construed this into a direct attack upon themselves. The judges rejected the motion, stating in the clearest terms that there were insufficient grounds for the action to be heard. The General's statement, they explained, was contained in a spiritual article setting up standards of conduct for the people of The Salvation Army, and could not be said to apply to any of the plaintiffs in the action in particular. The costs of the proceedings were to be paid by the plaintiffs, much to their chagrin.

Plotzensee Prison, one of the largest in the country, was visited in the autumn of 1912 by the Territorial Staff Band. This was the first time any German Salvation Army band had been granted such a privilege.

In Saxony, Bavaria and other German states only three religious denominations were recognized by law—the Protestant, the Roman Catholic and the Greek Orthodox. Baptist, Methodist and other Free Churches did not exist in the eyes of the law, so that tributes to the work of the Army from other than Free Church ministers were to be particularly appreciated. Professor Dr Adolf Harnack, whose name was well known throughout the world, and who, in his

Militia Christi, gave the Army a good recommendation later, wrote in glowing terms :

The Salvation Army is in no need of testimonials ; its work is its own testimonial. It has through its work disarmed the mockers and turned its enemies into friends. Not every Christian can be a soldier of The Salvation Army, but every Christian ought to be grateful to it, and can learn from it.

And one of the leading Liberal pastors, Professor Dr Freidherr von Soden, Pfarrer Dean of the Jerusalem Church in Berlin, said this :

I hail The Salvation Army on German soil not only because she saves so many lost ones, but also especially because our German Evangelical Church can learn so much of her. More communion, less fuss ; more deeds, less doctrine ; more of going into realities, deeper into the people ; more work of all for all ; more organization which places all in the front.

Pastor Walter Nithak Stahn, who officiated at the favourite church of the Kaiser, the Kaiser Wilhelm Memorial Church in Berlin, had this to say :

The Salvation Army is a Christian work of great ideas, sprung from pure love to fellow-men. It differs favourably from other religious sects and organizations, firstly by the unassuming bearing of its proclaimers, who do not claim to be the " only believers " ; then by the absence of any fanaticism towards the " world " and the " Church " ; thirdly and chiefly, by Christianity of action, shown especially towards the " fifth class," the poorest and fallen of the people.

Pastor Clemens Schultz, of the Parish of St Paul, Hamburg, aptly sums up the relationship of the Army to the Churches, previously much misunderstood :

The Salvation Army has always placed itself in the service of the parish ; it has never disturbed the relations of pastor and people, has never wanted to form a special community of saints within the community, has never clashed with the State Church, has never entered into dogmatic disputes, has never *demanded* the true faith, but has always *brought* that true faith which is active in love.

In *English Pictures viewed in German Light*, Pastor Otto Funcke had expressed a very unkind opinion of the Army,[1] but only a few weeks before his passing he repented in this generous confession :

In spite of all its shortcomings, The Salvation Army has given me an impressive penitential sermon. It has shown me that in my public life I should have done many things differently. It gives me deep pain that I can hardly start in new ways now, in the closing days of my office and earthly pilgrimage. I think, however, I may ask my younger colleagues to perform their office in the spirit of Jesus, the Good Shepherd, and to seek the " lost "—those whom none else seek.

Another unkind criticism had been published in the first edition of *Present Day Churches and Sects*, but in the second edition Pastor Lotze wrote :

Great by eloquence, more of deeds than words, by his prominent organizing talent, we may say by his art of strategy, by his glowing devotion to his work, General Booth certainly deserves a place of honour among the benefactors of humanity.

Prominent German statesmen also gave unstinted acclamation to the work of the Army, although, as Graf Artur Posadowsky-Wehner, Imperial Minister of Home Affairs, wrote, they could not identify themselves with its tactics and methods.

As in many other countries during this period of the Army's history, a remarkable spiritual awakening broke out unexpectedly in 1912 at Elberfeld—where within weeks more than 375 seekers, including wonderful trophies of grace, were registered—and spread throughout the territory. The Oberburgermeister of Elberfeld gave permission for Captain

[1] *The History of The Salvation Army*, vol. iv, p. 18

Schmidt to hold open-air meetings in certain parts of the town, a concession of no mean kind. One of the converts, Paul Küll, was once a member of a gang of thirty desperate bandits who terrorized the countryside.

The German Staff Band was formed in 1910 under Ensign (later Colonel) Percival Treite.

From a train at Cologne station, all alone and unrecognized, Commissioner George Scott Railton was promoted to Glory on 19 July 1913, after forty years' service. He, who had once been in charge of Army work in Germany and could speak six languages, had travelled 325,000 miles in pioneering and prospecting.

It is significant that sixteen months before the First World War broke out on 4 August 1914 Commissioner Oliphant, then Territorial Commander for Switzerland and Italy, being interviewed by a *Christian World* reporter concerning religion on the European continent had this to say regarding Germany :

In Germany you come face to face with rationalistic influences, permeating not only the schools and universities, but showing itself in the Church.

CHAPTER THREE

ITALY

The religious bias of Italy caused the Army's chariot wheels to drag heavily in the early years of the twentieth century, and the mixture of racial elements often put the Salvationist in a quandary, for the north and south were as different from each other almost as two nations. Open-air meetings as such were not allowed, but being permitted to advertise and talk of their wares gave Salvationists a splendid opportunity to explain to the great crowds that gathered around them, at the fairs and in the market-places, the purpose and contents of the *War Cry*, to sing a song and to read extracts from its pages. "We like your religion because you never criticize either in your meetings or in your paper," was the general comment. Nevertheless, in 1907, Lieutenant-Colonel Albin Peyron, who was in command of the Army's work, was fighting an uphill battle, and as he and his comrades passed through the streets of some towns, they would hear such cries as "Down with the Salvationists! Down!" The Colonel was succeeded by Brigadier Constant Jeanmonod.

Thousands of young Italian men and women emigrated to the United States every year and returned to their native land with a changed outlook, Americanizing even the remotest hamlet. Converted in New York from drunkenness and gambling, young and illiterate Luigi Cuzzone returned in 1904 to Ariano di Puglia dressed as a Salvationist and with the soul of an apostle. He hired and furnished a hall and advertised a meeting, but on the first night doors, chairs, benches and lamps were broken by powerful opponents. No meetings being possible Cuzzone commenced to win souls one by one, his first convert being Gabriel Riccio, a tavern-keeper, who in turn won over his brother. These three banded themselves together and went about preaching. Soon a young married woman, Antoniella Fierro Consolante, joined the group, and became the means of her husband's conversion just prior to his death. One Sunday morning Gabriel Riccio's brother felt constrained to sing in the church after mass had concluded. The police were summoned and a few weeks later Gabriel was sentenced to nine months' imprisonment, with the option of a fine of 1,000 lire, and Cuzzone to seven months.

The prayer of these friends, that the Lord would let them see The Salvation Army firmly established in Ariano, was answered when headquarters decided to send officers to reinforce the trio. Accordingly, Captain Gallia opened a hall and swore in a little band of soldiers. Cuzzone eventually returned to America, and Antoniella Consolante entered the training-home. A revival broke out in Ariano in 1908, no fewer than 200 converts being recorded.

While many who attended Army meetings in Italy yielded to Christ few became Salvationists, there being an understandable prejudice against an open acknowledgement of the religious truth proclaimed by the Army. At Torre Pellice, capital of the Waldensian Valleys, many of the 500 factory girls, who belonged to a class which no other religious body had succeeded in contacting, came to the fifteen days' tent meetings held in 1908 and, risking a threat of the direst penalties, continued to attend the meetings of *Esercito della Salvezza* (The Salvation Army) at the hall. The officers taught them to knit, sew, mend and sing salvation songs, the girls, as a rule, being rough, untameable and with little time to learn domestic duties. In this town of 2,000 people there were no fewer than twelve parish churches and a hundred clergy, but the fight was more against infidel than Church influence.

Through another returned emigrant from America, Vito Mastri, the spiritual fire burst into flame even more gloriously in Faeto, a Roman Catholic town of 3,000 inhabitants high up in the Pouilles Mountains in southern Italy, three and a half hours' mule journey from the nearest railway station. A corps was established and officers sent in to maintain the work. Later the first hall was turned into a school where reading, writing and arithmetic were taught to both young and old. Eventually a band was formed and several young people became officers. Yet another corps, Faiano, near

Naples, was opened as the result of newly enrolled Salvationists returning from the United States. Superstition was rampant at Faiano, and those who identified themselves with the Army were at once subjected to persecution. In life they were beset with petty hindrances and in death were denied burial, until the bishop had the over-zealous priest of the district removed.

Despite these occasional outbursts of spiritual flame, the General was not happy about Salvationism in Italy, and wrote to his son on 30 March 1908:

From what I hear about Italy I am not sure whether we should not gain immensely by dropping the preaching altogether and go in for rescue homes, criminals, shelters and the like.

In the latter part of 1912 Staff-Captain (later Lieutenant-Colonel) Virginio Paglieri went on a mission to establish the Army's work in Rome, where years before it had been represented by Major Vint.[1] The headquarters were at this time situated in Milan, where Brigadier (later Lieutenant-Colonel) and Mrs David Miche were in charge. It was a great discouragement in those days that converts would kneel at the Mercy Seat and then go off to confess their " sin " to the priest. An English officer, Adjutant Mary R. Smith, having trouble with some of the people who attended her meetings in Milan, would keep order by walking up and down the aisle while delivering her message.

When, on the night of 28 December 1908, sudden destruction overwhelmed the city of Messina and hundreds of surrounding villages in South Calabria, the Army quickly dispatched to the scene a relief party under the direction of Commissioner Cosandey. In recognition of these services, which lasted several months, King Victor Emmanuel of Italy, in November 1909, conferred upon the Commissioner the

[1] *The History of The Salvation Army*, vol. iv, p. 10

distinction of Cavalier of the Corona d'Italia. Brigadier Jeanmonod and all other officers who participated in the work received a medal and diploma.

CHAPTER FOUR

HOLLAND

The salvation war was forging ahead under Commissioner Thomas Estill when the General visited Holland in October 1904, although not having the privilege of holding open-air meetings was a great disadvantage. At Utrecht and Leyden, however, the burgomaster consented to such gatherings being held twice a week, and thereby actually shut his eyes to the law which forbade religious open-air activities. The enterprising officer at the Hague No. 1 corps hit upon a novel way of satisfying official regulation. He hired a stall in the great Saturday-night market and sold Army literature and polishing wax, made in an Army industrial home. At the same time he pressed home the claims of God to the seven or eight hundred people who stood around him. On another occasion Utrecht 1 corps obtained permission from the burgomaster to hold a demonstration during the annual and historic Fair Week. A large screen was hung over the canal, from one side to the other in front of the town hall, and pictures were thrown on to the sheet by an electric apparatus mounted on a car standing on a bridge. That night, for the first time, an Army flag was hoisted in the centre of the city. A crowd estimated at 10,000 attended the gathering and the head of the police congratulated the Salvationists on the venture. That a band was permitted to play at the railway station reception to the General in both The Hague, the very centre of officialdom and respectability, and Amsterdam was an encouraging sign of the time. Bands were also allowed the exceptional privilege of playing in the streets in connection with the national festivities celebrating the birth of Princess Juliana in 1909.

During a holiness campaign conducted in 1906 by Colonel (later Commissioner, D.D.) Samuel L. Brengle, of the U.S.A., hundreds of men, women and children yielded to Christ, although soul-saving in the country was characteristically slow and difficult. Quite a number of Jews became Salvationists, and in certain quarters doctors were so enamoured of the Army that they attended Salvationists free of charge.

The Queen Mother, who, as with Queen Wilhelmina, had contributed to the funds of the Social Work, paid a visit to the Children's Home at Naarden-Bussum, near Utrecht, in October.

Towards the end of 1906 an imposing building, formerly an hotel, near to the Central Station in Amsterdam, was acquired as a territorial and trade headquarters and printing works. A most unusual acquisition to the Army's properties was a large and historic Roman Catholic building known as the Old Paradise Church, centrally situated in Rotterdam ; at the back was the bishop's residence. Commissioner William Ridsdel, who succeeded Commissioner Estill in the summer of 1907, purchased this at a comparatively low figure to relieve the pressure on the Men's Social Work, and for the purpose of providing accommodation for homeless families. At this time one-third of Holland's six million inhabitants were Roman Catholics, and the priests were saying to their parishioners : " Yes, The Salvation Army is right ; but it is only for the drunkards and bad people ! " Yet another historic property was originally the birthplace of

Dr Kuyper, a former Prime Minister ; this was purchased as a hall and quarters for the corps at Maassluis. The quaint old hall and quarters of Amersfoort corps dated from 1618. At one time it had been a cloister for Catholic nuns, and for 200 years a bakery. Antiquarians from all parts of the world used to visit it.

By 1910 fighting at the doors of halls and interruptions of meetings were rare, but in 1911 Brother Walraven, the father of eight children, was murdered one Sunday evening at the door of The Hague slum corps by a man who had been disturbing the meetings and had been ordered out by the officer. In his rage the man plunged a knife into the Salvationist's breast. A feature peculiar to Holland was that men would often enter Army halls puffing at a cigar, and sometimes would actually light up during a meeting, this being due to the fact that almost all men and boys were inveterate smokers.

A sensation was caused in educated circles by the conversion in 1909 of one of the most popular writers in Holland, the wife of an influential Member of Parliament. She attended the meetings at Leyden. Equally great was the stir aroused by the conversion at The Hague of Kloosterman, a widely known anarchist agitator and lecturer. Royal recognition of the Army's work came again in 1910 when H.R.H. Prince Hendrik, Consort of Queen Wilhelmina, visited the Army's Farm Colony at Lunteren.[1]

In this same year a great move forward commenced when Commissioner Ridsdel introduced a National Staff Band under Ensign (later Lieutenant-Colonel) J. P. Rawie. This was a travelling combination, and the bandsmen received 5s per week and bought their own uniform, which was similar in design to that of the International Staff Band. The seventeen men travelled for sixteen months, visiting every

[1] *The History of The Salvation Army*, vol. iii, p. 183

corps in the territory. When the Dutch Staff Band ceased to function, five of its number became officers, among them Colonel Douglas Ridsdel, son of the Commissioner, and Brigadier François Bulterman, the Deputy Bandmaster, who died in a railway accident in 1936.

Holland contributed officers to the work in South America, England and Indonesia, and in 1911 two women officers who were to achieve distinction, Brigadiers Johanna van de Werken and Bertha Gugelmann, left for service in India; the former became a Commissioner and the last-named a Lieutenant-Colonel.

A long-cherished idea of William Booth was to have a number of missionary boats moving along the innumerable canals of Holland holding meetings among the waterside population and ministering to their spiritual and temporal needs. In due course a suitable barge of 120 tons was purchased by Commissioner Ridsdel. This had been the temporary meeting-place of the Groningen 11 corps while its hall was being renovated, and during which some striking conversions had taken place. The *tjalk* (barge) was known as *Hoop voor Allen* (" Hope for all "). Captain Wijnholt, the skipper, held a master-mariner's certificate for both inland and ocean-going navigation. The barge contained a hall capable of accommodating 180 persons. Commissioner Railton conducted a meeting on this vessel. Baptist ministers sent their young people to " The converting shop," as the barge came to be called. " You will get them converted," said one minister, " and go on your way, and they can come to my church ! " The police declared that the converts' meetings on the barge were wonderful.

The twenty-fifth anniversary was conducted during the Whitsun of 1912 in the Amsterdam People's Palace, Holland's largest hall, by the Foreign Secretary, Commissioner T. Henry Howard. On the Monday Commissioner Ridsdel celebrated the fortieth anniversary of his first appointment as an officer. There were then 94 corps, 336 officers, 1,559 local officers, 344 bandsmen and 334 corps cadets.

CHAPTER FIVE

DENMARK

Colonel (later Commissioner) Charles Sowton, for some years in charge of the Army's Scandinavian work in the United States, was appointed in November 1904 to succeed Colonel William J. Richards in the command of Denmark. The day of opposition and misunderstanding was then long past. Permission had been freely given for the Army to hold meetings in the open spaces of most of the towns as well as in the woods, and to march the streets headed by its bands ; but it was not until the Congress of 1907 that Copenhagen saw Salvationists processioning gaily through the capital on their way to hold a Sunday-afternoon meeting in its central park.

In this same year the General was received by Their Majesties the King and Queen of Denmark in special audience in the Palace at Copenhagen, the interview lasting for seventy-five minutes.[1] His Majesty had previously visited a shelter and the rescue home in Copenhagen, and the Tsaritsa of Russia invariably forwarded a donation to the Army's work when visiting the land of her birth. Several of William Booth's books had been published in Danish, and 88 centres, 43 outposts, ten slum posts and two batteries were in operation. The batteries were caravans which travelled from place

[1] p. 148

to place, finally fixing upon a centre where it was hoped a corps might be established. The institution of " Christmas pots "—an American custom—by Acting-Commissioner Sowton proved a decided success at the outset, and for several days officers, soliciting help for the poor, stood in the streets by great cauldrons resting on tripods. The Dorcas League, comprised chiefly of officers' wives, mended old garments and made new ones for distribution to the needy.

An event of considerable importance to the Army in later years was the acceptance of Dr and Mrs Wilhelm Andreas Wille as cadets. They entered the International Training Homes in May 1906. The doctor, who had been a Salvationist for some time, visiting his patients in his uniform, gave up a flourishing medical practice in Køge with the hope of proceeding to India as a medical missionary, his wife also possessing valuable medical qualifications ; but it was in Indonesia that Dr Wille eventually established a far-reaching reputation as an eye-specialist.

In 1908 the King and several members of the Danish Royal Family, including Queen Alexandra of England and the Empress Marie of Russia, were among the contributors to the Self-Denial Fund in Copenhagen.

Staff-Captain Peter Andersen, Bandmaster of the Danish Staff Band, capable speaker, gifted singer, expert pianist and adept at playing various wind and string instruments, was smitten with blindness in his twenties, but when forty years of age, in 1910, he became a spiritual evangelist and band instructor for Denmark. With commendable tenacity he had learned the Braille system of reading and writing and, with the assistance of his wife and the officers of the various corps he visited during his campaigns, he wrote out the whole of the Bible in Braille, completing this colossal task in three years. His work was contained in fifty bulky volumes. The Staff-Captain was a convert of Major (later Lieutenant-

Colonel) Robert Perry, who had commenced the Army's work in Denmark.[1]

In May 1912 the Army in Denmark was to celebrate its twenty-fifth anniversary, and the Territorial Commander, Commissioner Mrs Lucy Booth-Hellberg, proposed a National Day of Celebration in which a special effort would be made to raise sufficient money for securing a badly needed training college ; but for such a purpose permission had to be obtained from the King himself. Not only did His Majesty approve of the National Day, but gave instructions that every Governor in the country was to see that it was observed within his territory. A few weeks later His Majesty died unrecognized while staying in Hamburg, Germany, on holiday.

No fewer than 500 committees throughout Denmark undertook to help with the collection. The students of one of the capital's theological seminaries were sent into the streets by their principal to sell the little floral badge that was handed to every donor of 10 öre (sixpence). A military band played outside Copenhagen's Town Hall, the programme opening with the " Jubilee March," specially written for the occasion and dedicated to the Army by the famous Danish composer, Fini Henriques. Thousands of people attended this *al fresco* concert. In another town the colonel of a regiment ordered his band to play in the streets to remind people of Jubilee Day. 50,000 kroner (£2,500) was raised by this effort, in which many distinguished citizens took part. The Silver Jubilee celebrations were conducted by the Foreign Secretary, Commissioner T. Henry Howard, and Queen Alexandra, who was staying in Copenhagen with her sister, the Dowager Empress Marie of Russia, received the Territorial Commander, Commissioner Mrs Booth-Hellberg.

[1] *The History of The Salvation Army*, vol. iv, p. 20

CHAPTER SIX

CENTRAL AMERICA AND WEST INDIES

JAMAICA

" Salvationists may be this or that, or may be not this or not that," said *The Jamaican Times*, in 1904, " but there can be no doubt with those who watch them closely that to them it is a vital, ever-present truth, the truth by which they religiously live, move, and have their being, that ' The blood of Jesus Christ cleanseth from all sin.' To the theories of sceptics they oppose the facts of changed lives, of converted drunkards and harlots and thieves. They believe and live." Thus was the work of sixteen years summed up by the island's press. " Changed lives " meant, among other things, that many couples living together as man and wife, some for upward of twenty years, a quite common occurrence, had entreated the Army officers to unite them in holy matrimony.

In that same year, and for a few months previously, the " Isle of Springs," as Jamaica has been called, experienced a period of misfortune and distress caused by the ravages of a hurricane which blew down seven Salvation Army halls and damaged several others. Further damage was done in January 1907 when many halls and social institutions in Kingston were wiped out by an earthquake and fires in various parts of the metropolis. All forty officers escaped without serious injury, but all were homeless, as were 20,000 other people. Lieutenant-Colonel (later Commissioner) Bruno Friedrich was sent from International Headquarters by the Chief of the Staff to assist in arranging distress relief. Again, in November 1912, Jamaica was visited by destructive wind-storms and tidal waves, which resulted in much loss of

OVERSEAS
PIONEERS
of the
PERIOD

1 & 2 Captain and Mrs Kono (Manchuria) 3 & 4 Robert and Annie Hoggard (Korea)
5 Anna Knuttel (Palestine) 6 Joseph Hammond (Port Said) 7 Thomas Frisch (Paraguay)
8 Frank Smith (Brazil) 9 Isaac Unsworth (South Sea Islands) 10 David Leib (Panama)
11 Matilda Hatcher (China) 12 Jens A. H. Povlsen (Russia) 13 Joseph P. Rauch (Panama)
14 Eduardo Palací (Peru)

A momentous occasion in the history of The Salvation Army in Korea. The stone-laying of its first property, Seoul 1 Hall, in March 1910

The first Salvation Army hall to be opened in Austria, at Gablonz, in 1906, with Captain Paul Hühner (standing behind the cycle) and Lieutenant Zochler (taking notes). Note the officers' peculiar headgear

life and material damage in the towns of Savanna-la-Mar, where the corps hall was totally destroyed, and Lucea. Bluefields hall was also wrecked, and in the district of Montego Bay a large number of Salvationists were rendered homeless. Some time previously when news was received at Montego Bay that the officers were farewelling, a request signed by the Member of Parliament, local magistrate and leading townspeople was sent to Headquarters praying that they might be allowed to remain, so highly were they respected.

In 1909 Commissioner (later General) Edward J. Higgins led the Congress celebrations in Jamaica, spending twelve days on the island. Ensign Miller, the corps officer at St Ann's Bay, commenced in 1910 and successfully continued a day school with an average attendance of fifty, thereby remedying an evil at the wharves, which had been pestered with truant and mischievous children. Another school was opened at Louisianna for the rising generation living among the mountain banana plantations, by a woman-officer who had been a teacher. The opening and dedication, at Kingston, of a new block of buildings, comprising the territorial headquarters, Central Hall for public meetings, training college, officers' quarters and a men's hostel was one of the most important functions of the Congress celebrations conducted in 1911 by Commissioner Richards. A newly formed brass band participated. Thousands were unable to gain admittance to the Central Hall. The former buildings had been destroyed by the earthquake of 1907.

While on tour in 1912 Brigadier (later Colonel) George Souter, the Divisional Commander responsible for the work in Jamaica, dedicated to God [1] no fewer than 160 infants.

When Colonel Charles Rothwell was the Territorial Commander, His Excellency the Governor of Jamaica,

[1] Equivalent to christening in the Church

Brigadier-General Sir William Manning, K.C.M.G., presided at one of the 1914 Congress gatherings held in the Ward Theatre and spoke highly of the Army's work as he had seen it in India.

BRITISH GUIANA

Despite the general financial depression in " The Magnificent Colony," the Army's work pushed forward steadily in British Guiana (Demerara). In 1911 the already erected gallows were cheated of three victims, plantation hands, through the persistent pleading of Staff-Captain Ghurib Das (Alexander).[1] They had been arrested on suspicion, tried for murder and condemned to death on purely circumstantial evidence. The Staff-Captain was not only convinced of their innocence, but collected a budget of evidence to substantiate his contention, which included the victim's dying confession to a nurse that his injuries were self-inflicted. The men were reprieved within three days of the date of their expected execution, but it was not until after two years of unceasing effort that Ghurib Das succeeded in securing their unconditional release from prison. By this time he had pointed them to Christ. Mrs Staff-Captain Bennett who, with her husband, was a government-appointed probationary officer, was instrumental in securing the release of a woman who had served eleven years of a life sentence for murder. Convicted in 1900, she had been sentenced to be hanged. Staff-Captain Bennett was in charge of operations among West Indians.

A particularly encouraging feature in Georgetown was the work carried on among East Indian children under the direction of Staff-Captain Ghurib Das and his wife.

[1] *The History of The Salvation Army*, vol. iv, p. 34

ST LUCIA

A sentence of fourteen days' imprisonment pronounced upon the officer stationed at Castries, in St Lucia, for playing a cornet in an open-air meeting, was cancelled after an appeal to a higher court. In October 1907 Captain Wiggan erected a palm leaf " barracks " at Mahaicony for special meetings, in his anxiety to have a Salvation Army hall in the village, and also to consecrate the site.

BARBADOS

Provincial headquarters were set up on the island of Barbados in March 1907, under the control of Brigadier Nehemiah Glover, whose responsibilities also included Trinidad, Grenada, St Lucia, St Vincent, the Lesser Antilles, British Guiana and Antigua. In 1912 a number of small movable halls were built for work among the peasantry, most of whom were engaged in fishing at certain seasons of the year.

TRINIDAD

When the legislators of Trinidad were considering the introduction of a law to deal with itinerant street preaching, police authorities pointed out that such restrictions as were proposed might prevent The Salvation Army from continuing its open-air work, and this was not desired, as in certain of the worst quarters of Port of Spain, the capital city, such meetings exercised a healthy influence on the lawless and were of assistance to the police in maintaining good order. At Kingstown the worst drunkard in the town was converted after eighty convictions. " If the Army did no more good than making 'Dissy' sober and respectable, it deserves the thanks of the community," said the local newspaper.

PANAMA

Thousands of navvies from Jamaica and other West Indian islands being employed in the construction of the great Panama Canal, in Central America, Staff-Captain (later Brigadier) David Leib, of the West Indies Territory, visited the newly established Republic in the summer of 1904 to enquire into the possibilities of the Army opening up work among the men. He was everywhere kindly received. Dr Manuel Amador Guerrero, President of the Republic, granted him an interview ; the officials of the railroad company gave him a first-class pass over their system ; and General G. W. Davis, United States Governor of the Canal Zone, agreed to provide the Army with land or buildings.

Work was commenced on the Isthmus during the autumn of the year by Adjutant and Mrs Jackson, the first corps was opened at Cristobal in the Canal Zone by Lieutenant-Colonel (later Colonel) Joseph P. Rauch, the Territorial Commander, and soon more than fifty conversions had been registered and a second corps opened in Colon. The first meeting there, attended by a large and influential crowd, was held in a pavilion made of coconut-palm branches that had been specially erected by the Panama Government for speech-making in connection with the first anniversary of the Independence of Panama from Colombian rule, and the taking over of Canal affairs by the United States of America. Meetings were conducted in both English and Spanish. Panama City and Empire corps were started a few months later. A rest house was opened at Cristobal in 1907 to provide shelter for men awaiting employment.

Outside British Guiana, Panama was the only country on the American continent south of Mexico where open-air activities and marches were freely permitted.

ST VINCENT

Work in St Vincent was commenced in the summer of 1905, but for reasons of economy officers were withdrawn five years later ; nevertheless, a little band of seventeen converts, some of whom had been notorious characters, kept the flag flying by conducting both open-air and indoor meetings, and were still enthusiastic Salvationists when the Territorial Commander, Lieutenant-Colonel (later Colonel) Sidney Maidment, and his wife visited the island in 1912.

ANTIGUA

An island with a population in 1904 of 37,000, Antigua first saw The Salvation Army in the person of a Captain Grant, who became an officer in Jamaica, and who was visiting his relations. His uniform immediately attracted attention and he was asked to hold meetings in St John's, the capital. So much success attended his efforts that he took upon himself the responsibility of continuing them, and in a surprisingly short time he was able to report that he had won 250 converts and numbered hundreds of people in his congregation. Soon he had 100 recruits ready to be sworn-in as soldiers. Lieutenant-Colonel (later Colonel) Joseph P. Rauch, the Territorial Officer, thereupon sent in officers to consolidate the good work. His Excellency the Governor expressed his sympathy with the Army's activities, as also did the Colonial Secretary, the chief magistrate and the inspector of police.

BRITISH HONDURAS

Following repeated appeals from some of its 33,000 inhabitants, Staff-Captain Leib visited the island of British Honduras in the summer of 1906, but the work was not commenced until 1915 by Adjutant Trotman, who worked first among the lumbermen in the hinterland, later transferring to the capital city of Belize. An immigration officer, who is still living, arranged for a Methodist minister to vouch for the authenticity of the officer in Salvation Army uniform. The place in Belize where most open-air meetings were held was called " Battlefield " by the pioneer officer, and the city square is still named " Battlefield " to this day.

COSTA RICA

Leaving Hadleigh Farm Colony in 1896 for Costa Rica, one of the loveliest countries in the Western Hemisphere, Brother and Sister Mrs Fred Moules took over the management of a large market and flower garden in San Pedro ; but soon after their arrival were bereft of their employer, who had been interested in the Army, and found themselves practically alone in a strange land and unable to speak Spanish. Later, another Salvationist arrived from Hadleigh, and together the trio jogged along, hoping that the Army flag would one day wave in the country of their adoption. Then, in 1907, Major John H. Clifford, General Secretary of the West Indies Territory, called at San Pedro, while on a visit to San José, the capital, and discovered the Moules, who asked him to conduct in their home the first Army meeting to be held within the vicinity of the capital. The population of the republic was then 309,000.

Toward the end of the year Major Clifford, accompanied by Captain Eduardo Palací, a Peruvian, and Lieutenant George Stewart, a Jamaican, who became the first corps officers in the country, arrived in Port Limon from Jamaica to commence operations officially, and from the first the meetings were well attended. Open-air work was not allowed, but Salvationists had liberty to conduct meetings in the *piazza* (veranda) of any house, or in any yard where the owner had given permission. A mission hall on the outskirts of Port Limon, and the land on which it was built, were handed over to the Army by a Jamaican lady.

The Major secured an interview with the President of the Republic, Don Cleto Gonzalez Viquez, who had read and heard of the work of the Army and promised to accord him any facility he needed. The president of the Northern Railway gave the Major a first-class pass to whatever point he wished to travel, and passes were later issued to all officers.

CUBA

Brother Alexander Hay, a Jamaican, who had served for six years with the West India Regiment in West Africa,[1] had been living in Cuba for some time. Finding no Salvationists there, he started meetings himself at Santiago in 1902 in the house of Mr Robert Dixon, of St Kitts. Later, Hay went to work on the railway and conducted Saturday meetings in Guantanamo, giving his testimony in English; a friend translated it into French, which Spanish-speaking people were able to understand. Hay then obtained employment in the United States naval yard and obtained permission to hold meetings in the camp, an American foreman at

[1] See p. 72

Boqueron lending him a tent and eventually a wooden building.

Adjutant Elmer Johnson, of the United States, did pioneer work in Havana in 1912, but operations were not officially commenced until 1918.

CHAPTER SEVEN

NORWAY AND ICELAND

In June 1905 the Norwegian Storting (Parliament) in Christiania (Oslo) revolted against the aged King Oscar II, who refused to sanction its Consular Law, and declared the dissolution of its country's union with Sweden and the cessation of His Majesty's rule. Prince Charles of Denmark, who was married to Princess Maud, daughter of King Edward VII of England, was invited to occupy the Norwegian throne, and in June of the following year he was crowned in Trondhjem, the ancient capital, as King Haakon VII. The Salvation Army was officially represented by Lieutenant-Colonel (later Colonel) Sidney Maidment and Staff-Captain Kristian Kristoffersen, who participated in the ceremony by forming part of the Order Guard.

About the time of the Dissolution a wave of revivalism was sweeping through Norway, having come, strangely enough, by way of The Salvation Army in America. Albert Lunde, a young Norwegian who had emigrated to the United States, became converted in an Army meeting in Chicago. He never enrolled as a soldier, although he continued to attend the meetings, but was greatly used in the salvation of souls. Returning to his native village some years later he began to preach. Soon the largest halls were too small for his congregations and the clergy of the State Church opened their doors to him. Then, the churches being too small, the Calmeyergaten Mission Hall—the largest in Scandinavia—was taken, and night after night was crowded with some 5,000 people. The revival had its influence upon the Army, especially in the smaller corps, many of which took on a new lease of spiritual life. Lieutenant-Colonel (later Commissioner, D.D.) Samuel L. Brengle, who was to become the Army's great exponent of holiness, was sent over from the United States of America in 1906 to conduct a four months' campaign in Scandinavia, which resulted in 1,955 seekers after this blessing, 371 of them in Norway. Commissioner and Mrs William Ridsdel were Norway's leaders at this period, they having been in charge for five years, during which a new training home was erected. The Commissioner, who found it essential to travel extensively, was granted a first-class free pass on the principal ships of the various steamship companies, a privilege not enjoyed by any other traveller. The Ridsdels were followed by Colonel (later Commissioner) and Mrs Johan Ögrim.

The year 1907 commenced with a new wave of revivalism sweeping the country and centring in Christiania and, the question of sanctification being given special emphasis, Colonel Brengle was sent over for his second and last visit. Within four weeks the seekers in his meetings in the capital numbered 1,017.

" Working his way toward Bergen . . . Brengle achieved victory in virtually every town where he campaigned," writes Clarence Hall in his biography, *Samuel Logan Brengle*. At Bergen he championed the cause of orthodoxy in a great gathering of the intelligentsia of the city arranged by the astute corps officer, Adjutant (later Commissioner) Theodor Westergaard. His " Atonement " address on that occasion Hall considers as " the outstanding platform achievement of

Brengle's career," and all he used to guide his thoughts were a few scribblings on the back of an old envelope ! More than 600 seekers were registered during the Bergen campaign, and 3,000 all together. The employees of Norway's largest flour mill requested their manager to close down for two hours that they might attend the Colonel's morning meeting. They made up the time lost by commencing work at 3.30 a.m. This was in the little town of Vaksdal.

The General visited Norway in this same year and King Haakon not only received him in audience at the Royal Palace, but attended one of his public meetings. Her Majesty the Queen showed her personal interest in the Army by consenting to a motor-boat being named the *Queen Maud*. This vessel was used for missionary work in both summer and winter among the remote islands in the Helgeland district, situated to the north of the Norwegian coast. Its headquarters were at Oksningen. Some idea of the difficulties of travel in these parts is furnished by the experience of a woman who gave up going to church because on the last occasion that she did so she was unable to return home for more than a week owing to the tempestuous weather and the non-arrival of the steamer.

A mild sensation was caused during King Edward's visit to Norway in 1908 when for the first time a Salvationist in uniform was seen at a reception given at the Palace. This honour was accorded Brigadier (later Colonel) Othilie Tonning, Secretary of the Women's Social Work in Norway, and a member of the Christiania City Council. The Brigadier was later awarded the Gold Medal of Merit by King Haakon in recognition of the Army's work among women and children.

The Norwegian Staff Band was formed in February 1909, its first Bandmaster being Captain (later Commissioner) Tobias I. Ogrim.

The salvation lifeboat *Catherine Booth*,[1] which accompanied the cod-fishing fleet on most of its excursions, and kept watch on the stormy seas lashing the treacherous Lofoten Islands, had rescued no fewer than 370 boats—fourteen of them in one week—and saved more than 1,500 lives during the ten years of its service, reported the *War Cry* for 8 January 1910. Adjutant (later Brigadier) Emil Ovesen remained the skipper until 1913.

Björnstjerne Björnson, the famous Norwegian writer, passed away in the summer of 1910. He had been a warm friend of the Army, and had spoken on its behalf during times of misunderstanding :

We ought to be thankful to the Salvationists because they have come to our town to show us the real state of our young people and, instead of blaming The Salvation Army, we ought to help it. Speaking for myself, I declare that I admire the courage of these young women who so bravely stand to proclaim their good tidings.

The most northerly Salvation Army corps in the world, at Hammerfest, which lies within the Arctic Circle, was visited by Colonel (later Commissioner) Henry Bullard in 1910. The first Army flag to be hoisted in this latitude was made by a persecuted convert from odd pieces of yellow, red and blue cloth. Another corps the Colonel visited was that at Kirkenes. This small mining town of 600 people, on the most northern border of Russia, had come into existence some three or four years previously as the result of the discovery of rich iron ore in the grey mountains which surround it. Considerable excitement was caused while the Colonel was there by the loading on the ss *Bengal* of the first shipment of iron. The crew were among the crowds which packed the Army hall, but two days later the heavily loaded vessel, following in the wake of the ship in which the Colonel was

[1] *The History of The Salvation Army*, vol. iv, p. 42

travelling, foundered during a severe storm and the eighteen members of the crew were lost.

Commissioner and Mrs Ögrim were followed in the command of Norway by Colonel (later Lieutenant-Commissioner) and Mrs J. A. H. Povlsen in 1912, and in the following year the meetings of the Silver Jubilee of the commencement of the Army's operations in the " Viking Kingdom " [1] were led by Commissioner Ridsdel in Christiania ; Commissioner Hanna Ouchterlony, the pioneer officer, Major Peter Thunell, the first Captain in Christiania, and the evangelist, Albert Lunde, participated. Colonel Jens Povlsen was then the Territorial Commander.

ICELAND

Twenty-five years after he had established the Army's work in Iceland [2] Major Christian Eriksen passed to his Reward, happy, doubtless, in the knowledge that in this isolated northern island five corps were in operation among its greatly scattered 85,000 inhabitants. The officers of the smaller corps supported themselves by conducting day schools for children, and this was considered to be a quite satisfactory arrangement. In a speech made some years later by Mr Gislasen, the representative of the Danish Home Mission in Iceland, he said :

The doctrine of The Salvation Army was quite new to us. Nobody ever spoke of salvation through the Blood of the Lamb, of conversion and living a new life. Prayer meetings were never held. To take a collection in a meeting, or to solicit subscriptions from others on behalf of the poor and poverty-stricken, was considered worse among us than to live in hidden or open sin and vice—but The Salvation Army taught us otherwise.

[1] *The History of The Salvation Army*, vol. iv, p. 38
[2] *The History of The Salvation Army*, vol. iv, p. 43

During his visit to Iceland in 1907 King Frederick of Denmark greeted Ensign Marie Wind, in Thingvalla, with a handshake and assured her of his interest in the Army. Major Theodor Westergaard, who conducted the anniversary meetings in 1912, was privileged to give a lecture on the Army in Reykjavik Cathedral. When writing of his experiences on this occasion, he said :

The Army does not enjoy the same sympathy and help from the legal authorities as in other countries. The Icelanders have an idea that the presence of the Army in their country lowers them in the estimation of other nations !

Evidently the Althing (Parliament) thought highly of the work being done, for in 1914 it contributed 1,000 kröner toward the cost of the new headquarters.

This is what the Divisional Officer, Staff-Captain Neils Edelbo, wrote to *All the World* in December 1913 :

To bring an Icelander down on his knees and get him to pray is a great victory in itself, but to see him turn back and give God the glory is, I regret to be compelled to say it, almost a miracle, which, alas ! hardly happens with one in ten. If you have got them so far as to kneel and pray, then they consider that God, as well as men and their own souls, ought to be satisfied for a long time. You often see people for the last time in your meetings, when you have seen them come to the penitent-form and this in spite of visiting them in their homes and making other efforts to help them. .... And yet we have seen results of our work so beautiful and so glorious that the tenth part of it would be quite enough to recompense us for all our hardships, efforts and sacrifices.

Among the "glorious results" was the conversion at Akureyri of a sea captain and all the members of his crew. There was then at Reykjavik a little brass band comprised entirely of women, with the Staff-Captain as the bandmaster.

CHAPTER EIGHT

FINLAND

Although Finland experienced a political explosion in the summer of 1904, during which the Russian Governor-General was assassinated, The Salvation Army remained uninjured, a splendid tribute to its constant and single-eyed devotion to God and the people. The annual Congress meetings were conducted soon afterward in Helsingfors (Helsinki) by Commissioner Railton, and in these two officers were dedicated to commence Finnish work within the Arctic Circle. The first officer to leave Finland for the missionary field was Captain Hanna Heinonen, who went to India in 1905.

Colonel (later Commissioner) and Mrs Johan Ögrim were then in command, they being succeeded in 1906 by Lieutenant-Colonel (later Commissioner) and Mrs William H. Howard. Colonel Ögrim divided the country into three districts and a division, and appointed leaders for each. Open-air gatherings were permitted for the first time in 1905, a demonstration taking place during the summer in Kaisaniemi, a park in the centre of the capital. A year later full permission was granted the Army for both the holding of open-air meetings and marching through the streets in almost every town in the country, thus ushering in a new era.

That the excellent work the Army was doing was winning new friends every day was also evidenced in that Lieutenant-Colonel Howard and his secretary were provided with free passes on the State Railway, so that the most distant corps could be visited with the minimum of expense. Both Lieutenant-Colonel and Mrs Howard visited the two corps situated beyond the Arctic Circle, the most northerly being

Kittila, some 200 miles from the railway. To reach it eight days were spent on the road in an open cart. The State church at Tammerfors was placed at the disposal of the Army for a Divisional Congress in 1909, this being the first time a Lutheran building had been used by Salvationists in Finland.

When, at Christmas-tide 1910, some provincial police-officers hesitated about permitting Salvationists to set up their collecting-pots in the streets—in aid of the funds for helping the poor—without a special edict from the Governor-General, an officer from Headquarters called upon His Excellency at his private residence. The Governor-General, dispensing with form and ceremony, at once saw the officer, listened to his request and then immediately ordered messages to be sent to all provincial governors. An hour later corps officers in many towns were surprised by a visit from local officials who came to apprise them of the Governor-General's instructions that they were to " hang out their Christmas collecting-pots."

Remarkable advances were noted during the stay of the Howards. The Men's Social Work was founded by the opening of the first shelter [1] in Helsinki in 1907, when also the first Summer Colony was instituted and the first children's home opened. Within two years of the General's visit in 1909 [2] officership had improved by 20 per cent, soldiership by $12\frac{1}{2}$ per cent and local officership by 40 per cent, while the number of bandsmen had doubled, as had both the numbers on the young people's roll and the attendances. Corps income had increased by 20 per cent, as had the soldiers' cartridges.[3] Attendances at meetings were 25 per cent higher.

Colonel (later Commissioner) and Mrs Karl Larsson, of

[1] *The History of The Salvation Army*, vol. iii, p. 117
[2] p. 149
[3] *The History of The Salvation Army*, vol, ii, p. 82

Sweden, were appointed to the command of Finland in 1912. Some little time later, while the Territorial Commander was away on an extensive tour, a couple of policemen called at the quarters after dark, demanded entrance and made a systematic search, confiscating letters, documents and copies of the *War Cry*. At midnight the police forced Mrs Larsson to accompany them to Headquarters, where a similar search was made, various papers seized and the door sealed. It was several days before the Colonel and his staff were permitted to enter their Headquarters again, but some months elapsed before a caller arrived to hand over two devotional books which had been taken. All the other material had been burned by order of the police.

At the end of 1913 there were eighty corps in Finland, 300 officers and fifty-two candidates for the next session of cadets. In one town the police-master kept a grace-before-meat box[1] in his office and demanded an extra charge of 25 penni (twopence) for the Army's work from every man sentenced for drunkenness. It did not take long to fill !

CHAPTER NINE

BELGIUM

One of the most densely populated countries in the world, Belgium crowded 7,000,000 people into its 11,000 square miles at the time this volume opens. The Roman Catholic Church was more vigorous then, perhaps, than in any other country of Europe, and there were more public-houses in proportion to the number of residential houses than in any other Continental country. The sanctity of marriage was

[1] *A specially-designed collecting box usually placed on the dinner table.*

The coloured frontispiece of the illustrated supplement to *Le Petit Journal*, showing an attack made upon the Armée du Salut in the streets of Paris

A reduced facsimile of the front page of the first issue of an eight-paged periodical printed in Russia and published in St Petersburg

An automatic machine which produced a glassful of hot milk. It was presented to the Army by its Swedish inventor for the use of the poor of Stockholm in 1906

Taken at Alton, Hampshire, this photograph gives an idea of the great crowds that used to gather to hear William Booth during his Motor Crusades throughout the British Territory

but lightly esteemed by many, so that often the legalizing of their union was one of the first duties of those who sought salvation, and in 1905 whole families were being converted in Army meetings, as also were a number of anarchists. A man charged with murder in 1900, and discharged through lack of evidence, was among the converts, and immediately gave himself up to the police, confessing that he had indeed committed the crime.

Brigadier (later Lieutenant-Colonel) and Mrs Fritz Malan had the direct charge of forty officers in twenty-five corps and outposts, a rescue home for women and *hôtelleries* for both men and women, but Commissioner Cosandey was the territorial leader of the Army's operations in Belgium, France and Italy also being under his command. Spiritual work was then, and always has been, hard going in Belgium. Although the Salvationists had perfect freedom at the beginning of the century and full co-operation from the police, the forces of bigotry, anarchy, atheism and indifference to religion were rife. Here one met also with the rankest superstition, the blankest ignorance and the prevalence of drunkenness and vice.

The work in Brussels was greatly hampered by the division of tongues, the majority of meetings having to be conducted in French, even in entirely Flemish parts of the city. One might address a man in French but, although he understood every word, he would not deign to reply until spoken to in his own tongue. There was no love lost between the French and the Flemish population, and although meetings were conducted in Flemish by Dutch officers stationed in Antwerp and Ostend, their presence was not really appreciated. French, Dutch and English copies of the *War Cry* were sold in Antwerp. Unlike the procedure in most countries, officers and soldiers held open-air meetings *following* the Sunday-morning meeting, and then visited the public-houses with the *War Cry*. This arrangement proved most effective throughout the country.

"The way in which a corps is opened is interesting," wrote Lieutenant-Colonel (later Commissioner) Mildred Duff. "We take a small house—a little two-storied affair—renting it by the month. Meetings are held in the largest room. As the work prospers we move out at the end of the month into a larger house and so on." Those who became Salvationists were generally outstandingly enthusiastic. For instance, a Salvationist shopkeeper with two establishments wished all his serving assistants to wear uniform, and requested that his twelve travellers should do likewise on their rounds.

Brigadier David Miche was the provincial officer for Belgium from 1905 to 1911, and Brigadier Constant Jean-monod from 1912 to the outbreak of the First World War.

CHAPTER TEN

SOUTH AMERICA

ARGENTINA

Writing in *All the World* for April 1905, the Rev. A Stuart Pennington, Rector of the English College, Buenos Aires, pays tribute to the Army :

In the whole country there are forty-five officers of various nationalities. Over these is Brigadier [later Colonel] Maidment,[1] a cheerful, active and intelligent commander. . . . One great secret of the Army's influence is the methodical, business-like administration which characterizes its every department, and

[1] p. 101

gives confidence to those from whom it asks for means to carry on its work.

At the Congress conducted in April by Brigadier Frank Smith,[1] more than fifty officers were present, they being drawn from many nations—Swiss, German, Belgian, Scandinavian, Spanish, North American and British. Although the Argentinian Republic had been in a " stage of siege " and the cities had been under certain restrictive regulations, one of which was the prohibition of outdoor assembly, the Army had permission to hold its open-air meetings. Brigadier Smith visited all the corps and outposts. In some places as many as 1,000 people were assembled for his meetings.

1907 was a good year for spiritual results from seed sown in the rocky soil of this country, for nearly six hundred people professed conversion in the Argentine and Uruguay, including eighty-six seamen. Brigadier (later Lieutenant-Colonel) and Mrs William Bonnett were the officers-in-charge.

" The South American Territory," said Commissioner Ulysse Cosandey, who was appointed in 1909 to the command of an area comprising eventually Argentina, Uruguay, Chile, Paraguay and Peru, " with its vast distances, its manifold perplexities, its financial difficulties, and, above all, its lack of officers, is a problem indeed to solve." And at that time Great Britain had more than £450,000,000 sterling invested in Argentina, and Germany was interested to the tune of £175,000,000. In the following year the Commissioner prospected in Bolivia.

Certain officers of an adventurous disposition were appointed as outriders in Argentina and Uruguay, their duty being to visit *estancias* (ranches), which they did, travelling many miles by boat, train, bicycle and on horseback, often having to wade through swiftly rushing rivers and find their way across wide stretches of country as best they could.

[1] *The History of The Salvation Army*, vol. iv, p. 372

Sometimes they would be away from headquarters for as long as three months at a time. Many of the *estancias* belonged to Britishers.

A notable venture during this period was the opening of a tramps' and beggars' home in Buenos Aires, in 1910, when the Army was specially empowered by the authorities to clear the streets of such people for the celebration of Argentina's centenary as an independent republic, with many visitors attending from overseas. The first building erected by the Army in Buenos Aires was opened in 1911 as a night shelter for men, in the Calle Copahué, the Municipal Band playing outside the shelter at the opening ceremony.

Colonel (later Commissioner and Chief of the Staff) Henry W. Mapp, then the Territorial Commander, conducted the Congress in 1913, during which he was invited to the house of the Vice-President of the Republic, who evidenced a keen knowledge of the Army's efforts. The entire territory of South America then comprised but 103 officers, 38 corps and outposts, 57 local officers and 14 social institutions.

Lieutenant-Colonel (later Lieutenant-Commissioner) William B. Palmer was appointed Chief Secretary in March 1912 and was virtually in charge of the territory until the arrival of the new Territorial Commander, Colonel Mapp, toward the end of that year. When the Colonel left in 1914 his Chief Secretary was appointed to succeed him. Colonel Palmer's term as Territorial Commander covered eight of the ten years he spent in South America.

URUGUAY

When Brigadier Frank Smith had conducted the 1905 Congress in Argentina he visited all the corps and outposts in

Uruguay, where he was sympathetically received by the Prime Minister, who, he discovered, knew a good deal about the Army.

Adjutant David Thomas, a former Welsh sailor, was the divisional officer for the country in 1909. He had four corps and five outposts under his supervision, in addition to the seamen's home at Montevideo, where his headquarters were situated and where he had been converted some years before.

At Salto, the second largest city of Uruguay and the centre of learning and culture, Dr Asdrúbal Delgardo, a distinguished lawyer, and other friends bought and gave to the Army in 1911 a piece of land, 1,000 square metres in extent, for the erection of a citadel and officers' quarters. In connection with this corps there was a splendid outpost at San Eugenio, a day's journey away by train and on the Brazilian frontier. Here Envoy Henry Hollidge, manager of the railway engineering works, and his wife had begun meetings in their own home. Among their several converts were some from Brazil.[1] When, as Territorial Commander, Commissioner Cosandey visited Salto in 1910, the finest hall in the city was placed at his disposal, the regimental band played selections at the entrance and rockets were fired to announce the meeting.

PARAGUAY

Salvation Army operations in Paraguay were commenced at the beginning of 1910 by Adjutant Thomas Frisch, a native of Uruguay who had married an Englishwoman. His first meetings were held in a hall in Asunción, the capital ; the population was then nearly four million scattered over an area of some 142,000 square miles. Almost immediately

[1] p. 12

upon his arrival he was received by the President of the Republic, who expressed himself in kindly terms concerning the Army. Later in the year His Excellency gave audience to Commissioner Ulysse Cosandey, the Territorial Commander.

By 1912 another corps had been opened at Villa Rica, and a fruit farm purchased in the vicinity, this to rehabilitate the wrecks of humanity who came nightly to the shelter for the homeless. Schools, a hotel and a crèche were also opened. At Sapucay were two aged saints who had belonged to the Army and had known the General forty years before in London.

During the revolution in February and March 1912, Staff-Captain Frisch was asked by the White Cross Society to go as an assistant doctor with the first expedition it was sending to the north. The Staff-Captain had had great experience in similar work in the Uruguayan Revolution of 1904, so left within three hours with Lieutenant Eloisa Velasco and another young woman who took over the nursing of the wounded. Later the Staff-Captain was placed in charge of a first-aid station in Asunción.

CHILE

From time to time pressing calls came to the Army to begin work in the Republic of Chile, and Brigadier (later Lieutenant-Colonel) and Mrs William T. Bonnett proceeded there from the Argentine, in September 1909, being presented with a flag for the use of the first corps by Commissioner Cosandey, Territorial Commander for South America. Previously copies of the *War Cry* in French, Spanish and English had been despatched to people living in Iquique, and a British Vice-Consul had made an offer of some premises in which meetings could be held, conveying to Headquarters the interesting news that " already there is a Salvationist here who was converted under General Booth more than forty-five years ago."

On the day that the pioneer party landed in Santiago an important meeting had been organized by the archbishop of that city with a view to combating drunkenness. All the prominent citizens had been invited to the meeting, among them Senator Walker Martinez, formerly the Chilean Minister in Washington. The senator, who had not the slightest idea that the Salvationists had actually arrived in the city, spoke of the great and effective work accomplished by The Salvation Army and of what he had himself seen in the U.S.A., particularly among drunkards. The very next day, to his intense surprise, he received a visit from Brigadier Bonnett. The first meeting was held in the open air in Plaza Echaurren, Valparaiso, on 26 November.

The first corps was opened at Santiago, the capital, with its half a million inhabitants, on the following day, the meetings being held in a renovated wine depository. The Brigadier, assisted by Mrs Bonnett, Captain D. Arn and Lieutenant Danielson, conducted a five weeks' special campaign, and within a short space of time thirty-three recruits were enrolled and six companies of juniors were in operation. The first public meeting in Chile created considerable interest and twenty-two seekers knelt at the Mercy Seat. Later the Brigadier visited Valparaiso accompanied by two newly arrived officers and Brother J. H. Honeyman, the English Salvationist. Here the Brigadier addressed a congregation of more than 500 at the invitation of the Rev. Dr Hoover.

The first Chilean Congress, lasting five days, was held in Santiago to celebrate the second anniversary of the commencement of the work, it being conducted by Commissioner Cosandey. Twenty-two officers, local officers and cadets were present and 150 soldiers. Nearly 1,000 people attended a lecture in the Salon de Honor of the Chilean University and Dr Fernandez Peña, President of the National Association for Education, presided. Also during the Congress the Commissioner and Brigadier Bonnett were presented to His Excellency the President of the Republic, Senor Barros Luco, at Government House. "For enthusiasm and religious spirit," said the Commissioner, " I know of no Latin nation that can beat the Chileans."

A new corps was opened at Concepción, an important commercial centre, on 11 December 1911. The newspapers were friendly and the following appeared in *El Mercurio*, one of the leading dailies :

During these days of the National Holidays we have seen passing along the streets, walks, and especially the places where the masses congregate, the members of The Salvation Army, with that faith and patience which is characteristic of the Apostles. . . . We cannot deny the fact that a work of morality and social uplifting is being accomplished.

La Union, while making some unfavourable comments respecting the meetings, said :

We must be frank: we sincerely applaud the campaign against drink which General Booth's disciples are realizing. They are doing a humanitarian work and supply a natural need. They deserve applause, which we do not deny them.

Two halls were then being rented in the capital and a number of open-air meetings had been held with permission from the authorities, but full liberty for open-air work had not been granted. 420 seekers had been registered and 131 had become soldiers. The official organ, *El Cruzado*, was being sold. A special " anti-alcohol " meeting was held in the Municipal Theatre in San Fernando, over which Dr Peña presided, the Municipal Band playing in the public square to attract people to the gathering. At another such meeting held in a school, some of the students provided an orchestra of twenty-one instruments, and 600 working men were present.

During his visit to Santiago in 1914, Colonel (later Commissioner and Chief of the Staff) Henry W. Mapp was invited to address an English congregation in the Union Church. Ex-President Theodore Roosevelt of the United States was present—he was touring the country at the time —and expressed to the Colonel his pleasure at seeing a Salvation Army officer occupying the pulpit. The Colonel was also received in audience by the President of the Republic, who promised his support.

PERU

Adjutant and Mrs David Thomas, with Lieutenant Zacarias Ribeiro, a Uruguayan, pioneered Salvation Army work in Peru, the " Land of the Incas," in the spring of 1910, commencing at the Port of Callao, half an hour's tram-ride from Lima, the capital. On their arrival the pioneer party was received in the home of Brother and Sister Mrs Eduardo Palací. Within a month a suitable hall was secured by Adjutant Thomas in one of the poorest districts of the town. At the opening, four pastors of different churches were present. Brother Palací was commissioned the first Corps Sergeant-Major and Mrs Palací the first Corps Secretary. Formerly an officer in the West Indies, Brother Palací re-entered the work and eventually became a Lieutenant-Colonel and Literary Secretary for South America.

The first open-air meeting was held in Lima at the end of August, and was the first ever to be conducted in the Republic by Protestants. This was considered to be a great victory, for religious liberty, apart from Roman Catholicism, did not exist. The Salvationists, however, had to refrain from praying in public—this would have been a contravention of the law—both in the open air and in the meetings held in the Municipal Theatre lent to the Army free of charge during the month's visit of the Territorial Commander, Commissioner Cosandey, with whom was Colonel (later Commissioner) Arthur Bates, the Auditor-General, from International Headquarters. The President of the Republic granted the Commissioner and the Colonel an interview, and the Army's incoming was enthusiastically welcomed in the columns of all the newspapers of the capital. *Variedades*, the most important weekly review in the country, dedicated several of its pages to the Army and included photographs. The Commissioner conducted meetings in Cerro de Pasco, one of the oldest cities of South America and rightly termed the City of the Clouds, as it is more than 14,000 feet above sea level and to be reached only after scaling the summit of a mountain 17,500 feet above sea-level.

Within the first six months a corps of about thirty soldiers was established, a number of recruits were raised and permission was given for the Staff-Captain to visit both men and women prisoners in the ancient Casamatas Prison in Callao.

Colonel (later Commissioner and Chief of Staff) Mapp saw the President of the Republic in 1914. His Excellency was anxious that the Army should take up social work. In that same year Parliament passed a Bill in favour of religious liberty to all denominations.

CHAPTER ELEVEN

RHODESIA

Lieutenant-Colonel Johnston, better known by his Indian name of Jeya Kodi, was appointed in September 1904 to direct work in Central Africa, organizing his operations from Salisbury, Mashonaland (Rhodesia), with the oversight of both that country and Matabeleland, the centre of which is Bulawayo. Staff-Captain and Mrs Bradley were then still building up the work on its enduring foundation, although it was slow and tedious.

The Mashona [wrote Lieutenant-Colonel (later Commissioner) Francis W. Pearce in 1906] is not naturally religious ; he is more of a heathen than most of the tribes. His life is very largely made up of eating, drinking, fighting, and—*begging* ; for the Mashonas are inveterate beggars. " What will you pay me if I get converted ? " is the extraordinary question often asked. It has meant no small amount of labour and patient toil to teach them that not only will they receive nothing for getting converted, but that, if they have the means, they are in duty bound to pay something for the support of the work.

An article in the March 1905 issue of *All the World* gives further particulars regarding the murder of Captain Edward Cass[1] :

His death was doubtless due to the restless tide of natives who swept in from other districts. Those who knew him loved him, and his sudden end was much lamented. When the living wave had spent itself and venturesome horsemen picked their way gingerly along the track the Salvationists and their friends had journeyed, they found the whitened bones of those who had fallen by the way. They also found the tunic and brass S's of

[1] *The History of The Salvation Army*, vol. iv, p. 62

the brave Captain. So were his remains discovered and laid to rest in the soil which he had consecrated with his blood.

An Anglican priest, the Rev. Douglas R. Pelley, conducted the funeral service when the bones were discovered some six months after the shooting.

Mashonaland's first cadet, whose surname was Shilling, walked all the way to the native training institution at Emlungisweni, a distance of 1,500 miles. Fifteen new cadets were publicly received during Acting-Commissioner Richards' visit in the summer of 1905. He was the first Territorial Commander to visit the country and to conduct a campaign. There was at that time no literature in the Mashona language except the Gospels of Matthew and Mark, and consequently no books for the school work at the Pearson Settlement,[1] although Staff-Captain Bradley, with great labour, made a grammar for himself on the basis of a Zulu text-book.

William Booth was " much exercised about Rhodesia " when writing to his Chief of Staff on 27 November 1905 :

These pages of report you have sent me don't say much. Still I can see that with a million or two sterling you might make the *New World* about which I dream day and night. Shall I go and see for myself ? I could start in January.

Then followed a Postscript which was to have poignant repercussions : " Nicol : He is a dear fellow. *There is only one such !!!* "

William Booth was never to visit Rhodesia.

[1] *The History of The Salvation Army*, vol. iv, p. 60

CHAPTER TWELVE

INDONESIA

Sent from International Headquarters in 1903 to inspect the work in Java, Colonel (later Commissioner) Isaac Unsworth wrote his reminiscences in an article published in *All the World* in 1911, and thus described his visit to a Chinese corps in Batavia (now Djakarta) :

Their soldiers turn up to the meeting as though they had just been pushed off an ironing board of a first-class laundry. Each man was dressed in snow-white duck, and some of them were great dandies in their way. Their golden buttons were made of English sovereigns.

The Colonel was introduced to a lady of rank whose brother was a man of great influence in the city of Batavia. She was Sergeant Toroet, of Semarang corps, and on her jacket, made of fine green silk, richly brocaded, she had worked in red silk the words " Bala Keselamatan " (Salvation Army), but her S's were of solid gold. It appears that her brother, shocked when he saw her brass S's, had them removed by a servant and found a goldsmith who quickly made replicas in the finer metal. The Sergeant was unaware of the fact that she was the only Salvationist in the whole world who wore S's made of gold. Another Salvationist the Colonel met in Semarang was the wife of the leading Chinese official and the richest merchant of the city. She had been converted many years before as the result of hearing the Army drum on the march, and had ordered her coachman to drive her to the hall, where she was the first at the penitent form. On this visit Colonel Unsworth was received by the Governor-

General at his palace in Buitenzorg, and given a free pass over the Government railways.

For some years under the control of the Australasian territory, Java was constituted an independent territory, directly under the supervision of International Headquarters, in September 1905, Brigadier (later Colonel) Peter D. van Rossum being placed in command. During a visit to England in July 1906 the Brigadier reported that many Dutch soldiers, who were serving voluntarily in Java, had been converted in the Army's military home in Semarang and at the corps in Batavia. These men, on their own initiative, had rented a house in Batavia and turned it into a military home. In this same year the Government decided to send to every corps officer a gratuitous supply of medicines and appliances for treating the sick, besides books and other requirements—with the exception of furniture—needed in the native schools connected with corps throughout ther island.

Commissioner Railton, who had visited Java in 1905, returned two years later. He found twenty-two officers on his first visit and fifty-two on his second. The women officers, from the wife of the Territorial Commander, Mrs Lieutenant-Colonel van Rossum, downwards, all went barefoot and dressed in Javanese uniform when out of town. The whole country was organized under national authorities, who had to be and remain Mohammedans, so that the difficulty of getting converts can be imagined. Java was at that time one of the most difficult missionary fields in the world.

The country itself [said the Commissioner] is paradisical. [But] the people seem no less cultured, in a way, than their rice-fields, for whatever else they may or may not know, they have been trained to such a humble and submissive attitude towards the white man that numbers will not even dare show themselves to one who meets them away in a countryside, but will stand almost hidden behind their bullock or cart till the stranger has passed by . . . we have yet to encounter in Java anything like serious opposition to any of our efforts, yet the whole story of our work up to the present is one filled with toil and suffering that cannot be represented by any adequate result.

At Kajen, in the heart of the *desa-dom*, or native villages, Captain Barrett, an Australian officer, was the only white person in the district, and was considered so important that every night at eight o'clock the *wedono*, the highest local government official, dispatched a policeman to sit in her quarters and guard her till daylight !

Toward the latter end of 1909 Colonel Gerrit J. Govaars was appointed to succeed Lieutenant-Colonel van Rossum, who endured much physical weakness during his command. Before he left Java the Governor-General expressed himself as delighted with the gratifying result of the labours of the Army on behalf of some of the 12,000 lepers on the island.[1] A brass band was formed entirely of lepers in the Army settlement at Pelantungan, which was under the charge of Staff-Captain and Mrs Scheffer. Among the many important features of this picturesque settlement, 3,000 feet above sea-level, were the hot sulphur springs and baths.

The Army took up the challenge of educating the young, and at Kedoeng Pani, formerly a home of rest, Adjutant and Mrs Thompson were appointed to the oversight of the first day school. Although wages in many cases amounted to not more than 5d. a day, a father was willing from this small sum to contribute 5d. a month toward the education of his sons ; but many of the scholars paid nothing. So impressed was the Sultan of Solo, one of the native rulers, by the Army's work in instructing the youth of the island, that he sent five young men to be trained in Army methods and usages, and met the whole cost of their maintenance. Colonel Govaars

[1] *The History of The Salvation Army*, vol. iii, p. 279

and Major and Mrs Clifford were provided with free passes on all the State lines in Java.

The *War Cry* stated in its 1 January 1910 issue that, during the previous nine months, Captain (later Lieutenant-Colonel) Dr Wille,[1] who was responsible for the Army's extensive medical work in Semarang, had given no fewer than 16,000 consultations to patients and had performed more than 500 operations, 150 of which either restored sight to the blind or prevented blindness. Among the Captain's patients were the daughter of an admiral, a native prisoner, who was in chains and wore a heavy iron ring around his neck, and the son of a sultan who came to the hospital wearing a golden crown in which sparkled a hundred diamonds. The Captain was looked upon as the most efficient eye specialist in the Dutch East Indies. Lieutenant-Colonel (later Commissioner) de Groot, who was appointed to the command of the work in Indonesia in 1913, was responsible for gathering the necessary amount, £2,500, to establish the William Booth Memorial Eye Hospital at Semarang.[2]

At the end of 1910 the unusual spectacle was witnessed in the Dutch Parliament in Amsterdam of the Colonial Secretary reading the Army's Articles of War. Objection had been taken to the action of the Governor-General of Java in issuing a notification that Javanese Salvationists would be legally recognized as Christians. The objector contended that, as they were not baptized, there was no guarantee that they were really converted from heathenism to Christianity ; whereupon the Colonial Secretary proceeded to read the Articles of War, at the close of which he asked, with emphasis : "Would anyone be bold enough to say that persons who had to accept those Articles were not to be recognized as Christians ?"

[1] p. 30
[2] *The History of The Salvation Army*, vol. iii, p. 282

The Javanese were great borrowers, and in the village of Rogomoeljo the Dutch officer in charge of the corps, Ensign Everdina Wunderink, realized that the simple peasantry were being swindled right and left by Chinese money-lenders, who extorted as much as 240 per cent for their loans. She thereupon resolved to checkmate their activities. With a capital of only 25 guilder she commenced as a people's banker, charging only 1 per cent on monthly transactions and 3 per cent on loans for three months and upwards. She loaned considerable sums eventually and got all her money back. The changed condition of the village was one result of dominating this little Javanese money market. So greatly appreciative of the services of the Ensign were the villagers that they wanted to make her the " headman." The village was originally called Rogobojo, " a place of trouble," but so changed did it become through the influence of the Ensign and her Lieutenant that it was altered to Rogomoeljo, " a place of goodness."

On 15 September 1913 Ensigns Charles Jensen and Hendrik Loois pioneered the work in Central Celebes, and a party of nine Swedish, four Dutch, four Norwegian, two Finnish and two Danish officers arrived in Batavia. On that same day, and for the first time in the city's history, a Salvation Army procession marched through the streets. When the party arrived at Bandung the brass band of the military garrison greeted it at the railway station. This band also supplied the accompaniment to the congregational singing at the welcome meeting in the Concordia Hall.

A military home was opened in 1909 in Kotaradja, at the northern point of the Island of Sumatra, but was closed after a few years. Lieutenant de Stigter was " splendidly received " by all classes when collecting for the Self-Denial Appeal in 1910, and Colonel Govaars was urged by every post to send officers to establish the work properly.

The first officers arrived on the east coast on 7 March 1914 and, in accordance with a contract made with the Health Department, took over, on 1 April, the management of the Pulau si Tjanang Leper Colony, situated near the port of Belawan, seventeen miles from the city of Medan. In this same year a piece of land, on which to build a children's home, was given to the Army, for a period of fifty years, by the Deli Maatschappij, which owned all the tobacco estates in East Sumatra.

CHAPTER THIRTEEN

JAPAN

The Russo-Japanese War of 1904–5 gave The Salvation Army opportunity to serve the nationals of both countries. Regular hospital visitation was undertaken among the tens of thousands of wounded in Tokyo and other towns throughout Japan, this being organized by the Territorial Commander, Colonel (later Commissioner) Henry Bullard. Russian prisoners at Nararshino and Sendai, prior to their departure for home, were addressed by Major Eriksen, a Dane, who was translated into Japanese by Ensign Yamada and from Japanese to Russian by a Russian priest. The Major had an hour's talk with General Liaponnov about the Army and later took breakfast with him. The general thought The Salvation Army was the very thing needed in Russia.[1] Both Commissioner Railton, who was visiting the country, and Colonel Bullard addressed prisoners at Nagoya, Railton speaking in German and being translated by a Russian soldier.

[1] p. 72

When the war ended in September 1905 William Booth, quick to gauge the needs of individuals and nations, made an appeal for the sum of £5,000 as a peace offering, to be expended on the extension of the Army's work in Japan, which country had emerged astonishingly as one of the great powers of the world.

Despite war conditions the circulation of *Toki-no-Koe* (*The War Cry*) reached more than 10,000 copies fortnightly, and what this meant may be judged from the fact that the usual circulation of religious papers was from 600 to 1,500 copies per issue. The reason for its popularity was because its letterpress was written in such an easy colloquial style, as compared with many other religious books and publications, which were produced in the ancient, classical language, cold and difficult for ordinary people to understand. Missionaries of other denominations used *Toki-no-Koe* as a " reader " when learning the language. Staff-Captain (later Commissioner) Gunpei Yamamuro [1] was still the editor.

By this time, within nine years of its commencement, the Army was kindly considered by the Government, which placed no restrictions upon either its financial or its evangelistic efforts ; indeed, prison officials gave the Army facilities not even accorded it in England. Japan was definitely ahead of many European countries in respect of the liberties she accorded the Army in its open-air work. During his visit Commissioner Railton, who was conducting a six months' tour of enquiry and inspection in the Far East, reported that hundreds of university students were attending the week-day meetings in Tokyo and seeking information regarding salvation at the penitent form ; subsequently students' homes were instituted. In this year, 1905, *Shikan Zasshi* (*The Field Officer*) was issued.

In 1906 *Shin-Koron*, a magazine for progressive Buddhists,

[1] *The History of The Salvation Army*, vol. iv, p. 69

referring to the zeal of Salvationists in the country, said : " What could not Buddhism do if we could only get going on these lines." In this same year a Japanese " life " of the General was published in Tokyo, and a general history of The Salvation Army was translated into the vernacular by Major Yamamuro, the first edition being sold out in a very short time.

A new training home was opened in Tokyo in June 1906 and the first public commissioning of cadets took place on 24 January 1907. The largest batch of cadets, thirty-seven in number, were commissioned in 1913, consequently nine new corps were enabled to be opened, the most in one year.

The Army's position in Japan was potentially strong, but numerically weak. It was still in the embryonic stage, and the work was crippled for want of leaders and money to erect suitable halls. Its influence, however, was immense, disproportionate actually to its numerical strength, the authorities recognizing the soundness of its social principles and many leading statesmen and soldiers admiring the Army's system of government.

One of the first results of the General's stay in Japan in the spring of 1907 [1] was his decision to form a league for the protection of Oriental women at home and abroad. He also arranged for several Japanese women officers to leave almost at once for London, where they studied the Army's methods on behalf of wronged women and girls. The work of rescuing girls placed in grave moral danger [2] continued all the time, particularly in the famine district of Northern Japan, some 150 being brought from their poverty-stricken surroundings and placed in good situations in the capital. One such girl, out of gratitude for what the Army had done for her, commenced a Sunday-school among the children of

[1] p. 155
[2] *The History of The Salvation Army*, vol. iii, p. 197

the district in which she lived, and in which the Army was not at work. Upward of 200 children were gathered together each week.

Lieutenant-Colonel (later Colonel) Mary Tait conducted a six months' campaign in Japan following the General's visit, which she discovered had produced an immediate and powerful impetus to soul-saving work. The Army's first property to be acquired in Japan, a hall at Yokkaichi, was presented by a convert, Envoy Hattori San, a chemist and postmaster, in 1908. In the July of that year Colonel (later Commissioner) and Mrs Henry C. Hodder were appointed to follow Commissioner and Mrs Thomas Estill in the leadership.

During his visit to London in 1909 Brigadier Yamamuro told of his having recently conducted the marriage ceremony of an ex-criminal who was formerly an inmate of the Army's prison-gate home. This man had murdered five people before he was thirteen years of age. After serving many years in prison he was released. The Army took charge of him, and as a result he became converted. Commissioner (later General) Edward J. Higgins paid his second visit to Japan in December 1909. So great was the success of *The Common People's Gospel*,[1] a simple story of the life and teaching of Jesus written in everyday language by Brigadier Yamamuro, that the thirteenth edition, consisting of 10,000 copies, was issued in May 1910. It has now sold more than half a million copies. The first Japanese Brass Band was formed in 1909.

Commissioner Hodder, interviewed during his visit to London in 1911, stated that

the Japanese are a sober, dignified and courteous people. A drunken man is a rare sight and I have never yet seen a drunken woman. It follows naturally that sordid poverty and misery,

[1] *The History of The Salvation Army*, vol. iv, p. 70

as such you and I would find in most of the slums of the large cities in this country, are almost unknown in Japan. Poverty and misery, of course, there are, but they are kept pretty well out of sight.

Smoking was forbidden by law to all under twenty years of age. The Japanese had a natural aversion to the idea of being "missioned" by foreigners, but nevertheless, during Lieutenant-Colonel (later Colonel) John Roberts's nine months' campaign in 1911, more than 1,000 seekers were recorded. Sunday was not recognized, consequently no meetings were held during the daytime, but evening gatherings often continued until long after midnight.

When Commissioner and Mrs Henry W. Mapp were appointed to Japan in 1914 more than seventy corps and outposts were in operation as against only twenty-six in 1908. Japan's first contribution to the missionary field was made in 1914, when Captain and Mrs Ishijima were appointed to Korea. Mrs Ishijima was a niece of Lieutenant-Colonel Yamamuro, the Chief Secretary.

CHAPTER FOURTEEN

WEST AFRICA

An article in *All the World* for June 1905, and written by Commissioner Railton, partly solves the mystery [1] regarding what purported to be the presence of The Salvation Army in West Africa at that time. He says :

So great has been the appreciation of the Army by all the West Africans who have seen it in visiting this or any other country, that they have spread its fame along the coast-line of two thousand

[1] *The History of The Salvation Army*, vol. iv, p. 74

miles ; and the opinion of all Africans with whom I spoke there, from missionaries to publicans, was alike favourable to our coming. Two African hotel-keepers offered me, and to any other officers, free and liberal hospitality. In several cases, after years of fruitless writing here, the people have taken our name, and are trying to do what they can to be worthy of it. One such " Salvation Army," of Creek Town, founded by the first convert from heathendom, and afterwards first native minister of the Eka nation, had, I found, amongst its rules besides one against intoxicating drinks, the following two :

> The Salvation Army wishes you to take good care of yourself, so that wherever you stand to proclaim Christianity nobody can reproach you. Wherever you go—whether farmer, trader, or what—there you must preach the Gospel. You will be suspended if you are not agreeable to obey orders for the honour of God and the good of the Society.

That Salvation Army, adds Railton, is already supporting some of their own men, who are carrying on missions in heathen towns.

What Railton did not know was, that early in the century a Cape Coast—a seaside town in Ghana—Methodist, visiting London and seeing the Army at work, returned to his own country and commenced an organization on similar lines, calling it " The Salvation Army Lodge." This " Army " was the first to use the drum in religious services in West Africa, and it has since become an integral feature of practically all the smaller denominations in the country. The Lodge had its own flag. Eventually, having no overseas contacts, it became merely a teetotal movement, with one or two branches, including that at Saltpond ; but after about ten years the majority of its members joined the Methodist Church and the Lodge faded out.

This information was obtained first hand by Colonel Haakon A. Dahlstrøm, the Territorial Commander for Nigeria, from a chief living in Akim Oda, who had been a member of the Lodge in his youth.

When the 1st Battalion of the West India Regiment went to Sierra Leone in 1906, some Naval and Military Leaguers, headed by Lance-Corporal Morrison, finding the Army almost unrepresented, commenced to hold meetings, with the result that a number of converts were made. Within twelve months the Salvationists had their own hall, but had to hire the Memorial Hall, the largest in Freetown, for the first anniversary celebrations, this hall being nearly filled. When the 1st Battalion left and the 2nd Battalion arrived, Sergeant J. F. Drayton, a coloured man from Barbadoes, took over and was the leader of a gratifying work in progress on the peninsula in 1910. Lance-Corporal W. R. King, who was recognized as the officer in command, was carrying on the work in 1914, and had a Sunday-night attendance of 200, and a good young people's corps.

CHAPTER FIFTEEN

RUSSIA

Bramwell Booth's chance encounter with W. T. Stead in a railway compartment in August 1908—the one on the way to Stockholm and the other to St Petersburg (Leningrad)— would, it was thought, be destined to live as one of the operating causes of the establishment of the Army's work within the Russian border. The Chief of the Staff, hearing that Mr Stead hoped to see M. Stolypin, the Russian Prime Minister, suggested to the editor of *The Review of Reviews* that he should broach the matter of the Army's advent into Russia.

Stead was fortunate in obtaining the interview he sought

and it was duly reported in four columns of *The Times*.[1] The Army's entering Russia was put to M. Stolypin, who asked whether the organization really did good work, if it meddled in politics and whether it could be relied upon not to inflame popular sentiment against non-Christians. Receiving satisfactory replies, M. Stolypin remarked that he saw no political reason why there should be any obstacle placed in the way of the coming of the Army into Russia. " It would at any rate interest the people," he said, " and might be useful. . . . But let me have a copy of their statutes, so that I can examine them before I give my final decision." A copy of The Salvation Army's statutes was submitted to M. Stolypin before the notes of the interview were authorized for publication. Commenting on this interview the General wrote in his journal :

This is itself important, but to have the open approval of the strongest, some say the only real strong public man in the Empire, and this chronicled in the leading newspapers of Europe, is something worthy of note.

According to the *War Cry* for 25 March 1905 Stead stated that

Verestchagin, the Russian painter, who went down with Admiral Makarov [during the Russo-Japanese War], told me that if once a bright, brotherly, social religion, such as he had seen at the Regent Hall of The Salvation Army, were to enter Russia, it would spread like a prairie fire.

Stead reiterated the story of this interview with Admiral Makarov in the August 1908 number of his *Review of Reviews*.

The *War Cry* for 15 August 1908 gave a whole page to Russia. " At last," said the sub-title, " the way is clear for the entrance of the Army " ; an appeal for immediate

[1] See Appendix A : " W. T. Stead's Interview with M. Stolypin regarding the Army opening up its work in Russia as recorded in *The Times*."

financial help was made for work in the Empire of Russia, which had "hitherto been practically a forbidden land to The Salvation Army." Many causes, it was thought, had contributed toward this agreeable change on the horizon of the Army's prospects—the general influence of the Army itself, reports of its progress, the General's world journeys and motor campaigns, accounts of which had appeared in the Russian press from time to time : Russian travellers had met Salvationists in different parts of the world, Russians in outposts of the Arctic borders of Norway, Sweden and Finland had come into touch with corps, Russian residents in Switzerland had examined the work, and scores of Russians had knelt at the penitent form in Paris. A friend of the late Tsar and a companion of the present Tsar had become a Salvationist in Paris and on her return to St Petersburg had testified to a spiritual change. It was reported that a Salvationist of Hull Icehouse corps, temporally falling out of employment, had obtained a berth as foreman on board a ship bound for Russia, and at Reval had contacted a Swedish evangelist. These two had secured a building, which was packed to hear the English Salvationist ; one person had travelled 100 miles to hear him speak and this man and twenty-three others had become converted. So effective was the seaman's testimony that immediately the meeting was over he was driven to a larger hall where no fewer than sixty seekers claimed salvation. Two further meetings were conducted by the Hull Salvationist and forty seekers were registered. In October 1908 it was reported that a young Russian, who was a Salvation Army Lieutenant in Germany, was recalled to his native land for military service : " Since his arrival there, he has conducted several meetings, at which more than sixty persons have professed conversion," said the *War Cry*.

Commissioner Railton, who had visited Russia accompanied by Major (later Colonel) Herbert J. Jackson in 1904, again visited the country in 1908, reconnoitring for two months and having " had more to do with titled people than in all my previous life." He conducted crowded meetings in the capital. Lieutenant-Colonel (later Commissioner and Chief of the Staff) Henry W. Mapp visited St Petersburg in October 1907, calling upon Baron Nicolay.

When, in March 1909, the General paid his first visit to Russia and spent two days in St Petersburg, he was received by the British Ambassador, Sir Arthur Nicholson. Then he drove to the Duma (Parliament), where he and his staff were given seats in the Diplomatic Circle. The General was welcomed by Baron Meyendorff, the Vice-President, the President having been hurriedly called to Moscow ; he also met Senator Miassoyedoff, whose daughter was an officer in Paris. Later William Booth delivered his first address in Russia in the home of General and Madame Sabouroff. Among the captivated audience was H.I.H. the Grand Duchess Constantini, an influential member of the Imperial family, with whom he conversed for an hour. Finally, after a visit to H.R.H. Princess Abamelek, the General drove to the Government offices where he saw the Minister of Finance, who was acting as Premier in the absence of M. Stolypin. Upon his return to London the General was received by the Russian Ambassador, Count Benckendorff.

A month later Lieutenant-Colonel Gerrit J. Govaars, of Holland, was selected by the General to prepare for the opening of the Army's work in St Petersburg, where he was most kindly received. Later still Colonel and Mrs Jens Povlsen lived and worked in the country, but despite all the high hopes of the General and his Chief of Staff the Council of Ministers decided in 1912 not to allow the Army to carry on its operations in Russia, and the Povlsens had to leave.

During the summer of 1913, however, the Army in

Finland, which became the foster-mother of work in Russia, took part in a hygienic exhibition held in St Petersburg and received a first prize for its exhibits. At this exhibition a leaflet, " What is The Salvation Army ? ", was widely distributed. Not being officially recognized in Russia, the Army's converts there were enrolled as soldiers of the Helsingfors 1 Corps. A monthly eight-page periodical called *Vjestnik Spasenija* (*The Salvation Messenger*), edited by Constantin Boije,[1] was printed in the Russian language. Though not officially an Army publication, it was entirely devoted to a description of the work in Finland and had a circulation of 8,000 copies. It was the publisher's vain hope that the paper would be widely spread and become a pioneer for the Army, permission having been given for it to be sold in the streets by Salvationists wearing red bands in their fur caps bearing the words " Salvation Messenger " instead of " The Salvation Army."

CHAPTER SIXTEEN

CHINA

In a letter written about 1887–8 from Chin-chu, China, describing a visit he had made to his missionary sister-in-law, Quintin Hogg [2] wrote :

After dinner we went into the drawing-room, had a little conversation, sang some English hymns, and wound up with prayers. I was anxious to see what hymns our Chinese guests would select, and perhaps it may be taken as a testimony in

[1] *The History of The Salvation Army*, vol. iv, p. 46
[2] Founder of The Polytechnic, Regent Street, London, W

favour of our friend, General Booth, that one of them turned to the Salvation Army Hymn Book and selected a hymn to the tune of "Annie Laurie." The words were full of meaning, sung in that heathen city, and as the dear old Scotch tune went up from that little room, I could see a tear gleaming in more than one eye.[1]

It might well be that these Chinese guests had become acquainted with Staff-Captain Bradley and Captain Bailey, whom Commissioner Booth-Tucker had sent to China to prospect in 1887.[2] Perhaps the first European Salvationist to visit China was Sister Elsie Patterson, of Christiania (Oslo) VIII, a servant in the family of the Consul for Norway and Sweden. She entered Chefoo with them in 1905 and remained there for five years. During the few years up to 1906 that the Army had been at work in Chinatown, San Francisco, and Pacific Grove, California, in the United States of America, more than 1,400 " Celestials," as the Chinese were then called, professed conversion, many of them afterward returning to their native land. There were also Chinese converts in Indonesia, Australia, the Hawaiian Islands and South Africa at that time.

Professor Fong Foo Sec, of Canton, left China in his youth to reside in California where, while a lunch-counter waiter, he was converted in a Salvation Army meeting. Eventually he became an officer, but feeling the call to benefit his fellow countrymen in the homeland by obtaining a thorough education, he spent eight years in study at the University where he graduated, afterward receiving his M.A. degree from Columbia University. At the time of the establishment of the Chinese Republic in 1913 he was a professor of languages.

On his way from London to Japan in the spring of 1906

[1] From *The Life of Quintin Hogg*
[2] *The History of The Salvation Army*, vol. iv, p. 77

Staff-Captain (later Major) W. H. Evans and members of his party conducted meetings in Shanghai. The projected visit, which never materialized, of the General to China while on his Far East Campaign was the occasion for Commissioner Railton to spend the Christmas of 1906 in Peking. He considered that the Army had there an infinitely better chance to become established than it had had even in England. When Staff-Captain (later Lieutenant-Colonel) Matilda Hatcher visited China in 1907 from Japan with a Japanese Lieutenant, she found the *War Cry* "lying about everywhere, certainly in most English houses." A Chinese woman brought her a picture of Mrs Booth, "who did so much for women," which she had cut out from an Army publication and carefully preserved.

Commissioner Higgins prospected in 1909, and in the latter part of that year cadets were commissioned and appointed to China, these including Nellie Harling (later Mrs Lieutenant-Colonel Charles S. Sylvester) who was the first woman-Lieutenant to be appointed, although the appointment was cancelled and she went to Korea instead. Colonel and Mrs Lindsay were appointed to the command of the first China Territory, to be established in Shantung, with headquarters at Chefoo, but nothing seems to have come of it.

Commissioner Lamb visited China in the summer of 1912 to investigate and report upon a native Christian movement desiring incorporation with the Army, its leaders having seen Salvationists at work in other parts of the East. "My visit to China did not make me desire to Christianize the 'Chinee,'" said the Commissioner. "On the other hand it was strongly borne in upon me that as soon as the message of 'Christ to the sinner' is brought home to his heart, the Chinaman will Christianize himself."

CHAPTER SEVENTEEN

SPAIN

On the eve of her wedding in 1906 it was stated in the daily Press in London that " by Princess Ena's special request King Alfonso will throw open Spain to the influence of The Salvation Army," but this must have been wishful thinking, for, after sixty years, Spain has not yet thrown open its doors to the organization.

THE PHILLIPINES

Brother Owen T. Quinn, of the New York 1 (U.S.A.) corps, having been sent to the Phillipines on government service in 1912, held Army meetings in the islands. The work was not officially inaugurated until 1937.

SINGAPORE

Although there were a few Salvationists, mainly Naval and Military Leaguers, in Singapore, the Army flag was not yet flying officially when Acting-Commissioner and Mrs Hoggard and a party of officers bound for Japan and Korea [1] arrived there in 1908. The Commissioner addressed the Leaguers in the hall in which they held their Sunday meetings.

[1] p. 1

CHAPTER EIGHTEEN

THE UNITED STATES OF AMERICA, MEXICO, THE HAWAIIAN ISLANDS AND ALASKA

The appointment in November 1904 of Field Commissioner Eva Booth, then in command of the Army's work in Canada, to succeed the widowed Commander Booth-Tucker and to take charge of operations in the United States, commenced a memorable era in that vast territory. An innovation was made in the parallel appointment of Commissioner George A. Kilbey as Deputy-Commander for the Western States, with his headquarters in Chicago. A few weeks later Eva wrote to Bramwell Booth describing the Army's Christmas effort in New York :

It is a stupendous affair—far greater in proportion and wider in influence than I had ever imagined. I suppose it is the mightiest thing of its kind on the face of the globe. . . . We gave away 5,500 baskets, and 3,000 sat down to a hot dinner at night. A free breakfast at the shelters provided for 1,000 more. Altogether 30,000 were fed on the one day in New York and 250,000 throughout the country. The papers here speak of it as the greatest Christian charity in the world. Then the abject poverty of the people was a revelation to me. I have seen nothing like it since leaving London ; in fact, I doubt whether London equals it in some respects. I personally gave away hundreds of the baskets, and the famished tattered specimens of humanity that came up for them were an eye-opener as to the nether world of the great city. Some of them were blind, some were lame and on crutches, some were so old they could hardly crawl, and nearly all of them looked starved. It was a bitter day, and yet those at the clothing stalls, where hundreds of bundles of cast-off apparel were thankfully received, told me that many of the women were clad but in a single garment. . . . At night the crowd stretched from 42nd Street to 47th. The police said they had never seen anything like it before.

In his *Soldiers without Swords*, Herbert A. Wisbey, Jr, describes Eva Booth as

striking in appearance, her bonnet covered a wealth of flowing auburn hair and framed a handsome face dominated by deep, flashing eyes ; her figure was tall—five feet ten inches—and slender. The first woman Salvationist to adopt the bicycle, an excellent horsewoman and an enthusiastic swimmer and diver. ... She had the temperament of an actress. Dramatic, imperious, headstrong, she would drive herself for weeks of strenuous work until forced to retire completely for a period of rest.

William Beacraft, of Guelph, Ontario, Canada, arrived in Flint, Michigan, in 1904, to work for David Buick, an internal combustion engineer, under whose direction he built the first now-famous Buick engine. Beacraft linked up with the little corps in Flint and became its first Sergeant-Major. When Buick wanted more mechanics, Beacraft engaged two Salvationists, Morse and Randall. This was the beginning of the Flint Citadel Band, which made quite a stir at the International Congress in London in 1914. When Beacraft became president of the motor division of the firm, he had 4,500 employees under his supervision. His noon-day factory meetings—at which those employees who were Salvation Army bandsmen played—became so popular that similar gatherings were commenced in other Flint factories.

The twenty-fifth anniversary of the Army's commencement in the United States was celebrated in something like a rising tide of national approval in March 1905. A " siege " proclaimed by the Commander took place between 5 February and 14 March and was outlined as a special campaign

to destroy every kind of evil work resulting from sin, such as drink, blasphemy, hatred, half-heartedness, shame, hypocrisy, cant, lukewarmness, jealousy, cowardice, fashion, pride, conceit, lies, and the other enemies of God and man.

The siege resulted in the conversion of 6,000 seekers, from which 2,000 were sworn in as soldiers, although soldier-making was difficult at that time. A new citadel costing $30,000 (£6,000) was opened at Uniontown, Pennsylvania, by Judge Umbel. Outrider work claimed considerable attention on the Pacific slope of the North American continent, and numbers of families living in complete isolation in the wilderness, forests, or on the mountains were contacted by officers on horseback. At Ten Strike, nothing better than an empty shell of a building, formerly used for a post office, could be secured for a meeting. Some borrowed chairs with two-inch boards laid upon them served for benches. A rough table came in handy for the lamp loaned by a saloon-keeper, and two bouquets of wild violets in whisky glasses decorated the building. Mosquitos somewhat spoiled the occasion !

During this decade the Army's growing social services came under repeated attacks. On 1 May 1906, at the National Conference of Charities in Philadelphia, Edwin D. Solenberger, general manager of the Associated Charities of Minneapolis, declared that the social work of the Army as carried on through its homes, lodging houses and other agencies was poorly organized and administered. He further asserted that the so-called charitable work of the Army was largely subservient to financial interests. Brigadier (later Commissioner) Alexander Damon was present to represent the Army, and within ten minutes had won " the hearty approval of a large part of the audience." The matter was temporarily dropped.

Three years later a major conflict broke out in Boston, prior to Thanksgiving Day, at which time the Army made a special street appeal for funds. The Board of Overseers of the Poor, a strong local organization, banned the Army from the streets, prohibiting collections, including kettles,[1] on public property, which the Board considered degrading and demoralizing. Said one of its members :

The method is spectacular and showy, directly opposed to the quiet, unobtrusive way in which the other charitable organizations, by personal solicitation and letters, collect for the poor. The spirit of giving charity before it is asked is *wrong*.

Without warning, the Boston press took over in a big way, the public being asked to

Send your checks to the *Journal* to aid The Salvation Army of this city in its great heartfelt, helpful annual charity for the benefit of the city's poor. One dollar today will be worth five-fold the day before Thanksgiving.

The Overseers of the Poor backed down, but too late to be of help. However, 3,500 dinners were taken to the homes of the poor and 1,500 were given at the People's Palace ; 3,000 toys were also distributed to needy children. " The Battle of Boston " was over, but other battles were to come, the Army being involved in 1913 in the Los Angeles charitable dispute. A millionaire, Dr Milbank Johnson, was the leader of the opposition, and Commissioner Thomas Estill defended the attack. The Municipal Charities Commission had been created and given wide powers to regulate all public appeals. Dr Johnson, the President, charged the Army with inefficiency, not meeting actual needs, and unwise handling of funds. The Army was cleared in 1915, but not before Major William Dart had been arrested and imprisoned for infringing the law.

Between August 1906 and August 1907 more than a million dollars' worth of property was acquired. A corps was operating within the walls of San Quentin State Prison in 1906, which, with its band, held open-air meetings in the

[1] A " keep the pot a-boiling " contrivance, consisting of a tripod and cauldron, into which the public contributed donations

yard. The Prison Sergeant was serving a life sentence. Commissioner Kilbey was bound for San Francisco when the news of the great earthquake which doomed the city was conveyed to him. This was on 18 April 1906. Upon arrival he found that Colonel George French had already established a shop in Fairmont Park, and was supplying relief to distressed families. Many Army halls and institutions were wiped out and many others seriously damaged. Commander Eva Booth was soon at the scene of desolation and taking control. Owing to the court-houses in San Francisco having been destroyed by fire,[1] Judge Carrol Cook for some time held his tribunal in the Salvation Army hall. The year 1907 was considered to be the greatest in America so far, in all branches of the work ; no fewer than 2,500 persons confessed conversion at Worcester, Massachusetts. Nevertheless, in Eureka, in the Southern Pacific Province, Salvationist lassies were forbidden to enter saloons to sell the *War Cry*. In February of this same year the tragic death of ten Salvationists —six captains, a lieutenant and three cadets—by the loss of the *Larchmont* off the American coast, *en route* from Rhode Island to New York, sent a thrill of pity and admiration through the hearts of all who read the newspaper accounts. A heavily laden cargo schooner crashed into the old-fashioned paddle steamer on the coldest night of the year ; panic followed, the lifeboats were rushed, women and children trampled under foot, and in ten minutes the ship had gone down with two hundred passengers. Only nineteen reached land. With remarkable fortitude the Salvationists knelt on the sinking deck and, with the icy spray dashing over them, met death fearlessly with songs of salvation upon their lips.

While spending a summer holiday in the United States, Meletois Golden, a high priest of the Greek Church, encoun-

[1] *The History of The Salvation Army*, vol. iii, p. 255

tered an Army open-air meeting ; later he attended a meeting in Los Angeles, California, where he confessed himself a sinner and knelt at the penitent form. He relinquished his priestly office soon after and, entering the Chicago training garrison in 1903, became a captain and visited England in 1908. At the beginning of this year Commander Eva Booth conducted a Nine-Day Siege in several large centres.

No country in the world is so cosmopolitan as is the United States of America. Indeed, it has been aptly described, from an emigration point of view, as " the melting pot of the nations, wherein flow diverse races to become amalgamated, producing, as the final outcome, the American." In one meeting alone, conducted by Commander Eva Booth during the Congress of 1909, penitents were dealt with in English, Swedish, Finnish, Danish, Russian, German, French and Italian ; and in this year the population of negroes numbered ten million. In the Eastern Province, with New York as the centre, there were thirty-one Swedish corps and one each of Italian, Dutch and Russian. The Western Province, the headquarters of which were in Chicago, also included thirty-one Swedish, two Norwegian, one Finnish and three Chinese corps. In Chicago alone the population included 384,000 Germans, 54,000 Bohemians, 52,000 Poles, 45,000 Swedes, 44,000 Norwegians and 12,000 French, besides thousands from many other nations.

The opening of the Russian corps in 1909 supplied another proof of the aggressive spirit of Salvationists, of whatever nationality. A converted Russian, John Reut, who emigrated to America, became a soldier at a slum corps in the worst district of New York in 1907, as did his wife and eight children. Longing for the conversion of his countrymen, this comrade held Sunday meetings exclusively for them. His compatriots flocked to hear him and many souls were saved. Eventually a corps was opened in the Russian quarter of the city. Envoy and Mrs Reut were placed in charge and a crude sort of *War Cry* was produced, every word and illustration being done by hand.

★   ★   ★

" The key which shall open to The Salvation Army the gates of the Celestial Empire, with its population of nearly one-fourth of the human race, *may* be found at 815 Sacramento Street, San Francisco, which is the heart of Chinatown, and where ' a handful of corn ' in the shape of the Chinese Corps [1] is already bearing fruit," says an optimistic article in *All the World* for February 1905. There were no fewer than 30,000 Mongolians in Chinatown. The great earthquake of 18 April 1906, however, reduced the hall to ruins.

A quaintly worded letter sent to the General by Brother Tom Gin, of the Chinese corps in Chicago, reveals his concern for his own country and undoubtedly had some effect upon William Booth's determination to commence operations in China itself :

Our Chinese soldiers and comrades most all time want to write to you, but the pen don't mind to them and give them what he want to say. Today our comrades told me must send you a letter, so I think I do best I can't write you a few lines. First I gone to thank you and your Officer for open Chinese Corps, in China town, in San Fransisco, because we have opportunity to find our Saviour, who save us from sin and brought us into the fight and happy. Sing for hallelujah ! . . . Dear General, as you know, we have 400,000,000 brothers and sisters in China. These long time stand in dark places, and tire of devil chain, and holla for help and wait for Saviour. We do not tire to hope and faithful.

During the period under review the Italian work continued, particularly in the red-light districts among the more than a quarter of a million Neapolitans in New York, in

[1] *The History of The Salvation Army*, vol. iv, p. 83

which there were five Italian colonies. The Italian corps officer, says *All the World* for 1905, regularly visited Italians in the Tombs Prison three times a week. Among comrades sworn in at the Italian corps was an ex-Catholic priest who was converted in a Salvation Army meeting. He was a Latin and Greek scholar, a teacher in a theological seminary and an editor of a religious paper in Italy.

At the climax of the Congress of 1911 and to the astonishment of the great audience, President Taft attended a Salvation Army gathering on a Sunday evening in the Belasco Theatre, Washington, in which Commander Eva Booth spoke on " The Grand March Past." The Rt. Hon. James Bryce, the British Ambassador, was present at an earlier meeting. Later the Commander, the Chief Secretary, Colonel (later Commissioner) Peart and Colonel (later Commissioner) Holz were received in audience at the White House.

A spectacular innovation, known as " Boozers' Day," was instituted on Thanksgiving Day, 1909. Colonel (later Commissioner) William McIntyre conceived the idea of making a special effort to aid drunkards, and twelve hundred of them, combed from the dives of the Bowery, filled the Memorial Hall, they being brought there by hired buses.

One unhappy man at the Boozers' Convention in 1910 was a former news proprietor who had slipped down to the level of a Bowery bum ; doctors at Bellevue Hospital had pronounced him an incurable alcoholic. He was Henry Milans, who was converted at a Salvation Army meeting and who never again touched liquor nor had any desire to do so. Until his death he conducted a lively ministry by writing and correspondence. Milans' case is probably the most miraculous result of this program, but there were other, less spectacular cases.[1]

A decisive legal victory was gained in 1912 when a rival

---

[1] *Soldiers without Swords*, by Herbert A. Wisbey, Jr., p. 151

organization known as " The American Salvation Army "
was forbidden to use Salvation Army titles and uniform.
Defendants appealed against the decision, but their appeal
was dismissed. This organization had appointed its own
" general " and conducted its operations in such a manner as
to confuse people and make it almost impossible for them to
distinguish between the two movements, thus causing Salvationists considerable difficulty. In giving his judgment the
judge said :

It is so clear as to hardly justify discussion that the purpose of the
defendant in assuming the name "American Salvation Army "
for its organization, and " The American War Cry " for its
paper, and its adoption of the military titles and uniform and its
whole scheme of procedure was to take advantage of the long-
established and widespread public knowledge of The Salvation
Army, and to receive for itself whatever benefits might flow
therefrom.

The defendant then appealed to the highest tribunal in the
United States, but with a similar result, the action being
again dismissed.

In 1913 the Commander dedicated an officer for work as
a missionary among the coloured people of the United States.
By that year 812 corps and outposts had been established.

The Territorial Staff Band, formed in 1887, and then
known as the National Band, visited Toronto in 1908 and
attended the International Congress in London in 1914. On
the voyage out on board the ss *Olympia* the band gave a
programme, among those present being Theodore Roosevelt.

Herbert A. Wisbey, Jr, says that the period from 1904
to 1914

in the history of The Salvation Army in the United States is
generally one of consolidation and advance along lines already
laid down. There were few innovations, and these were not of
enduring significance.

Colonel (later Commissioner) Samuel Logan Brengle became in 1914 the first Salvation Army officer to hold a D.D. degree, this being conferred upon him by his Alma Mater, De Pauw University, Greencastle, Indiana.

MEXICO

Colonel Edward Wright, of International Headquarters, prospected in Mexico in December 1908 and was granted a cordial interview by President Díaz. Later the General received a letter from His Excellency in which he expressed his pleasure at meeting the Colonel, offered his " friendship onward " and solicited " the favour of serving the General in any way " he could.

During the fighting between the Federal and rebel troops in 1911, Adjutant Hunter, of the El Paso, Texas, corps, crossed into Mexico, visiting every wounded man in Juarez, and being given authority to go where he pleased by the Minister of State, who placed his own horse, fully equipped for war, at his disposal. " Red Lopez," the leader of the *Insurrectos*, attended the Adjutant's meetings twice on one Sunday, and was anxious to be photographed with him.

Although it was confidently hoped that Salvation Army work would begin in the country almost immediately, twenty-eight years were to elapse before an official entry was made.

THE HAWAIIAN ISLANDS

During the summer of 1904 Major John Milsaps, the Divisional Officer, made a tour of the Hawaiian Islands and saw 303 people seek salvation within four months. Chinese,

Japanese, Spaniards, Puerto Ricans, Portuguese and many other races were here found intermixed in an altogether bewildering way. For years a solid work among Koreans had been carried out, and at Honokaa there was, in 1909, a corps composed entirely of Koreans. Perhaps in no other part of the world was such a strange mixture of words necessary in order to make oneself understood. The fewer the words used to convey the thought, the better these people understood, for many words tended to confuse. The following is a fair example of how one had to proceed in the open air :

Me before no gwin, too muchee kapukahi hana hana, all time no polopei inside. Bum-bye me kito Yesi, speak Yesu kohua me ; Ke inside all wask, gwuin clean. Me this time no gwin hana hana pau. Spose you like you can alsame, you like Yesu you speak Hananim kokua.

Major Milsaps tells the following story in the August 1912 issue of *All the World* :

The Hawaiian jailer at Lihue, a large-boned, jolly fellow, brought his prisoners out of the lock-up and made them sit in a semi-circle in the grassy yard. When the time came to invite those who wanted Salvation to go forward to an appointed spot near the leader, immediately the jailer responded, followed by the assistant-jailer. Both men knelt to be prayed for and to pray. They felt the need of a change of heart. Looking around after the earnest pleading of the Salvationists for more to seek Christ, the jailer discovered the semicircle of prisoners unbroken. Were himself and assistant the only sinners in that crowd ? Surely, this was a time to assert authority ! Addressing the immovable scalawags, he *commanded* them to seek Salvation. Backing that command was authority. There was an immediate response, and quickly the imperious jailer had plenty of kneeling figures around him !

In 1912 Lieutenant-Colonel Blanche B. Cox was appointed

to take charge of the work in Hawaii and the seven adjacent inhabited islands, which are situated some 2,000 miles from San Francisco. There were nine corps and thirty-eight outposts in the division in 1914.

ALASKA

Lieutenant-Colonel (later Commissioner) Bruno Friedrich was Secretary for the work among the Indians of Alaska—purchased from the Russians by the United States of America—and British Columbia in 1904, while Adjutant Thorkildson, a Dane, was in charge of The Salvation Army Indian Settlement at Glen Vowell, on the banks of the River Skeena,[1] he being the pioneer missionary. The next year the conversion of five Indian braves was the beginning of an awakening. An Ottawa official stated that " Glen Vowell was the cleanest native village I have beheld from the Atlantic to the Pacific." Adjutant Thorkildson for more than ten years—this was written of him in 1911—had been employed in advising and instructing the Indians in the successful cultivation of 1,260 acres of land, although at first they failed to see the necessity, being content to exist from their hunting expeditions. The Army hall was erected by the Indian Salvationists. The remarkable rise and progress of the Army's work among the Red Indians of Alaska, it is recorded, constitute one of the most romantic chapters of its history.

In 1909 eleven corps and nine outposts had been established, three day-schools provided for the educational needs of the children, and an industrial saw-mill, in addition to the farms, found employment for the men and women. In this year 1,000 acres at Andimaul were handed over to the Army as another reservation for Indian Salvationists.

[1] *The History of The Salvation Army*, vol. iv, p. 108

Among the converts at Skagway [1] in the famous gold-rush days of 1898 was a young princess of high standing belonging to the Kog-wan-ton Clan at Sitka, who joined the Army, foregoing tribal honours to devote her life to the salvation of her people, by whom she was greatly loved. With her husband, Captain Quick, she represented Alaska at The Army's International Congress in London in 1914,[2] wearing priceless native costumes of the early days.

CHAPTER NINETEEN

AUSTRALIA

Australia was exceptionally fortunate in having two out-standing and progressive leaders in succession during the years under review, for in the summer of 1909 Commissioner Thomas McKie, a Tynesider, was followed by Commissioner James Hay, a Clydesider. New Zealand was then included in the command, and the official notepaper used in Melbourne bore the somewhat imposing heading : " Territorial Headquarters for Australasia, Melanesia and The Eastern Archipelago."

One of Commissioner McKie's innovations was the formation in 1905 of " The Austral Lasses Band " of twenty-one players under Bandmaster (Captain) Ruby Baker, now Envoy Mrs W. Spiller. They wore khaki-coloured uniforms with chocolate-coloured facings. By 1907 they had travelled 16,446 miles, and in meetings conducted by their spiritual leader, Brigadier Frank Veal, some 500 seekers found Sal-

[1] *The History of The Salvation Army*, vol. iv, p. 90
[2] p. 202

vation. An International Music Competition was held in 1905, and Major Will H. Gore, son of one of the two Australian pioneers,[1] who contributed no fewer than 200 compositions to the *Australian Band Journal* during its existence between 1883 and 1913, won the prize march competition with " The Melbourne March," and thus became the first Australian to be awarded an international prize for a musical composition. Another well-known contributor to this journal was Bandsman (now Retired Band Inspector) Harold Scotney. Major Gore was placed in charge of the newly-formed Music Department in Melbourne in 1907, he being responsible for the production of a single sheet of music every fortnight. He did the arranging and editing himself, and stamped the originals with the steel discs from which the zinc plates were etched for printing. Gore was also manager of the Musical Instruments Department, Bandmaster of the Territorial Staff Band, Instructor of the Cadets Band and sole adviser on all Salvation Army music matters in Australia and New Zealand.

Queensland's sugar industry was commenced in the 1860s, and, lured by the prospects, thousands of kanakas (South Sea Islanders) from the many islands comprising Melanesia, were enticed to the state to clear the rich scrub-land and assist with the production of the cane. The black labour question, however, and the burning " White Australia " policy, brought about legislation which resulted in the complete abolition of coloured labour, and ruination faced many of the farmers. When different counsels later prevailed in Parliament, kanakas were once more imported, but under strict government supervision. In 1901 there was another reversal of the policy and the kanakas were deported wholesale ; some, however, owing to marriage relationships, were allowed to remain, and, by dint of hard work, launched out

---

[1] *The History of The Salvation Army*, vol. ii, p. 243

for themselves in the fruit-growing business. A colony of them situated five miles from Bowen was regularly visited by Captain John Hof, who won their regard and eventually was the means of the conversion of many of them to Christianity. In course of time they built themselves a meeting-place, and attention was given to schooling and dressmaking. Two kanaka boys entered the Melbourne Training College in 1907, in which year Commissioner McKie arranged for Ensign Edmund J. Inwood to pioneer the Army's work on the Island of Mai, the centre of small, but well-populated, islands in the New Hebrides Group. The Ensign had already had experience with kanakas on the sugar plantations, and he found on the Island of Mai a band of Salvationists who had recently been deported from Queensland and New South Wales, and who were being led by a kanaka named Tomkin. There were also deported kanaka Salvationists engaged in the pearl fisheries around Thursday Island, which lies about thirty miles from the farthest north corner of the Commonwealth. In 1914 Commissioner Hay was the first Territorial Commander to visit the island.

The last of the prosecutions for obstruction in Australia [1] took place at Sale, in Gippsland, Victoria, in the latter part of 1907, when the corps officers, Captains (later Brigadiers) Ed. Egan and Thomas H. Lynn, together with Mrs Lucy Angus, were arrested, convicted and fined £5 for what the magistrate agreed was but a technical breach of the bye-law. They refused to pay and their personal property was seized to cover the fines. Again arrested for speaking in an open-air meeting, the two officers were sentenced to fourteen days' imprisonment. Several women cadets had also been sent to prison a short time previously. Two of them had a congregation of but one adult and seven children at the time of their

[1] *The History of The Salvation Army*, vol. iv, p. 95

arrest for obstruction ! During the twenty-six years from 1881 to 1907 more than one hundred Australian Salvationists were either fined or imprisoned for street marching or holding open-air meetings.

The years between 1903 and 1910 were fat with exceptional prosperity for the Commonwealth, and in this happy state of affairs the Army shared. The Self-Denial Effort reached a record of £36,000, and the Army's property was valued at £340,000, in this 450 buildings being included ; a Collaroy (N.S.W.) property was given by Miss Elizabeth Jenkins, who was converted at Newtown (Sydney) Corps.

Anti-smoking and anti-gambling leagues inaugurated by Commissioner Hay reached a total membership of 42,000. *The Local Officer* became *The Local Officer and Bandsman* in January 1910 ; it is now *The Musician*. That year saw the passing of Mrs Poll Cott, one of the most notable trophies of grace to be won for God anywhere in The Salvation Army world. At the age of sixteen she had been transported to Botany Bay from Ireland for a minor offence in 1845. Becoming incensed when her baby died as the result of what she declared to be the doctor's negligence, she was imprisoned for the vehement statements she made against him. Upon her release she went immediately to his surgery and smashed everything she could lay her hands on ; thus she commenced a life of crime rarely if ever equalled by a woman. The next forty years she spent constantly in and out of prison, having received no fewer than 257 sentences. After her conversion in 1885 she remained a faithful Salvationist for twenty-one years, and died in an Army institution in Newcastle, N.S.W.

The year 1906 marked the commencement of Easter meetings held in a great marquee in Sydney's Prince Alfred Park, and which have continued since. For two years (1903 and 1904) these meetings had been held in a tent in Hyde Park, after which there was a break in 1905.

Although the population of Australia was little more than half that of Greater London in 1911, 134 cadets entered the Melbourne Training College, this being the largest number since it had been erected ten years previously. By July the bustling Commissioner Hay had travelled more than 46,000 miles by train, motor-car, boat, coach, buggy and sulky, calling at many places not previously visited by a territorial leader. The extent of the continent can be gauged from the fact that a lad-Captain in North Queensland had a command covering an area equal to that of England ! The officer at Winton had to travel 1,000 miles by coach to visit one small township in her district. At one place visited by this officer the town clerk obtained a bell and went around the town announcing her meeting. In this year, 1911, the Commissioner conducted the thirtieth anniversary of the commencement of the work in Australia, and at that time there were 1,400 corps and outposts, 2,000 officers and employees, 4,380 local officers and 2,500 bandsmen ; the periodicals had a total circulation of 90,000 copies per issue. An event of no great importance at the time, but one which later was to have world-wide significance, was the transfer to International Headquarters of the Australian-born Brigadier George L. Carpenter who, in 1948, became General.

In the course of an address given in Melbourne Town Hall in 1912 in connection with the Army's annual social meeting, the Premier of Victoria, the Hon. William A. Watt, said :

It was by a mere accident that I was not an officer in The Salvation Army. I was scarcely twelve years of age when Colonel Hoskin came down to the suburb I lived in as the converted footballer from Ballarat, and took charge of the " Death and Glory " band of North Melbourne. What struck me then, and what strikes me now, is that your organization, without neglecting the heart and spiritual objects of its existence, gets down to business in the most systematic way.

The Army presents a lantern show during Utrecht's (Holland) historic Fair Week. A large screen was hung over the canal from one side to the other in front of the Town Hall. A crowd estimated at 10,000 gathered for the event

The Chief of the Staff, Mr Bramwell Booth (wearing a white band around his cap), follows his father's example and employs modern transport during his visit to Scunthorpe. With the Chief are Brigadier Stanley R. Ewens, the Divisional Commander, and (extreme right) Adjutant James A. Morgan, the Chief's private secretary. Their host, the Vicar of Scunthorpe, stands behind the car

William Booth rides in a rickshaw during his visit to Japan in 1907. Colonel Edward J. Higgins is seated in the other rickshaw, and on the left (wearing cap) is the Territorial Commander, Colonel Henry Bullard

William Booth, speaking in the pulpit of Wimborne Methodist Church, Dorset, on Friday, August 24, 1906. Very few photographs were taken of the General speaking inside a building of any kind

Colonel William T. Hoskin was the first Australian-born officer to become a prominent leader in his own country, he being appointed Chief Secretary for Australasia in 1905. Colonel (later Lieutenant-Commissioner) Wiebe Palstra [1] became Chief Secretary in Australia in 1912.

In January 1913 His Excellency the Governor of Victoria, Sir John Fuller, opened a home for girls—the first institution in the Commonwealth to serve as a memorial to William Booth.

After five years of command Commissioner Hay had travelled 200,000 miles ; the soldiers' roll had been increased by 2,300, and 109 new halls had been built and from forty to fifty were under consideration. Brigadier Ernest Holdaway, who had pioneered the work among the Maoris in New Zealand,[2] passed away in 1914.

CHAPTER TWENTY

CANADA, NEWFOUNDLAND AND BERMUDA

Commissioner Thomas B. Coombs, who, twenty-two years before, had left England to take command of the Army's work in Canada, returned as its Territorial Commander in November 1904, following Commissioner Eva Booth's " record of amazing leadership and an impression for good upon the nation that lingers to this day." [3]   Within twelve " furious " months he had twice toured from the Atlantic to

---

[1] *The History of The Salvation Army*, vol. iv, p. 19
[2] *The History of The Salvation Army*, vol. iv, p. 139
[3] " *What hath God wrought ?* " by Arnold Brown (Salvation Army Printing and Publishing House, Toronto), 1952.

the Pacific, covered 35,000 miles and witnessed 3,000 seekers kneeling at the penitent-form.

A man who had persistently disturbed a meeting in Montreal was charged before Judge Sicotte, who dismissed the case, ruling that the defendant had been merely a dissenter and was acting within his rights. In the Court of the King's Bench, however, Mr Justice Hall reversed the decision of the Lower Court in December 1905 and fined the disturber £2, or alternatively he was to serve ten days in jail. After reviewing the evidence Justice Hall said :

No one ever questioned the right of The Salvation Army to occupy the streets, and they have ever since had what protection the police could give them. If the rights of the Army are thus established in the streets, how much greater are they in a room which they rent and pay for exclusively for their own people ?

The decision was received with approval throughout the Dominion.

Marking the opening in Winnipeg, Manitoba, of the first large Grace Hospital,[1] 10 June 1906 was a significant day for the Army in Canada. This event was a daring innovation, for it gave indication that the Army was going to compete with the highest standards of medical and nursing practice as exemplified in the general hospital field. Between 1904 and 1907 more than 40,000 persons were taken to Canada under Salvation Army auspices in connection with its emigration work,[2] and, in 1908, 25,000 were transported in ten chartered ships in twelve months. Arnold Brown says :

As the tide of immigrants swelled, Immigration Lodges ministering to the physical needs of the travellers sprang up across the land ; colonies were put into operation ; labour bureaux worked to improve the settlers' lot. In all 200,000 men, women and children crossed Atlantic waters and prepared to lay the foundations of

[1] *The History of The Salvation Army*, vol. iii, p. 168
[2] *The History of The Salvation Army*, vol. iii, p. 155

the future in every part of Canada—under the aegis of a Movement that in Canada was not yet thirty years old !

In 1908 there were in the Dominion 999 officers and nearly 450 corps or units of soldiers quartered together and commanded by field officers. 16,080 persons professed to find salvation during the previous year. Sixty cadets were in training for officership in Toronto in 1909, and a German corps was opened that same year in Regina.

Royal assent was given on 19 May 1909 to an Act incorporating the Governing Council of The Salvation Army in Canada, and a statement issued at the time declared :

Due to a great deal of misunderstanding, The Army will, as other religious societies in the Dominion, become a body incorporate, and all its property in the future will be controlled by The Governing Council of The Salvation Army, and not be in the name of the Territorial Commissioner, as formerly. Enemies of The Army have from time to time maliciously misrepresented the position to the public, and it is particularly to make the position more generally understood that The Army all over the world, in the fifty-three countries and colonies where it operates, is being incorporated similarly to the established churches.[1]

Commissioner Coombs, whose continued ill-health, it was stated, necessitated a lengthened furlough, was succeeded in January 1911 by Commissioner David M. Rees. In the following year Commissioner Railton visited French Canada, and, on returning to International Headquarters, stated that the fight for open-air liberty was still going on in Quebec, whereas in Montreal the open-air meetings were " the great redeeming feature." A three days' campaign inaugurated on 27 January 1913 by His Honour the Lieutenant-Governor of the Province of Ontario, to raise $100,000 (£20,000) toward the General William Booth Memorial Training College [2] was

[1] Arnold Brown, op. cit.
[2] p. 244

commended by the Governor-General of Canada, H.R.H. the Duke of Connaught. When the target was reached on the third day crowds cheered in the streets, and the whole city of Toronto manifested delight. When Colonel (later Commissioner) Henry Bullard made a seven-and-a-half-months' tour of Canada, he met at Cornwall, Ontario, an Indian Bandmaster who owned a considerable property in the reservation, and whose band included a number of English and Canadian bandsmen quite content to play under his baton. The Colonel stated that

One of the most interesting and undoubtedly the most difficult sections of our work is that among the men in the lumber camps. . . . We have no regular organized work among them, but a good deal of work is being done, nevertheless, by the corps officers, who visit these camps, and also by the special officers in some of the divisions.

At his personally expressed wish, the Governor-General inspected the Army's social institutions in Montreal in December 1913, and later declared that his visit had been " a positive sermon in philanthropy."

Perhaps the greatest tragedy in the whole history of The Salvation Army took place on 29 May 1914—" Black Friday" —when the Canadian Pacific liner *Empress of Ireland*, taking 200 Salvationists to the International Congress in London [1] was rammed by the Norwegian collier *Storstad* in a fog and sank in the Gulf of St Lawrence within a few hours of leaving Quebec the previous evening. Although fog signals were exchanged, these were misunderstood, and at about 2 a.m. the hull of the *Storstad* suddenly loomed out of the darkness and crashed into the side of the *Empress*, which went down within a quarter of an hour with more than a thousand of its passengers. Among the 167 Salvationists lost were the Territorial Commander, Commissioner David M. Rees, and

[1] p. 202

his wife and daughter, the Chief Secretary and Mrs Colonel Sydney Maidment, many other headquarters officers, soldiers and friends, and the Territorial Staff Band, whose Bandmaster was Adjutant Hanangan. Commissioner Thomas McKie was sent from London by General Bramwell Booth to take command of the Territory *pro tem*. The funeral service of sixteen of those who perished was conducted by the Commissioner in the Toronto Arena, where, it is estimated, some 1,000 persons were assembled. Commissioner Rees was not buried until several weeks later. The Territorial Staff Band had been formed by Commissioner Coombs in the spring of 1907.

NEWFOUNDLAND

" The Norway of the New World," as Newfoundland has been appropriately called, experienced a period of considerable development from the year 1894 and was, in 1904, more prosperous, more enterprising, and showed signs of a greater future than ever before in its history. Its staple seal- and cod-fishery continued to enrich the island, and its mining and lumbering industries were being rapidly expanded. The work of The Salvation Army at this time came under the supervision of the Territorial Commander for Canada, Commissioner Eva Booth, and commanded the respect and appreciation of all classes, from government officials and leading ministers of the churches to the poorest men in the street. Some sixty corps, seventy-five outposts and twenty-five day schools,[1] most of them subsidized by the government, were in operation. The schools were managed and the finances governed by boards appointed under the Education Act and consisted of five members, being in each case the

[1] *The History of The Salvation Army*, vol. iv, p. 105

Provincial Officer, two District Officers and two Local Officers. Newfoundland had no State system of education, the responsibility being distributed among the various religious organizations, but were under State control and patronage, the teachers being partly State paid. In September 1908 a Central College, equipped on entirely up-to-date principles, was opened by His Excellency the Governor of the Colony, Sir William MacGregor, in St John's, the capital, as a training centre for teachers, in addition to fulfilling the purpose of a day school, with an average attendance of 250. It was also a training garrison for cadets and the headquarters of the Provincial Officer.

During the cod-fishing season many Salvationists were included in the 30,000 Newfoundlanders who spent their time on the dreary inhospitable coast of Labrador, and who on Sundays told the story of salvation to the Eskimos. The following extract from an article in *All the World* for November 1909 gives a picturesque illustration of how the Army's work proceeded in the outlying districts :

Here is a settlement of thirty or forty families, with others stretched along the shore on either side. All are hard-working people, gleaning their livelihood from the sea, and bit by bit adding to their homes, boats, and gear. Occasionally there are bad fishing seasons, and money is none too plentiful. An officer has been asked for, and a Captain or Lieutenant is sent. A meeting-place, a quarters, and a school will eventually be needed, and in due time they are all erected. Not in one year, perhaps, or in two, but bit by bit the work will go on until all three are there—the material evidence of the handiwork of the Salvation Army officer and soldier. Each officer takes up the building where the other left off, and just as the limited funds will allow does the work progress. In many instances even the doors and windows are made by the officer, who builds by day and preaches at night, receiving sufficient to feed and clothe him the while. Many buildings thus erected would do credit to any city, and they stand as monuments to the devoted service of some of our bravest soldiers.

A national disaster overwhelmed Newfoundland on the night of 31 March 1914 when no fewer than 300 men engaged in capturing seals on the icefield were caught in an unexpected blizzard. Being quite unprepared for such extreme temperatures some were soon frozen to death. Others saved their lives by burying their heads and hands within the bodies of the animals, which they had cut open. Some of the men were frozen into the ice. The General forwarded a substantial sum of money to the Lord Mayor of London's relief fund as the Army's contribution. Most of the men came from Bonavista, where the Army had three flourishing corps, and a number of Salvationists were among the lost. The strong Salvationist force on the island was then under the command of Brigadier Morehen, who had succeeded Lieutenant-Colonel Samuel Rees. There were at that time 134 corps and outposts, with 156 officers, and fifty-six day schools with accommodation for 3,000 pupils.

BERMUDA

Four corps, with a combined membership of 200 soldiers, were operating on the islands of Bermuda in 1910 at Hamilton, St George's, Somerset and Southampton, and, in addition, at three outposts in Warwick, Dockyards and St David's. From this little Atlantic paradise, known as " The Land of the Lily and Rose," a dozen or so comrades had become officers.

CHAPTER TWENTY-ONE

FRANCE

Though the difficulties facing the Army in France in 1905 were all but insurmountable, and the problems almost inextricable, invincible determination on the part of the Territorial Commander, Commissioner Ulysse Cosandey, and those under his direction, enabled them to triumph when others less courageous would have been vanquished. In this year a new Territorial Headquarters was opened in Paris at the corner of the Rue St Augustin. The Commissioner, who was also responsible for operations in Italy and Belgium,[1] said of France two years later :

We have great incredulity all around us. We have here the " Red Fanaticism " of anarchy. We have free thought, but there is a certain *noyau* of believers who are seeking, and not ineffectually to stop the torrent. . . . French scepticism is largely on the surface. France is *blasé*—tired of a religion of form and superstition. . . . In every class of society people believe more and more in our methods and our work. I am told that the Prefect of Police in Paris has given to all the police commissioners orders to send the friendless provincial women whom they find in the streets to our Hôtellerie. . . . Many people in France rather glory in going to funerals with the red rosette, which means " no religion." And there are clubs in Paris organized to fight religion. At the same time, when they come in touch with the real thing, all this surface scepticism and free thought soon disappears.

But men and women were accepting Christ, among them a professor who, it is said, spoke seventeen languages. The majority of the converts, even the most godless, were imbued with Roman Catholic ideas, and still had the impression that

[1] p. 49

a visit to the penitent form was something like going to the confessional box of the Church they had so long neglected. One of the women converts, a terrible character, was so accustomed to the use of fiery words that, after her conversion, an officer prepared a list of words that she ought not to use !

A soldier of the *Garde Républicaine* of Paris, one of the crack military corps of France, became a Salvationist and eventually applied for officership. When he handed in his resignation at the *Garde Républicaine* office, first his captain, then the commandant, and finally the colonel of the corps urged him to postpone his intention for a year, stating that they needed him on account of his moral influence.

Only once a year, on " Independence Day," 14 July—sacred to all Parisians as the anniversary of the Fall of the Bastille—were *Salutists* allowed to hold open-air meetings, which they did under the trees of the Champs-Élysées. At the end of 1908, however, Colonel (later Lieutenant-Commissioner) François Fornachon, then the Territorial Commander, was able to announce a notable advance—open-air meetings were being permitted in many cities where formerly government regulations, although still existent, would not allow. When the Colonel arranged to conduct an eight-days' siege [1] at various corps, many pastors publicly announced the Army's meetings from their pulpits ; this also was a previously unheard-of thing. The woman Ensign at Bordeaux was brought before the police authorities on two or three occasions for holding open-air meetings, but each time succeeded in giving a satisfactory explanation regarding her transgression of the law. On the last occasion she calmly informed the police commissary that the Army had undertaken the " disinfection of the streets " of the town, which, she added, stood in sad need of the process. Convinced of

[1] A spiritual campaign

the truth of her words, the official issued orders that the Salvationists were to be allowed to continue their good work. In some cities officers and soldiers alike paraded the streets during stated periods, announcing their meetings as they went along, and this novel and tactful form of advertising awakened interest in the Army's movements and attracted people to the halls. When Adjutant Jenny Blanc, of Le Havre, was taken before the chief of police for conducting an open-air meeting in which Colonel Fornachon and the General Secretary, Brigadier Frederic Delapraz, participated, she was told that such meetings must not be held without permission from the mayor.

"But the law of France is on my side," pleaded the Adjutant. "I know the law. It is printed in every school for every scholar to read, and it states that no one can prevent a citizen from doing good."

The chief of police smiled. "You can go," he said, "but be very careful, for I shall be compelled to punish you, if you are caught. Be far from us—always!"

Overwhelming floods, a catastrophe which could not "be paralleled in the history of any European capital," caused damage estimated at £50,000,000, intense suffering and destitution to the city of Paris in January 1910. This was due to prolonged rainfall, snow and frost, alternating in thaws, distributed over the whole basin of the Seine and its tributaries; a great part of the centre of the city was inundated. The General despatched Colonel (later Commissioner) Francis Pearce, who had had considerable experience in similar calamities, to confer with Colonel Fornachon regarding the best methods for assisting those in misfortune. The Territorial Commander was himself obliged to leave his quarters and belongings hastily, and many other officers and soldiers were in a similar predicament. Financial assistance was forthcoming from International Headquarters and the men's and women's hotels and the home for theatrical girls were thrown open as temporary shelters.

CHAPTER TWENTY-TWO

SWITZERLAND

The days of bitter persecution in Switzerland, when Salvationists were cast into prison by the authorities, or maltreated by the populace, had long since gone by 1904. Instead, the flowing tide of public opinion was gathering strength every day, and throughout many of the miniature republics those in power, and the democratic inhabitants for whom they stood, testified to the splendid character of the work the Army accomplished.

Commissioner and Mrs Emanuel Booth-Hellberg were succeeded in the Swiss command in 1904 by Commissioner William J. McAlonan, Commissioner Booth-Hellberg being granted a sick furlough, which proved to be the beginning of a long illness from which he died five years later.

Commissioner McAlonan inaugurated ' Oster-Aufruf,' a national Easter Appeal in 1905, this depending largely upon contributions made by soldiers and their friends at the altar service held in every corps on the Sunday morning. The total amount reached 26,000 francs (£1,040), which was thought to be very high. In this same year, and for the first time, the Neuchâtel corps was permitted to hold an open-air meeting on the principal promenade of the town.

The International Staff Band, under Lieutenant-Colonel (later Commissioner) George Mitchell, paid an Easter visit to Switzerland in 1906 and received, a most enthusiastic welcome. Reporting the event, *The War Cry* declared that " viewed merely as a crusade of harmony the Swiss tour of the International Staff Band stands without parallel in all the wonderful history of Salvation Army music." After playing before the Federal House of Parliament in Berne, the band played in the capital's great French church at night, this being the first occasion upon which the Army had been privileged to occupy the building. Fifteen hundred people were present. Masses of cheering people were everywhere, a marked contrast to earlier years. History was created when the band played in Konstanz, the city in which John Hus was burned at the stake, for it was the first occasion upon which an English Salvation Army band had played within the borders of the German Empire. Switzerland had at this time a brass band composed entirely of women–cadets under Ensign Riedmaier. The Training Principal was Major (later Colonel) Franz von Tavel, formerly a doctor of botany and bacteriology at Zürich University.

A second visit to Switzerland was undertaken by the band in 1907, when meetings were conducted by Commissioner and Mrs Booth-Tucker. Brigadier (later Lieutenant-Colonel) Richard Slater [1] accompanied the band, this being the only time that he left England. This year also saw the first visit to Switzerland of Commissioner James Hay, who conducted a salvation campaign in the French section of the country. When the International Staff Band made its third visit in 1909, the public fountains at Chaux-de-Fonds were set playing in its honour by order of the authorities. Two years afterward, with William Booth's grandson, Captain (later Colonel) Bernard Booth, as a bandsman, the International Staff Band was present for the Ascension Day meetings held in a huge marquee by Commissioner W. Elwin Oliphant, who was then Territorial Commander for both Switzerland and Italy.

[1] *The History of The Salvation Army*, vol. ii, p. 122 ; vol. iv, p. 177

Later the band headed the first Salvation Army march through the streets of Milan, in Italy. A Music Department was commenced in 1908 by Adjutant (later Lieutenant-Colonel) Gottfried Gertsch. This year also saw the inauguration of the band congress in Zürich.

The old district governor at Orbe had no love for the Army and had not in the least relented that exactly twenty years before, in 1888, he had imprisoned Captain Charlotte Stirling [1] for 100 days in the Castle of Chillon for inviting a few children to a Saturday-afternoon meeting ; so that in 1908 the young commanding officer of the corps, Gustave Isely, who was to become a Lieutenant-Commissioner, was informed that he must not take up collections. A policeman witnessed the breaking of this embargo, and the Salvationists were fined 1 franc 50 centimes for the first offence. Each subsequent offence meant the doubling of the fine. Isely was away at the time, but when he returned he went to see the governor, who angrily bellowed : " You have no right to make an appeal nor, for that matter, to hold a service in the streets." Isely informed him that the right to hold meetings was granted by law. The governor thereupon shouted : " Collecting is in any case forbidden. According to the law, singing and collecting is following the trade of street singers, and you hold no licence for that ! " Isely insisted that the Army's singing was of a religious nature ; that services of all churches, Catholic, Reformed or others, contained four parts : prayer, preaching, singing and collection, and prohibition of a song or a collection was tampering with the liberty of religious services. He also dared to remind the governor of his outrageous treatment of Captain Stirling, but this did not shake the old man's obstinacy, and the fine, doubled on a number of occasions, reached the sum of a few hundred francs ; then, as Isely refused to pay, he

[1] *The History of The Salvation Army*, vol. iv, p. 113

was sent for trial. The court acquitted him, much to the governor's chagrin !

In an interview in 1910 Commissioner Oliphant said :

In no quarter is the change of attitude toward us more pronounced than among the clergy and members of the Protestant churches. Formerly, through ignorance, they treated us with coldness and suspicion. Now many of the churches are opened to us. . . . I believe I am right in saying that, in proportion to the population (3,000,000), Switzerland can boast of more bands than any nation in the world. This, I should say, applies also to the The Salvation Army, especially if you include string and reed bands.

CHAPTER TWENTY-THREE

INDIA

The village of Kalvillai, near Cape Comorin, in Southern India, was the scene, in 1905, of the destruction by Salvation Army officers of a substantial and commodious heathen temple and of the goddess Bhadra Kali. Ensign (later Lieutenant-Colonel) Deva Rubem (Heden), a Swede, had worked earnestly for the salvation of the people until all of them, including the last of the devil-dancers, had become converted. The villagers then decided that, having no further use for their Hindu temple and its deities, they should be demolished and a Salvation Army hall and school erected. The key of the building was handed to the Territorial Commander, Lieutenant-Colonel (later Commissioner) Sukh Singh (Blowers), and the work of demolition, in which several women officers took part, was accomplished. This was the first of many such happenings.

The fame of The Salvation Army was so widespread

throughout Gujerat, in Western India, that in far-distant districts, where the Organization had never worked, all missionaries were called " *Muktifauj* " by the people. Christianity in those regions had become synonymous with the Army. Several European divisional officers were granted licences by the government to perform marriages for Indian Christians. Every Territorial Commander in India had to be a matchmaker and keep up a matrimonial bureau so far as officers were concerned, for those who came mainly from the girls' orphanages and married Indian officers did better work than those who were single. It was essential, too, that every white officer had a simple knowledge of medicine, for upon arrival at a village to conduct meetings someone was sure to require treatment. Lieutenant-Colonel Blowers was especially noted for his prowess in extracting decaying molars.

Lieutenant-Colonel Joseph Hammond was appointed in May 1905 to succeed Commissioner Edward Higgins as Resident Indian Secretary in Bombay,[1] and was given the Indian name of Jang Singh. There were then 1,789 officers, cadets and employees, and 1,852 corps and outposts in the country ; and for the purposes of administration the Indian Command, which at that time included Ceylon, was divided into seven territories : Gujerat and Western India, the Punjab, North India, South India, Madras and Eastern India, Maharashtra and Ceylon. Colonel (later Lieutenant-Commissioner) Clara Case (Nurani) was appointed to the command of South India and, in the following year, 1906, Lieutenant-Colonel (later Colonel) Joseph S. Rauch (Himmat Singh) to Gujerat. A brass band was formed in the boarding school opened in this year at Nagercoil, the first taught to music. It ranked second in the Travancore State, the first being the Government brass and flute band in Trivandrum !

[1] *The History of The Salvation Army*, vol. iv, p. 122

Petty persecutions had been the order of the day for some years in the Batala Division, Punjab, but during the summer of 1905 two corps of officers and a soldier were falsely charged with breaking down an idol in the village of Yowra Singh. Actually the idol, Bali Shah, had been broken down by village caste men who had encroached upon a graveyard belonging to some Salvationists. However, the officers and soldier were arrested and marched off in chains to the police station. They were at first refused bail. The Hindu magistrate declared that he would never allow a Christian to win a case while he was in office, and the defendants were each sentenced to a month's imprisonment or a fine of 25 rupees, despite the evidence of four other caste men who voluntarily came forward to testify to their innocence.

In the autumn of 1907 Commissioner Booth-Tucker, the Foreign Secretary at International Headquarters, and Mrs Booth-Tucker revisited India. Twenty-five years before, the Commissioner had been imprisoned for street processioning,[1] but now he could write :

The Army is looked upon by all classes as a public benefactor. Government officials welcome its leading officers, and consult them as to the best methods for helping the people. All classes of Indians regard the Organization with affection and confidence.

While travelling in Travancore (now Kerala State) in January 1908 Commissioner Booth-Tucker—who was then the special representative of International Headquarters in India—determined to introduce the cassava plant, from which tapioca is obtained, into famine areas, and, after considerable delay, the leading railway companies admitted this accessory food to the same privileges as staple articles of the people's diet, instead of placing it among the luxuries denied to all but the well-to-do. Indian grain merchants also co-operated with the Commissioner, who received initial orders for a

[1] *The History of The Salvation Army*, vol. ii, p. 274

A pencil study of
William Booth drawn by
the Author from memory
during a telephone
conversation

William Booth at his desk.   He was a prolific writer

MUSICIANS AND SONGWRITERS

1 Arthur R. Goldsmith   2 Edward V. Saywell   3 Albert Orsborn   4 Charles Coller
5 Bramwell Coles   6 George Marshall   7 Oliver Cooke   8 Wilfred Kitching   9 William
Broughton   10 Elsie D. Zealley   11 Ruth Tracy   12 Henry C. Goffin   13 Elizabeth Cossar
14 Arthur Bristow   15 Fred G. Hawkes   16 Motee Booth-Tucker (Mrs Hugh Sladen)

large supply, and the merchants themselves secured cuttings for planting over a considerable area. Cassava was planted in the Army's Farm Colony at Muktipur, near Ahmedabad, in Gujerat, and in other places where it possessed land. Tapioca became a popular article of diet, for in its flour form, in which it was distributed, the universal prejudice against the use of tubers was overcome. Nevertheless, when it was discovered that tapioca was of doubtful food value, the planting of the cassava plant was eventually discontinued.

Being greatly concerned about the rapid increase in the consumption of intoxicants in Gujerat and Western India, of which Territory he was in command, Colonel Sukh Singh inaugurated in this same year an Anti-Drink Crusade, which proved very successful, particularly among the Bhils.

Not least among the difficulties which had been faced and, in a measure largely overcome by this time, were those of race and language, for the Army's messengers were at work among the following nationalities—Punjabis, Gujeratis, Marhattas, Bhils, Telugus, Tamils, Malayalim and Cingalese —to whom the gospel of Christ was proclaimed in nine Indian languages, each of which was spoken by from 2,000,000 to 100,000,000 souls.

The Bombay Central Training Home, accommodating thirty cadets, was opened in 1909 by Colonel Sukh Singh. During his visit to Nagercoil that year Lord Kitchener, the Commander-in-Chief of the Indian Army, congratulated the boys' brass band.

Village banks having been established by the Army on the lines of those on the Continent of Europe, to combat the exactions of the village usurers, the Government, being impressed by the idea, in 1905 passed a law on the subject, in consequence of which, by 1910, village banks on a similar basis to those belonging to the Army were set up throughout the country. In 1907 the Army advocated central banks to provide capital for the village banks, and this innovation was also adopted by the Government.

During a brief visit to London by Commissioner and Mrs Booth-Tucker (Dutini) in 1910, the Commissioner made mention of the conversion of a Dom hangman and public whipper. So far as is known this man was the first public executioner to be sworn in as a Salvationist under the Army flag. Toward the end of 1910 Booth-Tucker produced an unpretentious pamphlet called "What The Salvation Army is doing in India and Ceylon, Coronation Year, 1911." Following is an extract:

Out of 315 millions less than 10 p.c. live in cities; the other 284 millions live in villages. . . . We can take you to hundreds of villages where our work has been established from ten to twenty years. The whole character of the village has been revolutionized. Drunkenness has disappeared. Cattle poisoning has ceased. Stealing and lying have given place to honesty and truthfulness, immorality to chastity; there is an air of propriety, of thrift, of peace and of happiness, which marks the community out from those which surround it.

The Maharajah of Travancore visited officially the Catherine Booth Hospital, of which he was the patron, in the summer of 1912.

The largest missionary party to leave Great Britain at one time left in 1913. It was known as "The Memorial Seventy," to commemorate the passing of William Booth,[1] and was under the charge of Colonel Bullard, who remained in India for two months, covering some 10,000 miles of travel. The party was bidden farewell in the Sun Hall, Liverpool, in a meeting conducted by the General. When, in January 1914, 100 Scandinavian officers farewelled for missionary work, fifty were assigned to India.

[1] p. 234

A serious difficulty was encountered in connection with the Army's work among the Criminal Tribes [1] when a number of young men found themselves unable to obtain wives, the dowry demanded being exorbitant. Only by the commission of crime could the money be raised. A woman officer was thereupon appointed to find wives and negotiate marriages, with the result that during 1913 nine couples were happily married by Brigadier Melling (Dileri Singh) in one ceremony in Bareilly.

Some idea of the extent of the Army's operations may be gathered from the statistics given in 1913 :

2,747 corps and outposts ; 1,772 officers and cadets ; 3 hospitals ; 3 dispensaries ; 3 weaveries ; 15 industrial schools ; 2 normal schools ; 2 boarding schools ; 4 settlement schools ; 9 settlements for criminal tribesmen ; 2 workshops ; 1 labour bureau ; 1 prison gate home ; 3 farms ; 2 dairies ; 4 rescue homes ; 1 silk camp ; 1 receiving home and 15 banks.

A medical institution was erected, equipped and handed over to the Army at Chini, a village in the Basher State, in 1913, and a newly married couple, Captain (now Lieutenant-Colonel) and Mrs Albert E. Walker were sent to take charge. The village being on the bank of the Sutlege River, with Tibet on the opposite side, many Tibetans used to call for medicine. There being a scarcity of bridges, they sat in a sling on a suspended rope and pulled themselves across the river. Did one fall in he was never seen again !

No greater sign of the Government's appreciation of Commissioner Booth-Tucker's work for India could have been shown than his award that year by King George V, in His Majesty's Birthday Honours List, of the Kaisar-i-Hind gold medal. This was India's official seal of approval of its erstwhile obstructionist ! About this time Colonel Sukh Singh (Blowers) was appointed a member of the Munici-

[1] *The History of The Salvation Army*, vol. iii, p. 274

pality of Ahmedabad, an honour not previously conferred upon a Salvation Army officer.

CHAPTER TWENTY-FOUR

CEYLON

Although a thriving work had been in progress in Ceylon since 1883, the extreme north of the island was not touched by the Army until 1905, when Lieutenant-Colonel (later Lieutenant-Commissioner) Yesu Ratnam (Stevens) was in command. At that time there were fifty-six corps, 133 outposts, 179 officers and cadets, twenty-four day schools, two village banks and four social and industrial institutions.

A Hindu did not necessarily lose caste by becoming a Christian in the far north, and might even live in the same house and eat freely with his relatives. All, however, despised the low-caste people, and those of no caste at all. Even those who had been converted to Christianity seldom accorded them brotherly recognition. It was, therefore, with obvious pleasure that these low-caste and no-caste folk, most of them engaged in the fisheries around the northern coast, welcomed the Salvationist-pioneers.

The Divisional Officer was Adjutant (later Lieutenant-Colonel) Anand Singh (John Tuley), whose headquarters were 300 miles from any Salvationists. Writing from Kenkasenturia, a village seaport, he said :

The people are extremely dark, and some of them quite mystified when we tell them they can be kept from telling lies and stealing. This is something very strange to them . . . just lately about fifty have decided to become Salvationists.

CHAPTER TWENTY-FIVE

SWEDEN

The appointment of Commissioner David M. Rees, Principal of the International Training Homes, to the command of the Army's work in Sweden, in November 1904, coincided with a radical change in the attitude of the national press, which had never seemed until then to have thoroughly understood the organization's aims and methods. Indeed, in some quarters the Press had lent itself to ungenerous criticism of the Army's internationalism. Now it began to praise instead of blame. Again and again it called attention to the beneficient efforts of the Slum officers in Kristianstad, in the south, and vigorously suggested that funds should be raised for their local operations, which suggestion was enthusiastically taken up by the public. The Press also called upon the city authorities to pay for the rent of the Slum settlement and to supply water free of cost, to which the city authorities agreed.

In 1905, however, a split was headed by Brigadier Kaleb Swenson, a divisional commander, who objected to the autocratic system of the Army and of William Booth's dealing with his officers, particularly with his own children. Swenson wanted corps to be self-governing, the sacraments to be introduced and other changes. Dismissed as an officer, he formed " The Swedish Salvation Army " with a number of officers and soldiers who followed him. This movement is still in operation, with a membership of some 2,000 and its own periodical, *Our Flag*.

At this time of anxiety, when a spirit, subversive and sinister, was looming over the Army in Sweden, and threatening to drive it into shoal waters, Lieutenant-Colonel (later Commissioner, D.D.) Samuel L. Brengle, of the United States of America, responded to an importunate call to visit the territory, he being a well-known exponent of holiness teaching throughout the whole Salvation Army world. In the spring of 1905 he arrived in Stockholm, accompanied by an excellent vocalist, Ensign Walter B. Mabee, and at the end of three weeks many new consecrations had been made by those readjusting their experiences at the penitent form. Prince Bernadotte, great-grandson of Napoleon's gallant marshal, and brother of the King, with the Princess and three of their children, were present at two of Brengle's Sunday meetings. In Uppsala Brengle won over the leader of the rival faction. The American evangelist described this Swedish campaign as " the greatest in my life so far." More than 1,000 seekers were registered. Brengle returned to Sweden early in 1906 for his second campaign in Europe, which resulted in 1,584 seekers in twelve weeks.

A new and almost unexpected concession was granted to Commissioner Rees in connection with the 1906 Self-Denial Effort, when the Stockholm chief of police permitted Salvationists to collect in the streets for three days. Neither the Army nor any other organization had previously been allowed this privilege in the capital.

A man who wished to provide a cheap and wholesome refreshment for night-workers during the bitterly cold weather invented an automatic machine which produced a glassful of hot milk by the insertion of a coin. He later, in 1906, handed over his machines to the Army in Stockholm. Until comparatively recently such machines were looked upon more or less as a novelty !

The year 1907 saw the largest number of Swedish cadets, 145, in training for officership. No other Training Home in the world, outside of Great Britain, could boast of so many. And in that same year, when the General visited the country to conduct the annual Congress, the Queen invited him to the Palace, His Majesty being regrettably ill. The General, it is stated, gave the longest public address in his career in Stockholm, speaking through a translator for an hour and fifty minutes ! A leading newspaper, commenting on the visit, began its report, " He came . . . he conquered." Colonel Henry Bullard campaigned throughout the country soon after, his tour embracing most of the large towns. In the hope of recruiting missionary officers he spoke mainly on his experiences in Japan. At this time open-air meetings were still not allowed, and marches took place at only two of the places he visited, while at another place the band was permitted to play only at the railway station at a public reception. " After the absolute freedom enjoyed in Japan in this respect," wrote the Colonel, " the denial of this privilege appeared to me to be peculiarly restrictive ; but the greatest respect was shown everywhere for the Army uniform." The first Divisional Young People's Secretaries were appointed during the Congress ; and at Christmastime pots, or kettles, suspended from tripods were used for the first time in the streets of Stockholm for collecting funds to provide free meals for the poor.

Permission was given for the Swedish Staff Band to play on the bandstand of a Stockholm city park at the conclusion of the 1908 Congress. Hitherto the bandstand had been used exclusively by military bands.

When Commissioner Rees farewelled after four and a half years, Commissioner Thomas McKie took over the command of 606 centres, ten divisions and 879 officers. Stockholm 1 was then the third largest corps in the Army world, with a roll of nearly 1,000 Salvationists. Within two years of McKie taking control, the soldiership of the Territory had increased by 1,200, and within the last four years the young people's work had been trebled. Jönköping had forty-four junior companies, as the Army calls its Sunday School classes, and in 1909, through the harvest of revival, became the largest corps in Sweden. Skansen was used for the first time at the Congress. Since then it has become the traditional meeting-place for the final Congress gathering of an enormous crowd.

Formal permission to hold open-air meetings was dispensed with by 1912 in Jönköping, and sometimes, when a meeting was held on an open space near to the County Governor's residence, the Army had no more interested auditor than the Governor himself, who listened from an opened window. In ten months no fewer than 300 conversions were registered, and the corps officer, Adjutant Erik Lund, was described as " The special friend of the rascals." Two years later, when Adjutant Oscar Janson was the officer in charge, the junior companies had risen to fifty-three, and on Good Friday, this was in 1914, 132 converts were publicly enrolled as soldiers, among them being some thirty to forty converted drunkards. In Malmö Slum and Rescue officers travelled free of charge on the electric cars, electricity was supplied to the home for women and girls, telephones were installed for officers at the lowest possible rate and Slum officers could obtain hospital training free. The publisher of an anarchist newspaper was won for Christ in the city, and when several hundred of his former comrades gathered round the open-air ring in an endeavour to kidnap him on his first appearance as a Salvationist, police had to escort him to the hall. On the Sunday afternoon of the 1912 Congress, a musical festival drew 7,500 people to the temporary Singers' Hall, the largest indoor audience up to that time. In 1913 the site for the present Training College was purchased in Skeppargatan, Stockholm.

General Bramwell Booth conducted a Scandinavian Missionary Congress in Stockholm within a few days of the opening of 1914. One hundred officers were dedicated for service in the Far East, fifty of them being Swedes. At the same time the General dedicated the site of the William Booth Memorial Training College. Later fifty Members of Parliament visited the Inebriates' Colony at Kurön.[1] The Prime Minister, Hjalmar Hammarskjöld, father of Dag, who was to become General Secretary of the United Nations, headed the delegation.

Lieutenant-Colonel Elisabet Liljegren, one of Sweden's most outstanding women officers, was suddenly called to her Reward in March 1914. Beloved, trusted, gentle and unobtrusive, she was for twenty-one years head of the Women's Social and Slum Work, and known from the highest to the lowest in the land as " The Colonel of the Slums." The Baroness Nordenfalk spoke at her funeral in Stockholm, and 5,000 stood around the graveside.

There are thousands [said a Stockholm newspaper] that mourn the loss, thousands who, thanks to her bright faith, her strong soul, and her burning love of men, have been enabled to carry the burdens and sorrows of life.

LAPLAND

At the close of the 1880s, officers stationed in the county of Jämtland often undertook long journeys to visit the Laplanders, but in 1897 Captain Erika Bäckström was especially dedicated to this work. Major and Mrs Andreas Wilks were Laplanders, and before he became an officer the Major was President of the Åsele-Vilhelmina Lap Union, the first " get together " to take an interest in the social and cultural life of these nomad people. Wilks was also the Speaker in the Lapland Parliament. Staff-Captain Ernst Lander was stationed among the Laplanders for longer than any other officer.

[1] *The History of The Salvation Army*, vol. iii, p. 190

CHAPTER TWENTY-SIX

SOUTH AFRICA

The first Salvation Army hall for Africans was opened in 1904 in the Barkerville Settlement, Bacaland, in the Transkei, Cape Colony, 1,000 miles from Cape Town, and Major (later Commissioner) J. Allister Smith,[1] Divisional Officer for Natal and Zululand, went up for the memorable occasion. He and his horse having made the night journey from his Headquarters to Richmond by train, the Major then rode the 200 miles to Barkerville. A congregation of 500 Africans filled the building, some of them with their faces painted with red clay. In promising to contribute donations, the prospective donors excelled themselves. The Major described the scene and the speeches. The following is an extract :

Mrali, amid much hilarity, said in an emphatic voice, as if he were angry : " Glad am I to be here today ; put me down for sixpence. Then I think of the wife I had before I had any whiskers, I give sixpence for her ; I give threepence for my boy, who will be taught at this school ; then take threepence for my girl, the daughter of my dead wife." . . . Then up jumped our brick-maker and said : " I give threepence to close the big Umfundisi's (the teacher or Major) mouth," meaning this to be a friendly challenge."

In this same year the first three African cadets entered the new Training Settlement at Emlungisweni, Mount Frere, East Griqualand ; and the poultry at the Social Farm at Rondebosch, Cape Colony, won as many as fifty-nine prizes in a poultry show. In November Acting Commissioner William J. Richards succeeded Commissioner Kilbey as Territorial Commander.

[1] *The History of The Salvation Army*, vol. iv, p. 133

The Government of Cape Colony recognized in 1905 the claims of Salvation Army officers to conduct weddings and appointed the Territorial Commander, the Chief Secretary, the Social Secretary and the District Officers as fully qualified Marriage Officers. Previously Salvationists in the Colony had had to go to other places of worship to get married. A proclamation in *The Cape Colony Government Gazette* made this innovation known to the public, and that same evening two Dutch officers were married under the Colours in Cape Town—Adjutant Solomon M. Ferreira and Lieutenant Johanna Rothwan—by Lieutenant-Colonel (later Commissioner) Francis W. Pearce. At the request of the authorities Captain Nelson, who had served among the Chinese in San Francisco, California,[1] was appointed to work among the 30,000 coolies employed in the mines on the Rand. A humane and enlightened measure known as " The Juvenile and Women's Imprisonment Bill," which was very largely the outcome of representations made to the Government of Cape Colony by the Army, was passed in the House of Assembly in the spring. The Bill provided " for the custody otherwise than in jail of certain persons." Mr Sampson, the Attorney-General, when speaking on the Bill, paid high tribute to the excellent work being done by the Army in South Africa. Officers were entitled to travel half-fare on all railways in Cape Colony, Natal, the Transvaal and Orange River Colony. A party of twenty-one officers left London for South Africa in May. During a period of three months in this year some 200 men sought salvation in meetings held in Paarl Jail, while over the Easter week-end a remarkable revival took place in the prison at Kroonstad, Orange River Colony.

In Zululand in 1906 a rebellion broke out, and in the Ixopo district, where it started, Adjutant and Mrs Carleton,

[1] *The History of The Salvation Army*, vol. iv, p. 83

who were stationed at the Miriam Booth Settlement, were forced to flee for safety. At the Hulett Settlement, where Captain Robert Chard and Lieutenant Cezula were in charge, the surrounding population was enthusiastic for the uprising, which was against a poll-tax of a pound placed by the Natal legislature on every male adult. The rebels demanded of Chief Mashwili that the Captain should be put to death, but the Chief, who had been treated by the Captain for various sicknesses, would not agree, and advised him to ride away on his horse immediately. The Lieutenant was hidden in a large beer barrel by a woman Salvationist until the danger was over. Lieutenant Sifalafa Ngcobo and his wife fled to the Nkandhla Forest, but were discovered by a force of " loyal " Zulus, who accompanied the Government forces. The Zulus killed the Lieutenant, tore the clothing from his wife and lashed a number of other Salvationists with a " cat-o'-nine-tails," although they protested that they were non-combatants.

New Training Homes for men and women cadets were acquired at Claremont, Cape Colony, that same year, and Acting Commissioner Richards was " able to give a satis-factory account of things " at the end of the year :

Our native[1] posts have been seriously disturbed, and their consolidation sadly interfered with, by the rebellion in Natal, though we have the gratifying reflection that our Zulu converts and soldiers behaved in a cool and Christlike manner. Our position in Johannesburg is stronger, a hall having been secured in the centre of the city.

It was said, and with truth, that The Salvation Army was one of the few religious organizations in South Africa, apart from their own Church, which had any considerable follow-ing of Dutch people. " Probably never in the history of the Army in South Africa has our position been stronger or our

[1] The word " native " is never used today, it being much disliked by the African people.

prospects brighter than at present," declared Acting Commissioner Richards in a *War Cry* interview in London in March 1907, and he quoted facts and figures to prove his statement.

Consequent upon his visit in 1909, the General decided that the African Work should be placed under the supervision of Brigadier Allister Smith. Within six months 400 Africans professed faith in Christ in Natal and Zululand alone, while 50 per cent of that number were enrolled as Salvationists. An African Training Home was opened at Tshoxa, near King Williamstown, and fourteen cadets took up residence.

Colonel (later Commissioner) Isaac Unsworth, the Editor-in-Chief at International Headquarters, in an *All the World* article published in January 1911, tells of his visit some years before to the Army's first African settlement by the Umvoti River on the borders of Zululand :

We found a number of natives in full uniform. This consisted of a red leather band round the arm with a brass S in the centre ! . . . We held our meeting this particular morning commencing at six. . . . Presently our interpreter read the lesson. It was the picture-prose poem the Saviour drew for the human race— " The prodigal Son." The young chief is present. He has never before attended a religious meeting, and is much inclined to look upon the whole affair as an entertainment, but the story impresses him. Every word has its effect. But he is of royal blood. His emotions, by constant practice have been so restrained, and must still be restrained if he is to remain a warrior. He bites his lip till we see the blood. The battle is surging within the man's breast. The truth is doing its work. Every eye is now riveted on the young chief. He cannot rest quietly in his place. He moves from side to side. Presently the wooing song rises, " Take my sin away " (*Susa zonk' izono zam'*). The sweet cadences break over the assembly. No one moves. Then a wonderful thing happens : the young chief comes forward and, dropping on his knees, he cries to God for deliverance. Tears are seen coursing down his cheeks. He is spoken to by the officers and pointed to Christ, and as the light dawns his rapture knows no bounds; he cannot be restrained ; he dances for joy !

The Colonel states that during his stay in South Africa he had been " promptly marched off to the common tronk " for taking part as a drummer in open-air operations at the Paarl. The case was brought before the Supreme Court, Mr (later Sir) James Rose-Innes being briefed as counsel, but before the case came on he was made Attorney-General in the newly formed Government, so his brief was handed to Mr W. P. Schreiner. The two judges—De Villiers and Buchanan—gave a verdict in the Army's favour, and the obnoxious bye-law, suspected to have been suggested to the authorities by the wine-farmers, was declared *ultra vires*. This trial proved a blessing to the Army, since the Government—Cecil Rhodes was then the Premier—through the Attorney-General, asked that Prison Gate Work, as operated in Australia,[1] should be conducted in South Africa, and a grant was made available. An officer was brought from Australia and every prison in the country was thrown open to the Army's ministrations.

When Commissioner Richards left South Africa in the summer of 1911, there were 119 corps and outposts, 414 officers and cadets and 511 local officers. Upon his arrival to take charge of the Territory in July, Commissioner William A. Eadie was warmly welcomed, Lord Gladstone, the Governor-General, personally expressing his gratitude for what the Army had done and was doing.

Writing in *Our War in South Africa* in 1902, Commissioner Railton says :

Among all the black and coloured peoples there is a great work to be done ; for very little can be accomplished without learning a language : Dutch, for the 280,000 coloured ; Zulu, for the 600,000 Zulus ; IsiXhosa, for the 600,000 Amaxosas, and other

[1] *The History of The Salvation Army*, vol. iii, p. 5

interior tribes ; SeSutho, for the 300,000 Basutos ; Sechuana, for the 600,000 Bechuanas, and so on.

In addition there were

a great number of Germans and Scandinavians, several thousand Malays, who were all Mohammedans, and 53,000 Hindus in Natal, with a sprinkling of Chinese coolies and men of many other nations, including Jews, all over the country.

At that time Lieutenant-Colonel Allister Smith had the responsibility for sixty-seven African corps and outposts worked by twenty-eight European and fifty-three African officers, 212 local officers and some 3,000 Salvationists. Among the African officers were Adjutant Mbambo Matunjwa [1] and Ensign Maqili, two of the Colonel's earliest converts.

A visitor to London in 1912 was an Afrikaner, Adjutant Martin J. Adendorff, who, with his wife, was in charge of the corps at Cradock, Cape Colony, where, within four years, no fewer than 600 conversions had been recorded.

CHAPTER TWENTY-SEVEN

NEW ZEALAND

Sixty years ago New Zealand was described as a working-man's paradise ; strikes were practically unknown, all disputes being settled by the representatives of capital and labour in accordance with the Conciliation and Arbitration Act ; old-age pensions were being paid, and education was free. At this time Lieutenant-Colonel Gilmour was the State

[1] *The History of The Salvation Army*, vol. iv, p. 62

Commander, with his Headquarters in Christchurch, under Commissioner McKie, who was the Territorial Commander for Australasia. The country then had a population of only 832,505, some 44,000 being Maoris and 3,000 Chinese. The Army's work was regarded as an indispensable adjunct to the country's well-being, and was held in the highest esteem from the Premier down. " I was a resident of this city when the Army commenced work here," said the Mayor of Wellington, " and if you were now to remove your organization it would be an irreparable loss." A novel and useful feature in connection with certain of the larger corps was the establishment of an ambulance brigade. There were then ninety-three corps, 146 outposts and 220 officers.

Missionary work commenced in 1903 on the Maori island of Matakana by Captain McCarthy, and resulted in drink being prohibited, gambling ceasing, smoking being disallowed among children, who were fast becoming confirmed cigarette addicts, and old feuds between Pakehas (white people) and Maoris being forgotten. Of the 110 adults, no fewer than ninety had become attached to the Army by 1907. During 1905 the island was handed over to the Army with all its inhabitants, including nine chiefs. Captain McCarthy, a Maori chief by descent, died in 1906 as the result of a chill following the capsizing of a boat, and his body was carried many miles by the Maoris to its resting-place behind the quarters. Among his converts was Hoani, a great warrior chief who had lost a leg in the Gate Pah battle, the chief's wife, Kauwhau, and their son Kareti.

A new administration system came into force in 1905, when the colony was divided into two provinces, the North and the South Islands, each under a Provincial Commander : Brigadier Ernest Knight, with Headquarters in Christchurch, and Brigadier Thomas Albiston, with Headquarters in Wellington, respectively. These officers were directly responsible to Territorial Headquarters in Melbourne in Australia.

An innovation for the Army was the establishment of a fishing industry for the impoverished Maoris at Tauranga, in the Bay of Plenty, seemingly a most inappropriate name ! Boats were purchased and every Maori on the island was set to work, the Army buying all the fish caught and marketing it in Auckland. As the business advanced a smoke-house for curing the fish and a refrigerating plant for preserving a particularly heavy catch were introduced. Another experiment at this time was the scheme on the Pakatoa Island, in the Hauraki Gulf, for the reclamation of habitual drunkards, who were committed there by the magisterial courts. The " father " of the Home of some forty-six inebriates in 1909, a year after its opening, was an octogenarian with 134 convictions. A second island for inebriates, Roto Roa, was purchased later, the men from Pakatoa being transferred there and the original island being opened for women. It was claimed in September 1910 that of 233 inebriates who passed through the Army's hands from 25 to 35 per cent were permanently cured.

The Austral Guards Band, which had visited New Zealand from Australia under Adjutant William Gore in 1904, again toured the Territory in 1906, following the successful visit in the previous year of The Austral Lasses Band.[1] These touring combinations produced a notable increase in the efficiency of the corps bands. An outstanding New Zealand band was that of the Auckland corps, which had reached a high standard of playing in the early years of the century under Bandmaster H. Tremaine and had undertaken a five weeks' tour of the North Island in 1907.

Colonel (later Commissioner, D.D.) Samuel L. Brengle, an American evangelist, conducted a six months' Australasian

[1] p. 92

Holiness Campaign in 1910, commencing in the South Island at Christchurch. The two months he spent in New Zealand resulted in more than 800 seekers.

The citizens of Christchurch dealt in a most effective and summary manner with an attempt to prohibit Salvation Army open-air meetings in the summer of 1911, when the city council passed a bye-law which had the effect of forbidding the holding of open-air meetings in the Cathedral Square, where the Army had stood for more than twenty years. Summonses were issued against the leaders of meetings who refused to comply with the new bye-law, but before the cases came before the court the municipal elections took place, with the striking result that all the councillors who had had a hand in framing the bye-law were defeated. Amid the deafening cheers of a great crowd of 8,000 people, the Mayor-elect, when returning thanks, said that it was the intention of the new council to rescind the obnoxious bye-law at its first meeting, and the election could be looked upon as " the funeral ceremony of By-Law No. 5."

Owing to the growth of the Army's activities in both Australia and New Zealand, it became impossible for one command to give adequate supervision, so Commissioner William J. Richards was appointed Commander for the newly constituted New Zealand Territory in May 1912, he being cordially received upon arrival in Wellington by His Excellency the Governor, Lord Islington, and the Prime Minister. Within three months the Commissioner had been accorded fifteen civic receptions, had conducted ninety-nine public meetings, seen 630 seekers at the penitent form, conducted twelve officers' councils, five councils for bandsmen, two for the Headquarters staff, ten for young people, and had inspected every social institution, including the inebriates' islands of Pakatoa and Roto Roa. Rangiwaihi Te Puni, the last chieftainess of her tribe, the Ngatiawa, passed away in the early summer of 1913. For twenty-three of her eighty-six years she had been a soldier of Petone corps. Her husband, Chief Eruine, was held in such high esteem that the Government erected a handsome monument to his memory. The first Chief Secretary was Lieutenant-Colonel (later Colonel) Alan Fisher, one of Pioneer Pollard's early converts.[1]

The year 1912 saw the commencement of an era of great progress in young people's work under Brigadier William Hoare, who had pioneered it in 1891 [2] and was reappointed to the country as Territorial Young People's Secretary.

Brigadier Ernest Holdaway,[3] pioneer of the Army's Maori work, passed away in Australia in 1913 at the early age of forty-nine.

The Government decided upon the inauguration of a scheme of compulsory military training for men and boys from the ages of fourteen to twenty-four in 1910, and a nine days' territorial camp was established for those between eighteen and twenty-four. Four years later, in May 1914, Commissioner Richards nominated four of his officers as military chaplains : Brigadier William J. Hoare, Staff-Captain Gunn and Adjutants Gray and Haywood ; they being duly gazetted with the rank of Chaplain-Captain in H.M. Forces. This was the first time in the Army's history that such appointments had been made in any part of the British Empire. Sir Ian Hamilton, General Overseas Inspector of Forces, visited the camps, and at Takapau, where more than 6,000 men were gathered, spoke most appreciatively to Brigadier Hoare of the work being accomplished by the Army.

A new and imposing training college, the William Booth Memorial, costing £13,500, was opened in Wellington in

[1] *The History of The Salvation Army*, vol. ii, p. 293
[2] *The History of The Salvation Army*, vol. iv, p. 140
[3] *The History of The Salvation Army*, vol. iv, p. 139

the spring of 1914 in the presence of the Premier of New Zealand. The first Principal was Brigadier (later Colonel) William Gist. Gisborne, with a population of fewer than 10,000, was the champion Self-Denial corps of the world, raising in 1913 £1,632, which caused quite a sensation throughout the Army's ranks. It was hinted that another town was likely to steal a march upon Gisborne, and the pride which the citizens of this little community took in its achievement is evidenced in an emphatic statement by the Mayor : " It shall never be said that during my mayoralty our town lost its premier place in the Self-Denial list." At this time there were 260 corps and outposts.

III WILLIAM BOOTH'S UNFLAGGING ZEAL

CHAPTER ONE

PIONEER MOTOR-CAR EVANGELIST

WITH the triumph of the 1904 International Congress still ringing in his ears, the General, a fortnight after its conclusion and applying old principles to new methods, commenced in August what the *War Cry* described as " one of the most daring exploits of his career." This involved a dash from the granite rocks of Land's End, in Cornwall, to the Granite City of Aberdeen, in Scotland, by motor-car, a hazardous journey of 1,200 miles ; something that no evangelist had ever before undertaken. The war-worn, but apparently not weary, seventy-five-year-old enthusiast was to visit sixty-two towns and conduct three, and sometimes four, meetings a day for a month !

" I want you to remember that my last words to you in the Albert Hall are, that you must make haste with the glad tidings of mercy," he had said in his farewell charge to the Congress delegates, and here he was, setting the pace for his world-wide Army by converting the motor-car into a war chariot or running platform of salvation. The Chief of the Staff, who was to meet him at important centres, thought that " the change from close travelling in railway compartments and meetings, often in a vitiated atmosphere, to daily ' blows ' on the road and comparative immunity from the stuffiness of halls, would have a most refreshing and recupera-

tive effect upon his father's physical and nervous system."
Any mechanical breakdowns, even when they occurred to
the detriment of the fixed programme, would but add to the
gaiety of the Campaign. When asked how and where the
idea germinated, the General replied :

The first time the notion occurred to me was at Banbury, twelve
months ago. I had never been there before, and probably never
shall go again. The whole place appeared to me to come out to
see me and bless me and touch me, and so I thought that if I
could get about quickly from place to place—especially to those
places it was not physically possible for one to reach by train—it
would be a source of legitimate pleasure to the people and
advantageous to the Kingdom. The motor-car suggested itself
as the readiest method. Since then the idea has fermented, until
now it has taken shape and form, and promises to be a success
when carried out.

The forthcoming enterprise was at first received with fear.
" They saw me landed in canals or pitched over a hedge,"
said the General, who had first boarded a motor-car in Paris.
With the sanguinity of an everlasting youth, or like the war
charger that tosses his mane with eagerness to rush into battle,
he was anxious to be on the trail.

One can scarcely realize in these days of the 500-mile-an-
hour racing-car that " the horseless carriage " was formerly
banished by law from the highways of Britain. A motor-car
could do the 200-mile journey from London to York in nine
hours and travel at the alarming rate of thirty-five miles per
hour when at full stretch—an incredible achievement sixty
years ago. The motor-car, fundamentally as we know it
today, was brought to England in 1895, and for long was
" too much the servant of the rich." The General's car was
considered to be a handsome and comfortable vehicle, seating
five persons, including the driver. Four cars were hired and
a fifth was placed at the Army's disposal by a ministerial
friend. One was set apart for representatives of the Press.

Mr Harold Begbie, who was later to write William Booth's official biography, represented the *Daily Mail*. Commissioners Coombs, Nicol and Cadman, who predicted " a campaign of dust, smoke, fire, salvation and victory," and Colonels Lawley and Eadie, " Captain of the Fleet," accompanied the General.

The campaign commenced on the rugged rocky peninsula of Land's End with the General quoting to Harold Begbie Charles Wesley's famous hymn, " Lo, on a narrow neck of land," which he had been inspired to write a century and a half before when standing on the same spot. No one else was present apart from the General's entourage, and the old man had drawn the younger man to the very brink of the cliff so that they stood alone together. Begbie thought the General to be nervous and tired.

The weariness of the old man made a more instant appeal than anything he said. One felt an infinite pity for him, and this feeling arose from the impression he made of unwillingness to be a chief figure, as though he shrank from publicity, as though he were ashamed of notoriety, as though he wanted to creep away and be a simple man of whom nothing was expected.

Then William Booth travelled to St Just to conduct the first indoor meeting of the campaign in the Wesleyan Chapel, the scene of his labours forty years before " when people cried for mercy by the thousands." The actor, Sir Henry Irving, looked intently upon the drama when the General was heralded to Penzance, where his son Herbert [1] had been born. Through the lined streets of wildly cheering villagers and townspeople in Cornwall he made his triumphal entry, on the third day, into Devon.

Writing from Liskeard on 11 August to Bramwell, he describes the terrors of the tour, which had only just begun :

[1] *The History of The Salvation Army*, vol. iv, p. 364

So far I have hardly spoken a word even to anyone when in the car. The speed—the hills ! ! ! ! the " chunting " of our engine and the crowds who expect a wave of my hand at every clump of houses absorb my attention. The hill ascents and descents are frightful—but so far I have been preserved from a scintilla of fear. Thank God for that ! But the nervous strain is terrible. I was asleep on the platform at night. We go past, often at a rate of 40 miles an hour. Oh, it is a WHIRL !

The tour now developed into something like a royal progress. He was welcomed by mayors, Church dignitaries and other leading citizens.

Writing *en route* to his officers and soldiers, the General says :

This is one of the greatest, grandest, and one of the most effective efforts I have ever been privileged to make. Some religious paper, they tell me, has been trying to belittle the effort by describing me as a showman. All right. I don't in the least object. I accept the application. For am I not flying through the land calling upon men and women to look at the accursed sins and vices that are eating out of their hearts and lives the peace and purity and plenty God wants them to enjoy ?

The General would not have the canopy put on the big open Humber. He sat exposed to the wind and the rain.

White macintoshed, with the folds of a motoring cap protecting his neck, the General even disdained to use an umbrella, and arrived at Piccadilly [Manchester] with a rain-washed face.

The unexpected greeting of the Lord Mayor, who waited uncovered in pouring rain, was, the *War Cry* wrote, " unique in his [the General's] remarkable history." At Harrogate the strange and cheerful spectacle was witnessed of the Mayor riding through the town with the head of The Salvation Army, preceded by the band of the local corps in a brake, and followed by nearly half a mile of carriages. In Newcastle upon Tyne Commissioner Nicol, who was reporting for the *War Cry*, was knocked face downwards on to the street by a horse, and miraculously saved from death by crumpling himself between the wheels of the bus it was pulling ; but the step on the back of the vehicle caught his body and turned him over and over. He was picked up unconscious, but apart from shock he was not seriously injured.

At Perth, Scotland, an impromptu function was resorted to which had rarely, if ever at that time, been associated with the reception of a religious leader into its domain, for the city council was convened in the early morning to welcome the General and the Chief of the Staff, who had joined him there, seated in their robes of office in the council chamber. Between Dunblane and Crieff the General, sitting next to the driver of his open car, was soaked almost to the skin by pelting rain during a violent storm. " The journey was weird and at times horrible," says the reporter, but the streets of the town were " as thickly laden with people as if the reception had happened in the full glare of a Highland sun beating upon the hills." Fittingly, the Earl of Aberdeen welcomed the General to the city of his name at the conclusion of this " real Hallelujah affair," and presented him with an illuminated address of greeting from 250 fisher-workers. All the important London dailies published lengthy accounts of the venture.

*   *   *

Not surprisingly the General embarked upon another and more extensive tour in the following summer, only two days after his arrival home from Australasia and the Holy Land. The Campaign started from Folkestone and finished in Glasgow, the General returning by way of the East Coast, the final meeting of the six weeks' effort taking place in the Royal Albert Hall. As in the previous year, the campaign was a prodigious achievement, a complete and gratifying success. It provided a wider and more commanding platform for the General than he had yet occupied, and that, perhaps, was the supreme result. It testified to the perennial youthfulness of William Booth, who, despite his years, seemed little affected by the weight of his responsibility, by the discomforts of the journey—for the cars of sixty years ago could hardly be described as luxurious, apart from their novelty and speed —or by the numerous addresses—many of them given in torrential rain—that would have taxed the mental and physical capacity of many a younger man. On this occasion W. P. Ryan, special correspondent of the *Daily Chronicle*, joined the fleet of six cars, and afterward wrote a book, *The Romance of a Motor Mission*, in which he likened the General first to an evangelistic Santa Claus and then to a modern Isaiah.

One of the many thousands who welcomed him to Folkestone on the first day of the campaign was Captain Care, an old fisherman who, during the troublous days of riots there, acted as captain of the skeleton army. This time the General, who was accompanied by the Chief of the Staff, used a big white Darracq with red wheels, and was himself attired in a dark green motor coat so that he could be the more easily located by the crowds waiting to cheer him as he hurried past. As before, he was greeted by the leading citizens of the cities and towns *en route*, and was heard by multitudes of people who dared inclement weather to attend the open-air gatherings. Indeed, the campaign assumed the dimensions of a national ovation to " the grand old man of England," as Mr John Henniker Heaton, M.P., had described him at Canterbury. At Barnsley he was met by three specially chartered trams filled with Salvationists. At Belper he referred to the fact that his father was a Belper man. At Ayr he addressed men and women prisoners before nine o'clock in the morning. It was estimated that 120,000 people gathered on Paisley Road to see the cavalcade pass by. Commissioner T. Henry Howard joined the General at York. The campaign closed with a picturesque and historic gathering of 10,000 people standing in pelting rain on Mile End Waste, where the Army had been born,[1] and later in the Royal Albert Hall, where the white car with the red wheels had a place of honour on the platform ! London had not seen the General since his return from the victories of Australasia and his visit to Calvary. This night he paid tribute to his eldest son, Bramwell :

I don't very often say much about him, because he is my son ; but because he is also the Chief of the Staff, perhaps I ought to say that he is by capacity, by his devotion, his courage, and his influence with men, well-fitted to be my right hand in the administration of the affairs of this great Movement. I could not wander about the world with the ease that I do but for him.

The remarkable organization of these triumphant campaigns was largely due to the genius of Colonel (later Commissioner) William Eadie, the Field Secretary, who was the " brains " behind the scenes, he being possessed of an unusual topographical and geographical knowledge of the country. It was a gigantic task, the calculation of the timing alone being of considerable importance. The enormous amount of advertising, the arrangements for the indoor and outdoor receptions and meetings, and the billeting of the General and his staff were superbly directed.

★   ★   ★

In the following year, 1906, the indomitable General decided upon a third Motor Campaign, the two previous undertakings having been so extraordinarily successful. This time the campaign was to start from amid the Highlands of Scotland, at Inverness, and conclude on 29 August in

[1] *The History of The Salvation Army*, vol. i, p. 45

Plymouth, and was to last a month. The line of progression was to be through a part of the country hitherto untouched by the previous expeditions. At Fort George he had the unique experience for him of preaching to two famous regiments of Highland soldiers, the Black Watch and the Seaforths. On the parade-ground 1,000 men stood, with military correctness, in the form of a square. Three resonant cheers, called for by the sergeant-major of the Black Watch, greeted the conclusion of the General's address. At Carlisle he spoke to the inmates of the workhouse. The *War Cry* reporter says that it was " a new thing under the sun, at least in this country," for the mayor and corporation to welcome the General on a specially erected platform in front of the market, to present him with an address and then to march to the town hall in a civic procession. Outside Fleetwood thousands of servicemen—Borderers and Royal Lancasters— blocked the highway, thus forcing the cars to stop, for the men wanted to hear the General. The Memorial Theatre at Stratford on Avon, never before leased to a religious organization, was generously placed at the General's disposal. At Bath, where the General's granddaughter, Captain Catherine Booth, was the Commanding Officer, Mr J. P. Whitney, the Premier of Ontario, gave striking testimony to the success and efficiency of the Emigration Department. Not everyone fell under the spell of the General. At least one mayor refused to countenance his visit, and a clergyman in a small Somersetshire town denounced him and the Army from his pulpit as being antagonistic to his Church ! The third Motor Campaign was concluded, as it had begun, in a prison, Dartmoor, where the General addressed 1,000 convicts, opening the meeting with " There is a fountain filled with blood " to the tune of " Auld Lang Syne " !

★   ★   ★

William Booth's desire for another Motor Campaign in 1907 revealed his insatiable thirst for getting down to the people. No sooner was his memorable visit to Japan concluded than the fourth tour was commenced in July, on the occasion of the celebration of the forty-second anniversary of the Army's birth. This Saturday ended with a veritable blaze of fireworks, in the midst of which the General struck out for the north. The tour began at High Barnet, near to the General's home at Hadley Wood, on the following Tuesday, continued through the eastern counties, across Yorkshire and Lancashire, around the coast-line of Wales, down to Brighton to finish in London. At Conway, North Wales, William Booth had the enchanting experience of speaking within the ruins of the twelfth-century banqueting hall of King Edward I's castle, one of the most magnificent piles in the United Kingdom. At Blaina the General's seventeen-year-old grandson, Bernard (later Colonel), delivered his first public speech. Nineteen years before, the name of Portal had been the symbol of hostility to The Salvation Army at Whitchurch, Hampshire,[1] but when the General entered the town he was welcomed by Mayor Spencer Portal and presented with an address of goodwill and God-speed by Sir William Portal. Here the Premier of Ontario again participated in a Motor Campaign meeting. Worthing had been a second Whitchurch twenty years before,[2] but now Mayor Linfield, who had himself sheltered, for a fortnight, two Salvationists from the mob incensed by hate and prejudice, presided at the General's meeting.

★   ★   ★

Yet another Motor Campaign was organized for the summer of 1908—a tour through Scotland and the heart of

---

[1] *The History of The Salvation Army*, vol. iv, p. 288
[2] *The History of The Salvation Army*, vol. ii, p. 179

England, commencing at Dundee and finishing up at the Crystal Palace. Colonel Eadie had been " skipper " of the four previous campaigns ; now his place was to be taken by Colonel Whatmore. How did this Grand Old Motorist, just about to enter his eightieth year, manage to keep in such extremely good health throughout these now annual and most strenuous of campaigns ? That was a mystery no one could elucidate, but look at his average day :

The General awakes by seven o'clock, and by eight has partaken of his toast, tea and hot milk. Between eight and nine interviews, autograph books, correspondence, and photography occupy his attention. At nine prompt his hands are waving adieus to the hundreds who cheer him on his way. At 10.30, after a dusty ride and a wayside meeting, he replies to a deputation from the Council, washes the dirt off his face, and takes his place on the platform. At 12.15 he is again waving that hand to the upturned faces and saying " God bless you ! " At 2 he is on the wheels ; at 3 expounding in a town twenty miles ahead the salvation of God and its fruits, and at 5.15 his fountain-pen is running over folio after folio. At 6 he is once more on the White Car, and at 7.30, after a couple of addresses, he is again in a new town, holding, by the spell of his sincerity, oratory, and personality, a crowd of people. At 9.30 the wheels of his human mechanism shows signs of wear ; but the last meal—the basin of milk—puts new life into him, and at 11 he is ruminating on the lessons of the day or the contents of a fat dispatch from I.H.Q.

In all these lengthy tours the General had the support of leading officers from time to time. Colonel John Lawley, his indefatigable A.D.C., was always at his side, and the irrepressible Commissioner Cadman was the leader of the innumerable overflow meetings. At West Stanley the General visited a dying corps officer, and at Knaresborough hundreds of children greeted him, as in many other towns. Accrington was like Mafeking night. At Oldham folk came out in their hundreds of thousands ; it was one of the great

*A familiar sight in William Booth's meetings: his A.D.C., Colonel John Lawley,
singing his own song, "Give them a welcome!" In his diary the General wrote:
"Lawley sang with delightful influence."*

emotional moments of any of the five campaigns. In Aylesbury Prison yard the General, standing in his car, addressed 127 women convicts. "They stood on a grass plot, dressed in blue skirts, white caps, white aprons and triangle-shaped handkerchiefs." At Reading the distinguished lawyer, Mr Rufus Isaacs, K.C., M.P. (afterward Marquis of Reading), in welcoming the General said : " The human race welcomed The Salvation Army as one of its greatest and proudest possessions." The band of the Argyll Highlanders serenaded the General's arrival at Chatham. The fifth Campaign ended at the Crystal Palace, the General in his white car making a triumphal entry through the north nave of the Central Transept, and being drawn by officers. The Army was then celebrating its forty-third anniversary. In all the General had travelled, during 165 days, approximately 8,000 miles ; he had held 495 indoor meetings, at which he addressed 500,000 people, and had spoken to 150 gatherings by the wayside. It was estimated that at least 9,000,000 people had seen him and, most marvellous of all, not once had the General missed an appointment, nor had his health been impaired.

★   ★   ★

The sixth Motor Campaign in succession started in July 1909 from the Congress Hall, Clapton, London, proceeded through the Eastern Counties and went west via the North and Midlands to South Wales. The car was a new and more powerful vehicle. Mr (later Sir) H. Rider Haggard, the novelist, spoke at the General's welcome to Bungay, Suffolk. " If the Government had only taken the General's advice," he said, " and had assisted in establishing colonists on the land, many of those who were now a burden to the State would have been comfortably situated and earning their own livelihood." The Duke of Portland presided over the Grand Theatre meeting in Mansfield. But at Pontypool came calamity ; the General was attacked by pain in the right eye, which had recently been operated upon for cataract, and his host, a medical man, sought the advice of a specialist, who ordered his immediate return to his oculist in London. He had suffered intense pain long before mentioning it. The campaign had to be abandoned after the General had spoken at Newport for an hour. The previous night he had stayed at the palace of Dr Percival, Bishop of Hereford, who had presided at the great Drill Hall meeting. " The General has, more than any other man, inspired thousands to work, and we are now welcoming the master-worker himself," said this lordship. On the following Friday Mr Higgens, the oculist, performed another operation on the eye, but this proved to be unsuccessful. It was thought that something from the road had entered the eye during the tour, for the General rode in an open car and seldom wore goggles.

★   ★   ★

To everyone's astonishment it was announced on 12 August 1911 that the General had decided upon yet another, a seventh Motor Campaign, to commence where the 1909 Campaign had abruptly ended, in South Wales ; and now he was eighty-two. The tour was to have commenced at Barry Dock only nine days later, and this time the General was to go north and conclude at Watford. " I feel it is going to be one of amongst the difficult enterprises of my life," he prophesied. The first week's programme had to be abandoned owing to the dislocation caused by the railway strike. As soon as this was settled, however, the General decided that the campaign should go on, now to commence from Leigh, Lancashire, on 27 August, continuing from Watford into the Midlands and concluding in Cardiff. The Postmaster-General, Mr (later Viscount) Herbert Samuel, M.P., presided at Guisborough. "I do not think," he said, "that history records in all her long annals the life of a religious leader who carried on his work for so long a period and over an area so vast as the General has done during his long life." The Rev. Dr Albert David, headmaster of Dr Arnold's famous school, was the General's host in Rugby.

Within a few days of completing his zigzagging rush 1,600 miles through England and into South Wales, this restless old soulwinner was off to Scotland for a full Sunday's meetings and a week of lecturing ! He now knew that he was growing blind and said so in the *War Cry*.

Chapter Two

EUROPEAN CONQUESTS

The General's journeyings became inseparable from his preaching and campaigning, and he was as famous a world-traveller as he was a reformer. Few, if any, men had so harnessed the forces of locomotion to the Gospel Chariot since Paul undertook his missionary journeys, during which he scattered the seed of Christianity throughout Southern and Eastern Europe. It was because the sins and sorrows of the world had burned themselves into his heart that he could not be still. He certainly did not travel because he enjoyed the experience, for even the most luxurious means of transport in his day were a long way short of what they are today, and his voice was generally affected by sea voyages and cessation from public work. He wrote to Bramwell on 13 March 1909 from Sweden :

I crawled out of the carriage at 4.30 p.m. half dead—with my bread, butter and cheese, &c., lunch, half or a quarter digested, to meet some 10,000 or 12,000 or more people—band playing—flags flying—carriage all ready for a platform, everybody ready but poor me. How to get a few sentences in any way equal to the opportunity I do not know—but I struggled through ten or fifteen minutes' talk.

The demands of his vast social and religious empire set the feet of William Booth marching, first to Holland, after the 1904 Motor Campaign. *De Nieuwe Courant*, one of the principal morning papers of the royal city, stated that such great crowds as welcomed him had rarely been seen at The Hague. "The Amsterdam week-end has been a glorious climax to the most remarkable campaign I have ever been privileged to conduct in Holland," he declared, although he admitted to being "more or less ill all the time, and am puzzled to know why." A few weeks later he was in Germany, conducting for the first time in Berlin a "Repentance Day" campaign in the magnificent Circus Busch, holding some 5,000 people, which was so often used by him in following years that it came to be known as the Circus Booth ! In the "most remarkable series of meetings yet conducted in the Fatherland" 420 seekers for Christ were registered. In some respects the lecture in the "New World" —one of the finest halls in the city—surpassed even the wonderful Circus meetings of the previous week.

In November 1905 William Booth was again in Germany, commencing in Cologne, where, in contrast to former days,[1] says the reporter,

The Catholic bishop and priests rather wish us well than otherwise ; but the best friends of the Army are the police. The press,

[1] *The History of The Salvation Army*, vol. iv, p. 2

judging by its fine, picturesque, and sympathetic reports, write about us without dipping their pens into inkpots of satire and prejudice.

From Mulhausen the General passed into Switzerland, opening his campaign in Basle and concluding in Geneva. Within four months he was back in Holland—50,000 people greeted him on his arrival in the Station Square of the capital. " Nothing during my wandering life has impressed me much more than the gatherings in the People's Palace, Amsterdam," he wrote. Toward the end of 1906 he was again in Germany, this time in connection with the national " Busstag " (Repentance Day) in the Circus Busch. " Often the roaring on the part of the savage animals mingled strangely with my introductory welcome,"he said, " from counts and countesses, merchant princes, university professors, clergymen, artisans, together with the rough and tumble sections of the community."

Royal recognition was granted the Army in the early part of 1907 when the General was received in audience by the King and Queen of Denmark, in the Amalienborg Palace, Copenhagen [1] ; King Haakon of Norway, in the Royal Palace in Christiania (Oslo) ; and Queen Sophia of Sweden, who received him on behalf of King Oscar, who was ill. William Booth's Scandinavian visit in this year was one of the most brilliant and important undertakings of his long and honoured career. A South European Congress of Staff Officers was held in the spring of 1908 in Berlin, where the General gave a remarkable exposition of Salvation Army doctrines and regulations in the Philharmonic Hall. When Lieutenant-Colonel Junker [2] had asked for the use of this hall some years before the manager threatened to kick him downstairs. At that time it was looked upon as sacrilege for

[1] p. 29
[2] *The History of The Salvation Army*, vol. iv, p. 7

the Army to use it ; now it had become a privilege. During the Repentance Day meetings in November William Booth made an eloquent appeal for the removal of suspicion between the Fatherland and Great Britain.

On the verge of his eightieth birthday, and during the rigorous winter of 1909, he again visited Scandinavia. At the conclusion of his lecture in Aarhus, Denmark, the Assistant Commissioner of Police spontaneously jumped to his feet and in a loud voice cried, " Long live the great General of Peace ! " The crowd yelled back its reply in hurrahs. The King's Chamberlain brought a welcome message from the King and Queen to his billet. In Norway he was " tired, but fighting grandly." His letters to Bramwell often speak of his tiredness :

What a whirl my life is ! [he wrote from Berlin in June 1906]. I am moderately located and miserably fed so far, but I have had an excellent night's sleep for me, that is, I have not woke above six times and got to sleep again on each occasion without any very long interval.

For the first time in the history of the Army a king was present at a meeting, and in his own capital. This was in Christiania where King Haakon rose to his feet in the royal enclosure of the hall in which the General was to speak to welcome him. In Sweden he was received by the recently crowned King Gustav V, whose brother, Prince Oscar Bernadotte, presided at the lecture. From Helsingfors (Helsinki), Finland, the General went to St Petersburg (Leningrad), this being his first time on Russian soil.[1]

Again astonishing his critics, the old man went off on a cheerless February evening in 1910 for another Continental campaign which commenced in Holland. He was then nearly eighty-one years of age and had but recently recovered

[1] p. 75

from an illness of the gravest character. He was still on the platform in Amsterdam at half-past ten on the Sunday night watching the seekers coming to the penitent form, and sometimes they came in their hundreds. Queen Wilhemina and the Prince Consort sent letters of apology for not attending his meeting at The Hague. In the November he spoke in Potsdam, Germany, where the royal residence was situated, a most unlikely centre for crowds, but the hall was packed, the audience including many royal personages. Three months later the General was on the Continent yet again. At Schaffhausen, in Switzerland, nearly 3,000 came to hear him ; on the previous occasion fewer than forty were present. In Italy the Lord Mayor of Rome received him and King Victor Emmanuel sent him a message of greeting. In Venice he added a gondola to his varied means of transport over the years. The summer of 1911 saw a Salvation Fleet of twenty-five steamers taking part in a brilliant demonstration across Lake Maelar to Sodertelje, in Sweden, where William Booth was the central figure of a wonderful field day. A fortnight of remarkable campaigning concluded in a " canvas cathedral " seating 3,000 people at Nimmerdor, Holland. The Rev. Dr Callenbach, of the State Church in Rotterdam, described the General in February 1912 as " a snow-capped volcano with a heart of fire." Another important week of staff councils for North European officers was held in Christiania in March ; the General was granted the honour of addressing a distinguished audience in the new University Hall ; and during the summer he spoke in Christiania Cathedral, something quite new for Norway. But the Continent was to hear him no more.

CHAPTER THREE

THE HOLY LAND AND AUSTRALASIA

On his way to Australia and New Zealand in the spring of 1905, William Booth decided to spend a few days in the Holy Land with the Chief of the Staff; however, Bramwell decided that they could not both be spared from London. Said the *War Cry*:

At first the General subordinated his inclination to utility, not quite seeing how he could get an adequate return, in the interests of the Army, for the expenditure of time and strength that such a visit would involve. However, being now convinced that there is a fair prospect of a journey to the Holy City being attended by some permanent good to the cause he has so much at heart, our Leader has agreed to disembark at Port Said on the voyage out to the Colonies, for the purpose stated.

Nevertheless, it was one of the desires of his life to see Jerusalem. The most dramatic incident of his first day (9 March) in the Holy Land occurred in the Garden of Gethsemane, where, profoundly moved, he threw himself on his knees beneath the shade of one of the venerable olive trees and called fervently upon God to bless the world. On Calvary an interesting episode took place—the signing of a moral encyclical addressed to " All who name the name ot Christ throughout the world," which the General had finished writing that day. This was published on a full page in the *War Cry*. The colours of the Army, unfolded in the Holy Land for the first time, were waved over the General's party as they recited the last verse of the hymn, " When I survey the wondrous Cross " commencing " Were the whole realm of nature mine." The General's visit to

Jerusalem "produced a small but potentially important revival" of religion among both Gentile and Jew, more than one hundred professing conversion in his meetings. In Jaffa forty converts knelt at the penitent form ; but the Turkish Government prohibited its subjects from attending the General's meetings. Says Bramwell in a private letter :

The secular press feels that a very large proportion of the newspaper reading public is interested in knowing what you are doing and discusses your movements and sayings day by day.

En route to New Zealand the General disembarked at Melbourne where in the Training Garrison he celebrated his seventy-sixth birthday. At Government House, Hobart, he was received by Sir George Strickland, the Roman Catholic Governor of Tasmania. The Australasian campaign actually commenced in Invercargill, New Zealand. When the General's train stopped at two stations which were "not on the programme," on the way to Dunedin, but where hundreds of people had gathered in the hope of seeing and hearing him, he gave instructions that henceforth he would speak at every station where there was a corps, whether on the programme or not. Protestation from his staff, who were anxious about his health, were of no avail. A Maori woman picturesquely supplicated Heaven's blessing on "the great grandfather of us all—the man with a thousand hearts in one !" In Dunedin, Bishop Samuel T. Nevill, the Primate, proposed to the General that The Salvation Army should unite with the Anglican Church in efforts for pushing on the social work. William Booth reciprocated this friendly spirit, referred to previous failures of the same object,[1] but said he would be glad to co-operate with any organization which left the Army free control. In Wellington he prayed at the opening of the Senate. The Governor of New Zealand, Lord Plunkett, and the Prime Minister, the Hon. Richard J.

[1] *The History of The Salvation Army*, vol. ii, p. 146

Seddon, welcomed the General, as did Sir Henry Rawson, the Governor of New South Wales. After a great meeting in Sydney Town Hall, the Archbishop of New South Wales said, " We have had a great time, and we are going away heartily ashamed of ourselves." A Salvationist M.P. in a red guernsey took part in " fishing " in the prayer meeting. Mr Carruthers, the Premier, invited the General to meet his Cabinet at lunch. Then followed luncheon with the Governor-General, Lord Northcote, and Lady Northcote, at Government House. Despite warnings of dengue fever— 100,000 of a population of 150,000 were stricken—the General persisted in going to Brisbane. Here again he lunched with the Cabinet. In Melbourne, the former Prime Minister of the Commonwealth, the Hon. Alfred Deakin, honoured the General with a flying visit, and the Governor of Victoria, Sir Reginald Talbot, attended his lecture in the enormous Exhibition Building; the Premier, the Hon. George Reid, invited him to meet his Cabinet at lunch. In Adelaide he was received at Government House by Admiral Sir Frederick and Lady Bedford. The Governor presided at his meeting in Perth. Altogether William Booth gave ninety-one public addresses, averaging an hour and a half each, preached fifty-six sermons, had sixty welcomes and saw 2,000 seekers at the penitent form.

When he left London in August 1908 for a three months' visit to South Africa, a waiting-room at Waterloo Station was placed at his disposal by the railway company, a saloon carriage was attached to a mail train and a special gangway was provided by the steamship company at Southampton. In the Market House at Durban he addressed 5,000 Zulus, some of whom had walked 170 miles to be present. Considerably altering his plans, he travelled to Salisbury, Rhodesia. He was received by the Governors of the various States.

CHAPTER FOUR

IN THE FAR EAST

The year 1907 was distinguished in the Army's history for, perhaps, the most interesting of all the General's wide-world travellings ; in the spring he visited Japan—where he stayed for a month—journeying via the U.S.A. and Canada, where, in Toronto, he was welcomed by the Lieutenant-Governor of Ontario (the Hon. William Mortimer Clark, K.C.) and the Premier, J. P. Whitney. The business of the Legislative Assembly was suspended in order to receive the General, who was conducted to the floor of the Chamber by the Speaker and Mace-bearer. The General spoke on emigration. In Ottawa he was the guest of Earl Grey, the Governor-General, and met Sir Wilfred Laurier, the Prime Minister. It was the Governor-General who, when he heard of William Booth's intention to visit Japan, had cabled to him to go by way of Canada. For the first time in the Dominion the stage of a theatre was used in the saving of souls ; this was in His Majesty's Theatre, Montreal, where more than 2,000 people were unable to obtain admission to the night meeting. Police-Magistrate Daly remarked that the General had received in Winnipeg a reception such as even the King of England would not get were he to visit the city. William Booth was made an honorary member of the Canadian Club, only the Governor-General also holding that privilege. " This will be one of the heaviest weeks of my life—eighteen important meetings in one week," he had written.

Following the Easter week-end in Seattle the General spent his seventy-eighth birthday on the *Minnesota*, which was flying the Salvation Army flag, in mid-ocean *en route* to

Japan, where he was received in the Imperial Palace by the Emperor, a rare honour for the head of a religious organization, following a welcome in Tokio in which 25,000 people participated. The *Daily Mail* described the occasion as one of " frantic enthusiasm." Etiquette required that conversation with the Emperor should be carried on in so low a tone as to be practically whispered. The General also offered prayer at a great Buddhist conference. At Yokohama he found Commissioner Railton awaiting him, and daylight fireworks were displayed to inform the port of his entry. The word " Hallelujah ! " in Japanese characters was produced in fireworks form for the first time in the history of the world. During the tour the General decided upon the appointment of Commissioner Eadie to take command of the Army's work in Japan in succession to Colonel (later Commissioner) Bullard, who had been in charge for the past seven years. One of the first results of the General's stay in Japan was his decision to form immediately a league for the protection of Oriental women at home and abroad. He also decided to inaugurate a campaign in Korea [1] under the supervision of Lieutenant-Colonel (later Lieutenant-Commissioner) Charles Duce. In Tokio the General was greeted in the Town Hall by some of the leading men of Japan, these including Field-Marshal Marquis Oyama, famous for his participation in the Manchurian War, who later invited William Booth to his own home. In Sendai 35,000 people shrieked " *Banzai !* " at the railway station, a welcome which " surpassed everything in my whole life's history." Of the great meeting he conducted, the municipal newspaper wrote :

If this man remains long in Japan he will change its religion, for he speaks not as the professors, but as a man with a soul in possession of secrets.

[1] p. 1

At the conclusion of the Japanese campaign Brigadier Yamamuro [1] was appointed as the Second in Command. Ten thousand university students were addressed at Wasida University at the invitation of the President, Count Okuma.

Summing up his impressions of Japan the General prophesied, and how rightly :

It is only a question of time when her industries will be tutored with the most expert direction, and packed with the finest machinery taken from all nations of the world, and I do not see what can prevent her producing the finest articles at the cheapest possible price.

William Booth returned to England after seventeen weeks to receive on 26 June 1907 the degree of Doctor of Civil Law from the University of Oxford and a great welcome home in the Royal Albert Hall on the following day,[2] when he wore his scarlet gown of a D.C.L. for the first and last time in public. Among the distinguished audience was Sir Arthur Conan Doyle, the creator of Sherlock Holmes.

CHAPTER FIVE

ACROSS THE ATLANTIC

William Booth sailed again for the New World on 13 September 1907. Earl Attlee was a passenger on the Allan liner *Virginian*, and in his book *As it Happened* he says :

Among the passengers was old General William Booth of The Salvation Army. I distinctly remember his going ashore at Rimouski crying, " Save your souls, save your souls ! "

[1] *The History of The Salvation Army*, vol. iv, p. 69
[2] p. 232

As the General touched Canadian soil after six days of " dirty weather," at three o'clock in the morning, was greeted only by Commissioner Coombs and his staff, and then was immediately immersed in enquiries and suggestions concerning the business on which he had crossed the ocean, according to the *War Cry* reporter, one is tempted to ask, " To whom did William Booth cry ' Save your souls ! ' *at three o'clock in the morning* ? " The noble earl's words savour of the melodramatic aurora that is frequently associated with memories of the first General. Such an incident, and certainly the wording of the cry, was quite out of character. During this journey the General lectured under the presidency of Signor Marconi, the inventor of wireless telegraphy, who spoke warmly of the Army's work and mission.

A body of brewers joined in the General's welcome to Rochester, and on the last day of his stay in Chicago he addressed 1,100 university professors and students, but he contracted a chill at St Louis and was too unwell to keep his week-end appointment at Cleveland. The *War Cry* reporter, Commissioner Alex. M. Nicol, found himself " as the poor substitute," but on the following Wednesday the restless leader, who very seldom missed an appointment through illness, was on the warpath again, speaking at Columba and Pittsburg. Within a few days he was lunching for the second time at the White House in Washington, D.C., with President and Mrs Theodore Roosevelt. The President expressed his opinion of brass bands, among other things :

There is no more effective method of evangelising a people than with a brass band. I confess I like brass bands, and I like your brass bands.

Philadelphia presented the General with the freedom of " the Quaker capital," an electric key being suspended from the arch of the City Hall—an honour, the *Philadelphia Ledger* stated, that no military hero had ever received. Governors of States welcomed him. The final farewell was held in the City Hall Park, New York, following an extended parade through the streets at 9 p.m., tens of thousands lining the route. President Roosevelt wired his congratulations. Said the *Hartford Times* :

General Booth is a steam engine in trousers. Although seventy-eight years old, he still continues to hustle, and his activities are as varied and as strenuous as ever. The idea of quitting work, tilting his chair, and taking things easy, never occurs to him. He is a bundle of energy, a keg of dynamite, an example of perpetual motion.

Although absent from International Headquarters for nearly four months, the General went direct to Germany, where, with the Chief of the Staff by his side, he conducted in the Circus Busch in Berlin yet another Repentance Day's meetings, which were attended by the Lord Mayor.[1]

Chapter Six

AT HOME

Although everywhere William Booth drew great congregations, and often had to listen to expansive eulogies from those who came willingly to preside, he was not spiritually satisfied, and wrote the Chief of the Staff on 8 October 1905 from Kilmarnock, laying bare his soul :

I feel very much impressed with these great crowds, and yet perplexed as to how to make the best use of them. It seems to me, as far as my knowledge goes, that no man was ever favoured

[1] p. 149

with such an opportunity of speaking to such crowds as has fallen to my lot. O'Connell, Gladstone and Bright had the chance of talking politics. Wesley and Whitfield drew immense crowds in the chief centres of population to hear about religion, but here I am, listened to with the profoundest attention by all classes of people on a combination of questions which the most nearly concern the welfare of the nation, and which ought to lie nearest to their hearts. And what complicates the thing still further is that I labour continually under the feeling that I do the work that Providence seems to have given me to do so imperfectly.

This part of the letter is typewritten, but, disappointed and dejected, he adds a postscript headed " Last thing," in his own handwriting, which bears evidence of his mood and weariness after a heavy day :

I have worked hard all day—*immense* audiences—*rivetted* attention —did not have a moment's freedom or helpfulness through the whole of the meetings. . . . My nerves are in a poorish way. I must get some sort of cessation from this whirl. But how can it be, I don't see. I am sick of this WORLDLY praise, &c. I am sure that it is unfavourable to the SOUL SAVING SPIRIT. I am writing jargon—I shall feel better tomorrow ! ! !

A few months later, from Paddington Station, he is again inwardly disturbed :

I wish I could have a little more time for MEDITATION about ETERNAL THINGS. I must not let my soul get dried up with these secular affairs—even if they concern the highest earthly interests of my FELLOWS. After all, SOUL matters are of most, are of infinite importance, and are most closely connected with earthly advantage. Oh, Lord, increase my FAITH and YOURS !

Writing to the Chief on 24 August 1906 from Dorchester, the General replied to Bramwell's frequent suggestion that he should take some sort of open-air exercise :

I shall be old [he was in his seventy-seventh year !] and infirm before I go driving for my health. It is very kind of you to suggest it, but I am a long way past that. The fact is that any occasion or recreation or anything else is a torture to me unless leading up to some useful end.

Almost every day he is entertained in a different household, where a generous hostess is prepared to feed him on " the fat of the land," but he steadfastly adheres to his austere dieting :

I am very comfortably billeted, and a beautiful supper was prepared . . . some kind of early salmon which looked very tempting and savoury, but I resisted the temptation and stuck to my toast and butter and apples.

In April 1906 William Booth was enthusiastically welcomed by the Mayor and Corporation of Eastbourne, of all places.[1] Said His Worship the Mayor, Stephen N. Fox, who presided over a huge gathering in the Hippodrome :

Time was when the finger of scorn was pointed at The Salvation Army. Time was when every cheap wit made it the butt of his clumsy ridicule. Who points the finger of scorn at this marvellous organization today ? . . . In days gone by some towns even attempted to shut their gates against the Movement, and I fear that Eastbourne itself was not blameless in this respect.

A few days before Christmas the General was speaking to a pathetic company of 1,200 blind men and women in Shoreditch Baptist Tabernacle. On 19 February 1907 he lectured at Salisbury House in the City of London, to a private gathering of City magnates, presided over by the Lord Mayor, Sir William Treloar. In June he spent three days at Clapton with 650 staff officers in council, his main cry being, " We must hold on to the Atonement ! " Each year he conducted deeply impressive memorial services for officers " promoted to Glory." In December 1907 the General had an interesting and picturesque interview in his home in Hadley Wood with three Swazi chiefs—Prince

[1] *The History of The Salvation Army*, vol. iv, p. 268

The Canadian Staff Band, with Commissioner Rees (centre, white cap) and Colonel Sidney Maidment (fifth from left), photographed prior to embarking on the ill-fated *Empress of Ireland* in May 1914. Only eight members of the group were rescued

General William Booth in his eightieth year

REPRESENTATIVE REVIVALISTS

1 Colonel Samuel L. Brengle 2 & 3 Adjutant and Mrs Clifford Boyce 4 & 5 Ensign and Mrs Joseph Henderson 6 Commissioner Elijah Cadman 7 Adjutant Kate Lee ("The Angel Adjutant") 8 & 9 Captain and Mrs Handel Booth

Melunge, and Chiefs Nogcogno and Nehemiah Vilakazi—
who had come to England to lay certain matters before
"The Great White King." The curse of the native races
was the drink traffic, and on this matter the General sounded
a strong note of warning ; then, after speaking of the
principle of righteousness, he prayed with them. Prince
Melunge later paid a Sunday-morning visit to Regent Hall
to hear the band, yet again visiting the corps on another
occasion for a meeting, this time accompanied by the other
two chiefs and Lady Blount. September 1909 saw the
General for the second time addressing for more than an hour
600 convicts of the Portland Settlement. On 2 May 1911 he
opened a Poor Man's Hotel at Nottingham, within a few
yards of the spot where he had been born eighty-two years
previously.

Major Jack Stoker, a member of the General's campaigning
staff, died in February 1911 at Leeds. Once a drunken miner,
of Blyth, described as being "as full of savagery as a bunch
of Kilkenny cats," he had become converted in 1880 and
had been a Salvation Army officer for more than thirty
years.

A "Living Pageant of Salvation Army Work and
Wonders" was presented at the Royal Albert Hall a week
later, the General, now nearly blind, presiding in connection
with the International Social Council, delegates from all parts
of the world having been invited. The Pageant was described
as "the most striking thing of its kind that London had ever
seen." This was followed by an All-night of Prayer and
Praise in the Clapton Congress Hall two days later. After a
heavy fortnight on the Continent in July the General commenced at Southport a new series of seaside campaigns. He
had come through an ordeal of terrible heat in London, but
"I am booked for Southport," he said, with emphasis to
those who tried to dissuade him, "and to Southport I go,

dead or alive ! " He was then in his eighty-third year. Lowestoft, Eastbourne (where the Mayor came to the station to meet him, and the Town Clerk, H. West Fouvargue, seconded a vote of thanks) and Ilfracombe were visited in succession.

The Good Friday of 1912 was, said the General, " The most remarkable Good Friday of all the Good Fridays of my life." He spent it at Clapton Congress Hall, and it was his last. Then he went to Torquay, where twenty-three years before his officers and soldiers had been often thrown into prison.[1] His last corps appointment was at Warrington, the commanding officer of which was Adjutant John Coutts, but who in the great crowds that attended those Sunday meetings dreamt that the corps officer's schoolboy son, Frederick, was, fifty-one years later, to follow in William Booth's footsteps as the Army's eighth General and its present Leader ?

The General's birthday was always the occasion for a great and enthusiastic thanksgiving service, except in 1907 when he was on the way to Japan. Although he was campaigning in Melbourne in 1905, his seventy-sixth birthday was celebrated in the Exeter Hall, London ; his seventy-seventh at the Crystal Palace, in 1906, when he was present ; and his seventy-ninth in the Queen's Hall, where he was also present. The greatest event of its kind was his eightieth birthday celebration in the Royal Albert Hall, which overshadowed all other events in the Army at that time, both at home and abroad. He was then in fine strength and vigour. Congratulations flowed in from all parts of the world, as usual, including messages from the Prince and Princess of Wales and the King of Denmark ; but his reception by Queen Alexandra and her sister, the Dowager Empress of Russia, at Buckingham Palace put the crowning touch on a memorable occasion for the Grand Old Man. In connection with these

[1] *The History of The Salvation Army*, vol. iv, p. 264

octogenarian celebrations the Army in the United States of America held its greatest exhibition. On his eighty-first birthday William Booth spoke for an hour and a half in the Congress Hall, Clapton, and received messages from Queen Alexandra and the Dowager Queen of Sweden. At eighty-two he was again at Clapton, and received congratulations from Queen Mary. Then came, if not the greatest celebration, certainly the most memorable, because it was the last. On the actual date, 10 April, he had tea with 800 officers at Clapton, and then addressed them, and the next day invited 300 young people to meet him at tea. On Thursday, 9 May 1912, with sightless eyes he faced his last audience at a festival of thanksgiving, when Commander Eva Booth brought him a message from President Taft of the U.S.A. The frail, weary-looking veteran made what was probably the speech of his life, his rasping voice, vibrant with the enthusiasm of his subject, needed no microphonic amplification to reach the topmost gallery. He was " going into dock for repairs " he told his 7,000 anxious listeners, concluding with, " And now, comrades and friends, good-bye ! " And it *was* good-bye, for he was never again seen on the public platform.

IV MAKING THE MESSAGE CLEAR
AND PLAIN

CHAPTER ONE

PERIODICALS

IN its 16 December 1905 issue, *The War Cry* announced that it had concluded arrangements with the Accident Insurance Company Ltd, by which purchasers would, free of all other cost, benefit by an insurance policy payable after death or in case of disablement. Beginning with the Christmas Number every subsequent issue would contain a coupon which, when signed, must be preserved ; then, following the signing of a further twenty-five such coupons, the holder or his widow, or her widower, or his or her legal representative, would, in the event of death or injury by accident, be entitled to certain sums in compensation. This Insurance Coupon, it was stated, possessed advantages over all other schemes, including £10 cash and 10s. per week for five years. The coupon had to be withdrawn in December 1907 owing to the insurance company declining to renew the contract ; but negotiations were completed with the Empire Guarantee and Insurance Corporation Ltd, which offered improved conditions with fewer coupons. Eight claims had been paid during the previous year. But the second insurance company declined to renew the contract, and the cryptic line appeared beneath the coupon in the 12 December 1908 issue :

" War Cry " readers should note that this Assurance Coupon will not appear after the present issue.

No explanation was given, and apparently the scheme died a natural death, never to be resurrected. At the beginning of the year a Welsh *War Cry* made its appearance, a revival of an earlier endeavour to publish *Y Gad Lêf* (the *War Cry*) in Caernarvon in 1889 and in Cardiff in 1906–7.

A new monthly magazine of thirty-six pages for promoting the moral, spiritual, physical and educational interests of young people between the ages of fifteen and twenty-one was issued in January 1906, and was called *The Y.P.* The name was changed in 1914 to *The Warrior and Life-Saving Scout*,[1] which today is known as *Vanguard*. *The Salvation Army Year Book*, a vade-mecum of information concerning the Organization's world-wide activities, was also issued for the first time in this year at sixpence; Brigadier (later Commissioner) Theodore H. Kitching was the editor for the first two years.

Described as " the latest addition to *The War Cry* family," a South African periodical produced in the latter part of 1904 in the IsiXhosa language was entitled *Intlaba Mkosi*. Of foolscap size and consisting of eight pages, the inner sheets were mimeographed, the cover being printed. In 1905 the South American *War Cry* was enlarged to eight pages and given a new name, *El Cruzado*, the Spanish equivalent for *The Crusader*.[2]

A new weekly newspaper, *The Bandsman and Songster*, now *The Musician*, appeared on 6 April 1907, Staff-Captain (later Colonel) Arthur R. Goldsmith [3] being appointed its first editor. In a foreword the General said :

It will tell of the last new Tune ; the latest wonderful March ; the last remarkably superior Instrument turned out at St Albans ; or the haul of souls that followed the last Musical Festival ; or

[1] p. 268
[2] *The History of The Salvation Army*, vol. iv, p. 56
[3] *The History of The Salvation Army*, vol. iv, p. 179

the last visit of the Staff Band to your native town. . . . " Who will write for it ? " do you ask ? Why, any number of people who are not expected to, and whom nobody thought could write, and who did not know they could write themselves.

The sixteen-page periodical, the front page of which was filled with advertisements and printed in red and black, was priced at one penny. *The Local Officer* [1] was incorporated with *The Bandsman and Songster* in January 1909.

A five-weeks' session of editors was held in the Staff Lodge, Downs Road, Clapton, in December 1906. Every Continental country in which the Army was working sent a representative. A flying midnight raid was made on Fleet Street, where, in the early hours of the morning, the *Daily News* was seen to press. Among the editors was Ensign Julia Hellquist of Finland, who was responsible for translating from English, German, Swedish, Norwegian and Danish no fewer than 520 songs for use in Finland.

The General's letters to soldiers, each to be read on a specified Sunday, commenced in April 1900,[2] were recommenced in the *War Cry* in 1907, continued for thirty-six weeks and included further subjects, from " Walking in the Light " to " Woman." They were later published in book form.

The Young Soldier celebrated its twenty-fifth anniversary in November 1909, and was described as unique as a religious journal for children. " It probably stands unequalled as the paper in which a child can write for Jesus for the good of other children."

Colonel (later Commissioner) Isaac Unsworth was installed as Editor-in-Chief at International Headquarters in November 1910. An event in March 1911 which was to prove significant in later years was the arrival in England

---

[1] *The History of The Salvation Army*, vol. iv, p. 174
[2] *The History of The Salvation Army*, vol. iv, p. 165

from Australia of Brigadier and Mrs George L. Carpenter, for the Brigadier, who was Literary Secretary in Melbourne and joined the I.H.Q. Editorial Department as "news editor" to the *War Cry*, was, in 1939, to become the General; Mrs Carpenter was to become the author of several books.

The year 1913 witnessed several important improvements and advances in Army literature. Notable among them was the enlargement of *All the World* [1] and *The Field Officer*,[2] which reverted to its original name, *The Officer*, and was enlarged from forty to seventy-two pages. The General decided that every English-speaking officer throughout the world should regularly receive the magazine, and that appertains to the present day.

A turn-about in the International Editorial Department was occasioned by the promotion to Higher Service of Brigadier Henry W. Walker, who lost his life in the *Empress of Ireland* disaster.[3] Lieutenant-Colonel (later Colonel) John Bond, editor of *The War Cry* in London, succeeded him as editor of the Toronto *War Cry*, Brigadier (later Colonel) Robert Perry becoming the London editor.

CHAPTER TWO

BOOKS

The amazing flow of Salvation Army books, and books about The Salvation Army, continued unabated during the period under review. The first to appear was No. 10 of *The*

---

[1] *The History of The Salvation Army*, vol. ii, p. 76
[2] *The History o The Salvation Army*, vol. iv, p. 174
[3] p. I

Warrior's Library,[1] *The Warrior's Daily Portion*, No. 2, being selections from the writings of the General arranged for morning and evening readings. A whole page of the *War Cry* for 20 August 1904 was given over to splashing this sixpenny production ! A book by Commissioner Booth-Tucker, *Colonel Weerasooriya*, a biography of the Singalese pioneer,[2] was published in the summer of 1905. At the end of 1904 came a further addition to *The Warrior's Library*, Lieutenant-Colonel (later Commissioner) Mildred Duff's *Hedwig von Haartman*, the life of the Finnish pioneer,[3] and later, *The Life of Jesus*. Mildred Duff was one of three prolific women writers on International Headquarters at that time ; the others being Brigadier Margaret Allen, who wrote *Bernard of Clairvaux*, *Fletcher of Madeley* and *Harvests of the East*, and Eileen Douglas, whose contributions were *The Fruits of the Spirit* and *The Whole Armour of God*.

Commissioner W. Elwin Oliphant wrote mainly on continental subjects. *Gerhard Tersteegen*, a life of the seventeenth-century German weaver, soul-winner and singer, was published in *The Warrior's Library* (1905) ; *The Life and Work of Oberlin*, the Alsatian pastor (1906) ; *Savonarola*, a life of the fearless Italian preacher and martyr (1906) ; and *The Story of German Song* (1909). Commissioner Railton was also busy, and from his pen came *The Life of Gideon Ouseley*, the Irish evangelist (1906) ; *Soldiers of Salvation*, pen pictures of work in many lands (1909) ; and *The Life of General William Booth* (1912). William Booth himself made a noteworthy contribution with *Visions* (1906), a collection of articles which had appeared in various periodicals. Then, in 1907, came *The Seven Spirits*, addresses to officers on Salvation Army doctrine ; and a most entertaining piece of

[1] *The History of The Salvation Army*, vol. iv, p. 167
[2] *The History of The Salvation Army*, vol. iv, p. 372
[3] *The History of The Salvation Army*, vol. iv, p. 45

purposeful fiction, *Sergeant-Major Do-your-Best of Darkington, No. 1* (1906), published first in *The Local Officer* as a series and described as " a literary cinematograph of corps life."

Colonel (later Commissioner, D.D.) Samuel L. Brengle, who was to become the Army's outstanding exponent of the teaching of holiness, had his first book, *Heart Talks on Holiness*, published in 1906. This was quickly followed by *The Way of Holiness*. Both were written in connection with the October holiness campaign and for " plain people." Other holiness books were *When the Holy Ghost is Come*, by Brengle, which commenced the new Liberty Library (1909), and *Standards of Life and Service* by Commissioner T. Henry Howard. In 1907 another woman author, who was later to write innumerable books for children, made her début with *A New Tommy Don't Know* and then *Jabez the Unlucky* ; this was Sarah L. Morewood, who wrote under the *nom de plume* Noel Hope. Bramwell Booth continued his writing with *Our Master*, thoughts for Salvationists about their Lord (1908), and Mrs Bramwell Booth had her first book, *Mothers of the Empire*, published in 1914. Mrs Colonel Brengle set forth anecdotal, biographical and intensely interesting chapters in *The Army Drum* (1909), and Muriel Clark, a Salvationist soldier, wrote *Sister Jeffries*, a novel of Salvation Army life from the inside, in 1914. The Red Hot Library continued its existence, as did The Warrior's Library, both of which were edited by Bramwell Booth.

Among several books written about the Army by non-Salvationists were *The Christianity of the Continent* by Jesse Page (S. W. Partridge & Co., 1906), which described how the work was spreading across Europe ; *The Romance of a Motor Mission* [1] by W. P. Ryan, the *Daily Chronicle* reporter of the 1905 campaign ; *The Romance of The Salvation Army*

[1] p. 138

(Cassell & Co., 1907) by Hulda Friederichs ; *Waste Humanity*, a review of social operations in Great Britain by F. A. McKenzie ; then, in 1909, the whole world was stirred by Harold Begbie's *Broken Earthenware*,[1] " a great book pulsating with passionate sympathy for the lepers of society, and with purpose stamped on every page." Begbie himself described *Broken Earthenware* as " A footnote in narrative to Professor William James's study in human nature, *The Varieties of Religious Experience* " ; but James was greatly impressed and replied : " I might as well call my book a footnote to his." Acclaimed by the Press of many countries, *Broken Earthenware* reached its sixth edition within a few months, and more than 200,000 copies were sold by 1911. Begbie wrote another book about the Army in this year, *Other Sheep*, the title of which was later changed to *The Light of India*, with a new and revised edition. It was a study of the people of India, which was described as even more wonderful and picturesque than that of *Broken Earthenware*, but it did not have anything like the same popular appeal. *The Great Idea* by Arnold White came out in 1909, and was a brilliantly written, powerful and clear-sighted exposition of the Army's methods and operations. Then came *Regeneration*, Mr (later Sir) H. Rider Haggard's independent view of the Army's social work. *The Times* published a striking leading article in reviewing this book, which was remarkable both for its outstanding opinion and warmth of commendation of the Army. Finally, in 1914, came *Handicapped* by David Lyall, another remarkable book in which the author treated of reformed women as Harold Begbie treated of " twice-born men " in *Broken Earthenware*. For the most part the book was related to Women's Social Operations.

But still there were fierce opponents in the literary world, and John Manson produced his *The Salvation Army and the*

[1] p. 192

Public in 1906. In his explanatory preface he quoted Professor Huxley as asking in 1890 :

Who is to say that The Salvation Army, in the year 1920, shall not be a replica of what the Franciscan order had become in the year 1260,

and, according to Huxley, it would then become, as had the Franciscan order within thirty years of the death of St Francis,

one of the most powerful, wealthy, and worldly corporations in Christendom, with their fingers in every sink of political and social corruption, if so be profit for the Order could be fished out of it.

It was Manson's hope that his religious, social and financial study would save the Army from this deplorable situation, in which it had never, and has never yet, found itself! Something of a sensation was caused when, two years after Commissioner Alex. M. Nicol's sudden departure from the ranks, he brought out a hefty volume, *General Booth and The Salvation Army* (Herbert & Daniel, 1910), in which he both praised and adversely criticized the organization in which he had rendered outstanding service for so many years. Nicol eventually returned to the Army in the United States of America, where he was commissioned an Envoy, which is equivalent to a local preacher.

CHAPTER THREE

MUSIC AND SONG

The Chief of the Staff decided that, as from 1 January 1905, the large songbook, *Salvation Army Songs*, was to be brought into regular use in every corps in the United Kingdom, and corps officers were instructed to familiarize themselves with the songbook and order a supply marked " Not to be taken away." This marked the institution of the songbook for congregational use. The *War Cry* might be used in two meetings a week, preferably Thursday night and Sunday afternoon. Where the young people's exclusive night was Thursday, *The Young Soldier* was to be used instead of the *War Cry*, otherwise *The Young Soldier* and *The Social Gazette* might be used on Wednesday and Saturday nights. *Army Bells*, the official songbook for young people's and children's meetings, was to be used in all young people's and junior soldiers' meetings excepting as previously stated.

A " striking departure " in March of that same year was the Chief of the Staff's decision to offer two prizes annually —£2 2s. and £3 3s. respectively—to Salvationists for (1) the best original melody for general Salvation Army use, and (2) the best original march for use of Army bands. The first prize for the melody was shared by Ensign (later Major) Charles Coller and Staff-Captain (later Major) William Gore, of Australia. Neither achieved any measure of popularity, but Gore won the march competition with his " Melbourne."

In the following year, 1906, the band-selection prize was won by Staff-Captain (later Colonel) Arthur R. Goldsmith.[1] The march prize went to Captain Robert H. McNally, of Australia. Bandsman (later Colonel and Head of the International Music Department) Bramwell Coles came third.

The works of scores of new writers of both songs and music appeared in *The Musical Salvationist* and the *Band Journals* between the years 1904–14 as in previous years, but much of the material, it must be confessed, was mediocre ; consequently it died prematurely. Some of the words were very good, but because the music was poor the song did not

[1] *The History of The Salvation Army*, vol. iv, p. 179

live. Sometimes a song lived because, although the words were poor, the music was good ; a truly successful song must be a happy marriage of words and music. A number of composers of song music later had compositions published in the *Band Journals*. It was exceedingly rare, and still is, for a composer to have his first work published for bands ; he has, it seems, to serve his apprenticeship with songster music.

The Salvation Army historian has, as it were, to be continually fossicking for gold among loads of earth ; sometimes a very wearying and monotonous task, not always appreciated by either his readers or critics. He has to ask himself whether certain material which he has discovered should be preserved or cast for ever into the limbo of forgotten things. In the matter of songs and music, for instance, if the versifiers and composers whose work has lived down the years to this present time are not mentioned in his History, there is no other volume in which their names could go down to posterity. If the slushy love songs of the beat groups of this modern age bring world-wide fame and millions in cash to their writers and performers, ought not the Army's historian to preserve the names of the men and women who wrote songs that are still being sung throughout the Salvationist world and which have brought innumerable souls into the Kingdom of God ? The answer can be only in the affirmative. Following is the list, then, of those—apart from names mentioned elsewhere in this volume or in previous volumes [1]—who contributed to the vast collection of Army songs and music during the ten years prior to the outbreak of the First World War, and whose work has survived.

Two future Generals made their début : Sergeant Albert Orsborn, of the Training Home, Clapton, as a maker of verse in 1906, and Deputy Bandmaster Wilfred Kitching, of New Barnet, as a composer of music to verses by his grandfather,

---

[1] *The History of The Salvation Army*, vol. ii, p. 107 ; vol. iv, p. 177

Auxiliary William Kitching, of Clevedon. Among those to become outstanding musicians, and whose names appeared for the first time, were Captain William Broughton, of Chicago ; Bandmaster Jules Vanderkam, of Belgium ; Captain Henry Goffin ; E. V. Saywell ; Captain Arthur Bristow ; Bandsman Richard Nuttall, of Blackpool ; Bandmaster John Pattison, of Seaham Harbour ; Bandmaster Harry Kirk, of Leeds ; and, perhaps, greatest of them all, Bandsman George Marshall, of South Shields.[1] Klaus Østby, of Norway, came into the picture in 1904, and by 1910 had produced 420 tunes, 118 songs and choruses, and forty-three songs for young people.

Enoch Kent had a gift for writing words to excerpts from classical music, and Assistant-Superintendent T. Jackson was adept in putting words to brass band marches. Typically " Salvation Army " songs, many of them of a rollicking nature, were to come from the pen of Bandsman Oliver Cooke, of Nunhead ; A. E. Hodson, of New Zealand ; and Captain A. Rayner (" That hat ! "). Women writers of words or music were Catherine Motee Booth-Tucker (now Mrs Commissioner Sladen), whose first musical setting was written to her father's words ; Private E. Aspinall (" Beautiful Christ ") ; Rosa Piggott, of Watford ; Marguerite D. Seiler, of the U.S.A., who wrote the music to Adjutant Fred W. Seiler's " With Christ in God " ; Brigadier Frances Forward (" Oh, glory to His name ! ") ; Mrs Lieutenant-Colonel (later Commissioner) Jolliffe (" Clear Skies ") ; and Mrs Major (later Colonel) Zealley and Mrs Bandmaster Cossar, of Newcastle upon Tyne, who both wrote a congregational tune which is in use today. Corps Sergeant-Major Ralph Johnson, of South Shields, was well known for the music of the lovely " Reckon on me," the words of which

[1] *Triumph of Faith*, by Arch R. Wiggins (Salvationist Publishing & Supplies 1958).

were written by John W. Bruce, of Jarrow ; W. Wells, of Reading 11, described as " King's Army Minstrel," for the words of " Who's that knocking at your heart's closed door ? " ; Lieutenant-Colonel Jack Addie for the words of " Just the same today " ; Bandsman E. A. Lambert, of St Albans, for the words and air of the striking Easter selection, " The way of the Cross " ; and Adjutant A. W. Bovan, father of Colonel Reginald Bovan, for his words, " A crown laid up in Glory."

Sergeant Gibby, of Pembroke Dock, wrote a large number of songs, as did Songster Leader James Greig, of Luton 1, who was no mean vocalist. Captain (later Brigadier) Archie C. Burgess, of the Training Home, Clapton, a concertina player of note ; Captain (later Major) A. G. Wolfe, a converted Jew ; Major Albright, of the U.S.A. (" I love him far better ") ; G. Logan, of Greenock (words) and Bandsman S. Howard, of Glasgow (music) ; L. J. Rowlands, of Australia ; and Sergeant (now Colonel) Albert Dalziel, of the Training College, Clapton ; all made their initial appearance in *The Musical Salvationist* with songs that were to live, or with songs that were to be precursors to songs that were to live. Ensign W. Ollis, Adjutant H. Mann and Bandmaster W. J. Stuckey, of East Ham, were specialists in children's songs. Adjutant Alex Neilsen, of Australia, wrote " Jesus died for me," a song that was to bring into the Army the whole Stevens family of Hawthorn. Harold Begbie, William Booth's biographer, also made his contribution, with the words of " Hymn of Service."

V THE BUSINESS SIDE OF SOUL-SAVING

Chapter One

THE TRAINING OF OFFICERS

AFTER eight and a half years as Principal of the International Training Homes, Clapton, Commissioner
David M. Rees farewelled in October 1904 for Sweden,
Commissioner T. Henry Howard being appointed to succeed
him. Among the 450 cadets commissioned in November
was the General's eldest grandchild, Cadet Sergeant (now
Commissioner, Retired) Catherine. She was also the first
grandchild of any officer in The Salvation Army to become
a Captain.

Considered to be one of the most significant advances
made by the Army in Great Britain during 1905 was the
opening by the Chief of the Staff of the first Staff Training
College, or Lodge, as it was sometimes called, at 55 Downs
Road, Clapton,[1] although it was unmarked by any public
demonstration and was unnoticed by the Press. Said the
Chief :

The Staff Training College is really an expression of the great
desire in every department of our work for greater efficiency in
its direction and control. . . . There has probably never before
been such a body of men and women raised up from the people,
inspired by a great passion for their salvation, and trained to
deal with some of the greatest problems of life. . . . Like much else
that is highly valuable and enduring, our Staff is an evolution. It
is a development—a growth.

[1] p. 189

The City of London stands silent for an hour and a half as William Booth passes through its vast crowds for the last time, on his way to rest in Abney Park Cemetery. General and Mrs Bramwell Booth follow immediately behind the bier

The new General and Mrs Bramwell Booth

Ensign Deva Rubem (Heden) sitting on the roof of the Hindu temple at Kalvillai, Southern India, which he was about to raze to the ground at the request of the villagers newly converted to Christianity

The second Chief of the Staff, Commissioner T. Henry Howard, who succeeded Mr. Bramwell Booth

The Salvation Army's first Commissioner —George Scott Railton

The Lodge was affiliated to and was part of the International Training Homes, and was under the immediate supervision of Commissioner Howard. The first course was devoted to more systematic and effective training of the Divisional Secretaries and "kindred branches of the minor staff of the British Territory," twenty in all. It consisted of three sessions, each of a month's duration, with intervals of two months in the Field between. It was intended that in future no officer should be promoted to staff duties until graduation in the Staff Training Lodge. A larger building, originally a fine old manor house, and to be known as the International Staff College, was opened in Upper Clapton in 1909, under the immediate direction of Commissioner James Hay, Head of the Training Territory.

An event of great significance and interest was the arrival at the International Training Homes in December 1905 of four men officers from Japan. In the Paris Training Home in 1908 was the daughter of a Russian Counsellor of State in Moscow, who spoke seven languages. She had heard the General while a student at Berne University. A rearrangement of sessions at the International Training College in 1910 brought Commissioning Day to May instead of it being held in November each year.

CHAPTER TWO

IMPORTANT APPOINTMENTS

Sweeping and far-reaching changes in the Army's government were announced in November 1904, when the General placed affairs in the United Kingdom more directly under the control of the Chief of the Staff, Colonel Hay continuing in the important position of Chief Secretary and Colonel Eadie remaining as Field Secretary, i.e. responsible for officers in charge of corps. Field Commissioner Eva Booth, lately in command in Canada, was appointed to take charge of the work in the United States of America, and in order better to secure the oversight of this enormous territory, the General took a new departure in appointing Commissioner Kilbey as Deputy Commander for the Western States, with headquarters in Chicago. Four years later he was succeeded by Commissioner Thomas Estill. Commissioner Coombs received the command of Canada. Colonel William Richards, for some years in command of Denmark, was appointed to succeed Commissioner Kilbey in South Africa. Commissioner Rees went to Sweden, from which country Commissioner McAlonan passed to the command of Switzerland, where he succeeded the Commissioners Booth-Hellberg, they going on furlough owing to the husband's ill-health. Colonel Sowton, for some time in charge of Scandinavian work in the United States, was promoted to the command of Denmark, with the rank of Acting Commissioner. Commissioner Howard took in hand the work at the International Training Homes at Clapton, and resigned the portfolio of the Foreign Secretary to Commander Booth-Tucker.

A Secretary for Welsh Affairs, Adjutant John Russell, was appointed in February 1905, " with a view to the opening of Welsh-speaking corps as rapidly as officers can be found for them." The new Welsh halfpenny *Y Plyg* (*The Fold*) was selling well. Colonel (later General) Edward J. Higgins, for nine years Chief Secretary in the United States, was added to the staff of International Headquarters to assist Commissioner Booth-Tucker, the Foreign Secretary, in the August, and Lieutenant-Colonel Minnie Reid (later to become Mrs

Booth-Tucker), following a long term of service on the Continent, was appointed to succeed Lieutenant-Colonel (later Commissioner) Robert Hoggard as Provincial Commander in Ireland. The nomination of a woman as a Provincial Commander on the British Field was described as " an interesting development." Commissioner Edward Higgins (father of the future General), who had been Resident Secretary in India for nine years, was made an International Travelling Commissioner in the same month. Brigadier Richard Slater was appointed Secretary of the Bands and Songster Brigades of the British Territory in the tail-end of the year. This was spoken of as " a new and important stage—perhaps an epoch—in our musical warfare." He was to retain the oversight of the Musical Department, and have a seat on the Musical Board. But the appointment did not materialize ! An interesting development, both at home and abroad, in October 1906, was marked by the General's appointment of Lieutenant-Colonel Stuart Roussel as Educational Secretary on the International Staff. It was to effect the numerous training homes, the advanced field training of officers in Great Britain, and to the increasing educational efforts which were then being made by the Army all over the world for the benefit of children and older young people. During the same month between twenty and thirty Continental editors and editorial assistants were brought to the Staff Lodge at Clapton for the purpose of receiving a four weeks' course of " higher training " in everything that concerned the management and editing of an Army journal.

A new leader for Japan, Commissioner Estill, of Holland, was appointed in May 1907, while the General was still campaigning there ; Commissioner Ridsdel, of Scotland, went to Holland ; Lieutenant-Colonel (later Commissioner) Friedrich, of Germany, received the command of the North India Territory, he succeeding Colonel Yudda Bai (Bannister).

In the following month Commissioner Higgins became Special Commissioner for Scotland, under National Headquarters, the country then being a Province ; but within three months he had passed away, and Commissioner Cosandey, in charge of the Franco-Belgian Territory, succeeded him ; this was in August. Colonel (later Lieutenant-Commissioner) Fornachon was switched from his recently unfulfilled appointment to the Danish Command to take charge of France and Belgium ; and Colonel (later Lieutenant-Commissioner) Povlsen, in command of the Eastern Province of the British Territory, was appointed to his native Denmark, a rare appointment at that time. Commissioner Booth-Tucker, the Foreign Secretary, had been reappointed to the control of all the work in India in July. He had pioneered the work there in 1882, being the first Army missionary,[1] and had been recalled in 1891 owing to the serious illness of his wife, the Consul. It was at the Commissioner's own request that the General made this reappointment. Commissioner Howard took over the Foreign Secretaryship for the second time, he being succeeded as Principal of the International Training Homes by Commissioner Hay in September. Lieutenant-Colonel Mapp, who in 1929 was to become the Chief of the Staff to General Edward Higgins, was appointed to the position of Assistant Field Secretary to the United Kingdom, following Colonel Whatmore, who became Field Secretary. He in turn had followed Colonel (later Commissioner) Eadie, who succeeded Commissioner Hay as Chief Secretary. Commissioner Booth-Hellberg, being in very indifferent health, went into temporary retirement in the same month, and Colonel (later Commissioner) Bullard was appointed from the command of Japan, where he served for seven years, to special service in connection with the Foreign Office.

[1] *The History of The Salvation Army*, vol. ii, p. 272

A most important advance in the administration of the British Field Staff took place in October 1908, when at one stroke of the pen twenty Divisional Officers were lifted to the rank and authority of Divisional Commanders. These men had, generally speaking, powers equal to those held by the Provincial Commanders, and had as their central staff a Chancellor, who had direction under the Divisional Commander of a certain class of corps, a Young People's Secretary and a Helper. Scotland received special consideration, Lieutenant-Colonel Byers being attached to National Headquarters as Secretary for Scotland, resident in Glasgow. Special Spiritual Campaigners were appointed in the persons of Brigadier H. L. Williams, Major Anker Deans and David Thomas and, in Canada, Major Richard Adby.

In September 1911 Colonel Whatmore was promoted Commissioner to succeed Commissioner Higgins as Assistant Foreign Secretary, the last named having been given the highly important position of Territorial Commissioner for the British Territory in June. Commissioner Higgins was the first son of a Commissioner to attain that rank. Commissioner Eadie became Territorial Commander for South Africa. It was reported that owing to the serious breakdown in the health of his wife, who had been a sufferer for a year, Lieutenant-Colonel Fritz Malan had been relieved of his command of the French-Swiss Province, and was to be succeeded by Lieutenant-Colonel (later Commissioner) Albin Peyron, of Italy. At the time of writing Mrs Malan is still living in Switzerland !

Following Commissioner Cosandey's request to be relieved of his command of the Army's forces in South America, owing to his state of health, he was succeeded in November 1912 by Colonel Mapp, who had been Chief Secretary in Canada. Commissioner Cosandey, upon his recovery, proceeded to Constantinople on a mission of enquiry regarding relief work among the various peoples then at war in the Near East. Colonel Unsworth, the Editor-in-Chief, was appointed Parliamentary Secretary at International Headquarters, a new position, for, at the time, several important measures, in which the Army was more or less directly concerned, were being brought before the House of Commons. Colonel Mildred Duff, with the status of a Travelling Commissioner, was appointed A.D.C. to Mrs Bramwell Booth, particularly in her campaigns outside of the United Kingdom. The office of Editor-in-Chief was not filled immediately as General Bramwell Booth decided to enlarge, to some extent, the powers of the officers responsible for the various periodicals, each of which worked in collaboration with Brigadier H. L. Taylor,[1] who was appointed Business Manager of the Department ; and the Editorial Council, the secretary of which was Brigadier (later General) George L. Carpenter. In November 1912, owing to the increase of the Army's work in other parts of the world, the Foreign Office at International Headquarters was reorganized, Commissioner Howard having been chosen by the new General to be his Chief of the Staff. The Foreign Secretaryship was divided among three Commissioners who were to be known as International Secretaries, each having certain countries placed under his care. The Emigration Department now being united with the Foreign Office, Commissioner David C. Lamb became responsible for both Colonial and Emigration Affairs ; Commissioner Whatmore for Europe and Asia ; and Colonel (later Commissioner) Francis W. Pearce for Southern and General Affairs, including South Africa, South America and the West Indies. The affairs of the United States of America, and those of the British Command which intimately concerned other countries, were specially reserved to the care of the Chief of the Staff.

[1] *The History of The Salvation Army*, vol. iv, p. 145

The position having been vacant for eight years, and much of the work involved having been directed by the General when Chief of the Staff, a new Chancellor of the Exchequer was appointed in the summer of 1913—Colonel (later Commissioner) George Mitchell, for many years Finance Secretary and Bandmaster of the International Staff Band. The Chancellorship was one of the most important and difficult positions at International Headquarters. Lieutenant-Colonel (later Commissioner) Samuel Hurren was selected as Personal Private Secretary to the Chief of the Staff. In a character sketch of Colonel Mitchell the *War Cry* stated that " in the United Kingdom alone the value of properties amounted to £1,500,000, while the annual revenue of £2,000,000 was required to keep going all the Army's machinery for the spiritual and social benefit of mankind throughout the world." The raising and economical disbursement of this large sum was the responsibility of the Chancellor.

He is an all-pervading influence in trading and financial matters. The great international trading concern at Judd Street, and the remote Salvation settlements in Zululand are alike affected by him. All financial matters come into his ken, and are co-ordinated by him into harmony with that iron-clad system of finance which a well-known publicist has declared to be as well managed as that of the London Joint Stock Bank.

Several important developments at International Headquarters took place in the summer of 1914 : Commissioner Whatmore became a Travelling International Secretary and Commissioner McAlonan, of Germany, was made an International Secretary, he being succeeded by Commissioner Cosandey, which position, however, he was never able to fill, owing to the outbreak of the First World War. Commissioner Mapp was despatched to Japan to succeed Commissioner Hodder.

CHAPTER THREE

POLICIES AND PREMIUMS

The Salvation Army Assurance Society obtained a legal victory in an action which it was forced to bring in July 1905 against the Pearl Assurance Company and R. Grahame Bruce. The action was to secure restraint and damages in respect of information, canvassing, etc., on the part of the defendants, Bruce having formerly been an agent of the plaintiff company. The High Court granted a perpetual injunction, ordered the handing over of all documents, etc., to The Salvation Army and awarded £35 damages and costs. The Society had again to take action against the Pearl Life Assurance Company, which had undertaken in May 1906 to forbid the distribution by its agents of a leaflet entitled *Another Glance at the Affairs of The Salvation Army Assurance Society*. This was a reprint of a criticism which appeared years before in *The Commercial World*.[1] It was, however, discovered later in 1906 that the leaflet was still being used. In the circumstances the Society, adverse as it was to litigation, felt bound to sue the Pearl Company for damages for libel and for an injunction against its repetition. The case was heard on 16 and 17 January 1908, and resulted in a verdict for the Society. The Pearl Company was required to pay £5 damages and the costs of the action, and had an injunction restraining it from repeating the libel. It was made clear to the jury that, although the libel was a serious one, heavy damages were neither sought nor desired.

An important action which had its effect upon all assurance societies was also won in a Scottish Court of Appeal,

[1] *The History of The Salvation Army*, vol. iv, p. 231

in August 1908. It having been discovered that the British Legal Life Assurance Society Ltd was receiving transfers from The Salvation Army Assurance Society without giving statutory notice, and the offending company insisting that the specific cases which were brought to their notice were not transfers within the meaning of the Collecting Societies Act of 1896, the directors of The Salvation Army Assurance Society were compelled to appeal to the courts for a decision. The action was brought in the Sheriffs Court of Lanarkshire, in Glasgow, where certain facts concerning the assurance of a family at Dunfermline were presented. The Sheriff-Substitute held that the transactions were not transfers as set forth in the Act, and gave judgment in favour of the British Legal Life Assurance Company. The Salvation Army Assurance Society appealed against this decision, which was reversed by the Court of Appeal. The action was remitted to the Sheriff-Substitute for him to convict the British Legal Life Assurance Company of the offence charged, and the Court found The Salvation Army Assurance Society entitled to the expenses of the appeal.

The Actuary to the Refuge Assurance Company, in a paper read at a meeting of the Sheffield and District Life Assurance Managers' Fraternal Association, and published in various insurance papers, and also in *The Insurance Mail Year Book* for 1911, alleged that while the General in his book *In Darkest England and the Way Out* had referred with concern to allegations concerning infantile assurance, that concern had had no effect on the policy of The Salvation Army Assurance Society, by which infantile assurance was practised in the usual way.[1] But an editorial in *The Insurance Mail* refuted the statement, pointing out that in its first prospectus The Salvation Army Assurance Society made plain its determination not to transact infantile assurance in the ordinary sense,

[1] *The History of The Salvation Army*, vol. iv, p. 229

and that later a table similar to those of other companies was issued, but in order to safeguard the interests of children and protect them against alleged evils the policies contained a special clause. Although a large number of infantile policies were issued, the Directors reported that in only one case had it been found necessary to enforce this special clause, which was thereby proved to be unnecessary and was subsequently omitted from future policies. *The Insurance Mail* stated that " there is no discord between the theories in General Booth's book and the practice of The Salvation Army Assurance Society."

Press congratulations to the Society on its all-round prosperity and advance were forthcoming at the beginning of 1912. *The Insurance Mail* wrote :

Turning to the present accounts, we find them to be as clear and clean as those of former years. The most carping critic—and the Society has many critics—cannot find a flaw in the balance-sheet. There is not one questionable or doubtful item. The auditors give a clean certificate.

The Annual Report for the year ending June 1913 stated that the most exacting critics had to admit that the progress made by the Society was truly marvellous. The Premium Income for the year in the Industrial Branch amounted to £257,412 6s 8d ; the Ordinary Branch Premium Income amounted to £72,208 14s 11d ; and the total income for the year amounted to £362,367 14s 1d. Editors of financial and insurance journals were again loud in their praise. Said *The City Review* :

In a comparatively brief space of time we find that the premium income has grown from the insignificant sum of £421 to the massive amount of £329,600, and the accumulated sums from £14,220 to over £881,000, and it is doubtful whether any other similar institution has made such great strides before reaching its majority.

THE SALVATION ARMY FIRE INSURANCE CORPORATION
LIMITED

So far as has been discovered, the first Salvation Army Fire Insurance circular was issued in 1899. In the following year the department was associated with the Assurance Society.[1] The present Corporation was registered by the Board of Trade on 11 January 1909, and henceforward issued policies to the general public, as well as writing the insurances on all buildings and contents belonging to The Salvation Army in the United Kingdom. The Corporation joined the Fire Offices Committee on 17 April 1913.

The Joint Board of the Health Insurance Commissioners intimated in June 1912 their approval of The Reliance Benefit Society. This had been formed by The Salvation Army for the purposes of the Health Section of The National Insurance Act of 1911, which was shortly to come into operation, and which meant that

practically every person between the ages of sixteen and seventy in the service of an employer, and whose salary is under £160 per annum, must be insured and must get a contribution card before July 15, either from the approved society of which he or she is a member, or from a Post Office, and produce it to his or her employer to be stamped on the first pay day after July 14.

The Society was soon overwhelmed by applications for membership far exceeding expectations.

[1] *The History of The Salvation Army*, vol. iv, p. 232

CHAPTER FOUR

HOUSES AND LANDS

In some parts of the British Field, even after more than forty years, many corps were housed in halls totally unsuitable for public worship, and Bramwell Booth determined that this unsatisfactory state of affairs should be gradually remedied. A five years' scheme to provide 250 new or improved buildings was put into force at the beginning of 1906. As a result 112 new buildings were opened in Great Britain during the eighteen months ending December 1907, and ninety others were in course of erection. One of the finest citadels erected was that at Barrow-in-Furness, described as unrivalled in the Territory, with seating capacity for 1,000 adults and 530 young people. It was opened on 20 August 1910. Another fine building was opened on 1 April 1911 at South Shields. On 29 June 1912 the British Commissioner opened Southampton's reconstructed citadel, seating 750 people, and a fine two-roomed young people's hall which accommodated 400 children. By this time 247 buildings had either been completed or were in course of completion in connection with Bramwell Booth's scheme.

The new Headquarters of the Women's Social Work at 280 Mare Street, Hackney, was opened by Mrs Booth on 6 May 1911. It was but a stone's throw from the previous headquarters at No. 259, which had been occupied for twenty-five years. Giving an idea of the work carried on at " 259," Mrs Booth stated that within twelve months no fewer than 1,573,595 letters were received and despatched.

The opening, though unpretentious, by the Chief of the Staff and Mrs Bramwell Booth of a hostel for the children of missionary officers at 55 Downs Road, Hackney, the former Staff Lodge,[1] was a new departure of world-wide interest in February 1912. Later in the year the Home of Rest for Sick and Wounded Officers was removed from Brighton to Bexhill after twenty-seven years.

CHAPTER FIVE

FINANCE AND TRADE

Almost from its inception the Army had its amateur financial critics,[2] but these must surely have been pacified by a convincing article which appeared in *The Grand Magazine* for April 1905 on "The Legal and Financial Aspects of The Salvation Army" by an eminent K.C., who, summing up, wrote :

So far as is humanly possible, there does not appear to be any ground for any reasonable apprehension for the property of the Army being diverted from the purposes contemplated by the original founders, and expressed in the trust deeds. Every penny received for the purposes of the Organization is strictly accounted for, a balance sheet is annually published, and all the receipts and expenditure are submitted to the audit of a firm of accountants of high repute and respectability.

Five years later, in his book, *Book-keeping and Accounts*, Mr L. Cuthbert Cropper, F.C.A., selected Salvation Army accounts, as published in the publicly distributed balance-sheets, as affording object-lessons in clearness and completeness :

[1] p. 176
[2] *The History of The Salvation Army,* vol. i, p. 266 ; vol. iv, p. 213

The accounts of The Salvation Army are kept upon modern and businesslike methods, and it is a matter of regret that the same commendation cannot be applied to the accounts of many other religious and charitable institutions.

Wrote the *War Cry* :

This fact should surely, once and for ever, " lay the ghost " of the ancient, worn-out, and unworthy suggestion that the Army does not publish balance-sheets. The Army not only publishes them, but they are so excellent that in this standard work on *Book-keeping and Accounts*, they are held up for imitation by business men desirous of having the latest system in their office.

The Army's Trade Headquarters, with its 150 van-loads of goods, was moved from the ramshackle building at Fortress Road, Kentish Town, in North London, to the central, newly erected and attractive corner building in Judd Street, King's Cross, which contained spacious showrooms, a warehouse, bonnet factory and dressmaking and tailoring departments. The building was opened on 1 June 1911. The Trade Secretary at the time was Lieutenant-Colonel (later Commissioner) John B. Laurie.

A new development in trade affairs came into force on 1 January 1913. This was the introduction of a method of profit-sharing for customers dealing with certain departments which thereafter constituted, and was to be known as The Salvation Army Supply Stores.

It is fascinating in these days to study the *War Cry* advertisements in 1905. A woman's cashmere uniform, " a marvel of cheapness," cost £1 1s complete. A woman's three-quarters uniform jacket and skirt lined throughout and made from all-wool serge cost 17s 6d ; red band tunics fully trimmed cost £1 5s ; a " made to measure " serge uniform suit was valued at £1 7s, but a cheaper one could be bought for 16s. Best uniform overcoats were £1 8s 6d.

VI EVANGELISM AND EVENTS

CHAPTER ONE

SPIRITUAL AWAKENINGS

NOTHING is less predictable than a spiritual awakening, or a revival of religion, call it what you will. It certainly cannot be produced by human effort, however highly organized or financially backed, as many a would-be revivalist has proved. Evangelists have been and are still innumerable, but revivalists are very few and far between. No man knows whether he will ever be a revivalist, and no man knows when, or where, or how a revival is going to blow up like a blast furnace. Christ said to Nicodemus : " The wind bloweth where it listeth, and thou hearest the sound thereof, but canst not tell whence it cometh, and whither it goeth," and this is the perfect description of a spiritual revival. This particular period in the history of The Salvation Army is remarkable for its tremendous spiritual upheavals in different parts of the world, but more especially in the British Isles.

The great Welsh Revival, in which Evan Roberts played the main part and Salvationists participated—700 conversions took place in the Cardiff Division alone—was in full swing when first evidences of the approaching spiritual upheaval in the Army throughout the British Territory came at the latter end of 1904 in Bulwell, where 386 men and women were converted within two months, including many of the most degraded drunkards, blasphemers, gamblers and wife-beaters in this Nottinghamshire mining town. The revival was born soon after Adjutant and Mrs Griffiths were appointed to the corps in the November. An eighteen-year-old company guard [1] dropped dead at daybreak without cry or warning as she was leaving home for work. This caused a sensation throughout the district and hundreds were turned away at her memorial service in the hall, where thirty-five seekers after Christ were registered. Such was the beginning of a long procession of converts. Strangely enough, the emotion that usually characterizes a revival was manifested only by the Salvationists ; there was no undue ecstacy about the repentant colliers and their wives. The question of "joining up" was almost dreadful in its importance. Among the converts were whole families and sixty married couples. There were also conversions in all the churches in the town. In March 1905 239 soldiers were sworn in and 150 recruits enrolled from 559 seekers.

At about the same time " a glorious work " broke out at Norland Castle, a corps in Shepherds Bush, West London, when one of the worst men in the neighbourhood became converted. A little later seventy-four seekers knelt at the penitent form on a Sunday night, and then, on 29 January 1905, the General conducted what the *War Cry* described as " a giant's day " in the Empire Theatre, when some 150 seekers were registered. Among the new converts was Teddy Pooley, who was to become world-famous as " Rags and Bones " in Harold Begbie's book *Broken Earthenware*. Ensign and Mrs Joseph Henderson were then in charge of the corps and numbered other notorious *Broken Earthenware* characters among their converts: Ginger Elmer, " The Puncher," Bill Rumble, " A Copper Basher," Alfred Nicholson, " A Tight Handful," and Alf Jacobs, " The Plumber." Some 400 converts were also registered. The

[1] The Army's term for Sunday-school teacher

revival fire was still burning in this very rough neighbourhood when, in May 1906, Kate Lee, " The Angel Adjutant,"
so named by Begbie, took charge. She remained for twelve
months and "captured," among many others, the depraved
itinerant newsagent, " Old Born Drunk," Joe Haisman,
" The Criminal " and " Lowest of the Low." Then came
Ensign and Mrs Jordan to stoke the fire further and to include
among their trophies Knap, the " Human Pin-cushion."
This man would strip to the waist, sew buttons to his skin
with a needle and thread and literally make a pin-cushion of
his body. He would also eat fine glass, put his head in a fire
and pull out a red-hot cinder with his teeth. Knap lost one
of his eyes through such an act of folly. Two brigades of
these extraordinary converts, each brigade being called " The
Terrible Ten "—Ensign Henderson's sobriquet—devoted one
day every week to visiting surrounding corps telling their
life-story, under the leadership of Band Sergeant Joe Cowlin,
who helped to " nurse " those who found it difficult at first
to stand firm. A crowded and keenly interested gathering
in the City Temple, London, listened with bated breath to
some of the original *Broken Earthenware* characters on a
Monday night in March 1912, they being introduced by the
Chief of the Staff.

The most amazing and longest-sustained revival was that
which burst into flame just before Christmas 1907 and continued for two years without a break at Ayr, a little seaside
town in Scotland with ancient and historical associations ;
Robert Burns, the poet, had lived there. The revival began
with a Saturday-night raid of drunkards outside public-
houses and the salvation of a gaolbird, his wife, brother and
two sisters. Adjutant Clifford Boyce, himself a converted
drunkard and gambler, was the commanding officer.
Within nine weeks no fewer than 864 converts—many of
them notorious characters—had been recorded. Three meet-

ings were conducted consecutively each Saturday evening and overflow meetings on Sundays. A *War Cry* special correspondent thus described a Saturday-night gathering :

The quaint " Scotchified " expressions of the converts were funnier than a pantomime, more thrilling than a tragedy, and as melting as melodrama. . . . It does not resemble the Welsh Revival in fervour. It does not bear any comparison with the Cornish and North-west Scottish fisher awakenings. For a parallel you have to imagine a cross between a Bulwell, and an Army opening in a dense industrial district, and a slum and hooligan corps. . . . Not since the remarkable happening at Bulwell, in which some of the most notorious characters of that district were transformed by the power of God, have we been able to chronicle so sustained and general a spiritual movement in a corps.

Although largely confined to the hooligan, slum and criminal elements in the poorer portion of the town, the revival was steady and continuous rather than sensational and spectacular. There was no emotion ; the decisions for Christ were demure, cool and deliberate. The 1,000th convert was one of the biggest drunkards in Ayr and had come out of prison that morning. Not a week passed without its miracles. Dan Christie, an ex-international footballer and a drunkard for thirty years—the converts were in the main whisky-drinkers—was an outstanding trophy of grace. Often, the Army hall being too small to accommodate the tremendous crowds, the Town Hall was taken for the meetings.

The *War Cry* published long reports every week. The Territorial Commander, Commissioner Cosandey, swore in 200 recruits as soldiers in one night ; 300 converts came from one street ; 1,250 attended a revival tea. " The Converted Comedian " had come home drunk and, in a fit of passion, had taken a knife, picked up his child, laid it across his knee and was about to kill it when his wife brought a poker across his arm and so prevented him from becoming a murderer.

Some of the stories that the converts had to tell of their unregenerate days read like fiction. The *War Cry* for 27 June 1908 contained a full front page of twenty-nine ex-drunkards, every one a miracle of grace. When the General visited Ayr during his motor tour that year, the governor of the prison was accompanied on the platform by thirty of his former charges, every one in an Army guernsey. All through these remarkable happenings Clifford Boyce went on with his preaching. He was not " a son of thunder " ; he preached simply and of nothing but the love of God. After eighteen months he and his wife, who was just as much " with it " as was her husband, farewelled and the town clerk attended their last meeting publicly to thank them for their work. They were succeeded by Ensign and Mrs Garry Morrell. The work continued with steady persistency, and by 13 November 1909 there were nearly fifty companies, or classes, in the junior corps, and 2,500 cases of conversion had been registered, hundreds having been made into soldiers.

Nelson saw 306 converts in six months ; Abertillery shared in the Welsh Revival, recording 450 within a month, as did Tredegar with 69 in seven days. In Scotland there were 226 conversions within five months of the opening at Stenhousemuir, an obscure little town without a railway, cut off from " the madding crowd's ignoble strife " ; 168 were recorded in seven months at Bridgeton, 220 during sixteen weeks at Clydebank and 130 within three months at Newmilns. In Ireland, at Bessbrook, an outpost of Newry, the congregation figures went up from 11 to 400 ; and at Ballynafeigh, an outpost from Ballymacarret, 72 adults and 59 young people professed conversion. The salvation of the worst man in the town was the beginning of a revival in quiet Ballymena, a most unlikely place for such an event, but where 50 new soldiers were added to the roll. At Leeds 111 whole families were converted, and the 160 seekers within

ten weeks included some whose stories were almost unbeliev-
able. A family of four professional concertina players was
numbered among the 200 converts in two months at
Tunbridge Wells, where Adjutant and Mrs Bobbie Edwards
were in command. Similar happenings took place at
Hollinwood (Manchester). As a result of the General's visit
to Dudley during his Motor Campaign in 1905 there were
500 conversions and 120 new soldiers had been made within
nine months. The Norland Castle revival overspilled into
Hammersmith, a neighbouring corps, where a number of
pugilists and gaolbirds sought Christ. One convert had run
through £1,000 in drinking and horse-racing in a very short
time. The landlord of one of the public houses was so
impressed by what was going on at the Army that he left his
business one Sunday and sat on the hall platform to listen
to the testimonies of his former customers. He declared his
visit to be " the most astonishing thing in my life." Penge,
in South-East London, counted 246 converts in three weeks
during its second awakening in 1912.

The Leyton revival was second in its length and results to
Ayr. Some of the worst characters in this East London
district were among the eighty converts between November
1907 and February 1908. Dick Punchin, a professional boxer,
had been drunk almost every day since his marriage eighteen
years before. The " Drunken Coalie " had served five years'
penal servitude. Just before his conversion the judge had
enquired of the clerk of the court if there were any previous
convictions. " Yes, my lord," replied the clerk, " we can
supply bushels of them ! " The Lion and Key public house
became known as " The Army Recruiting Shop," and the
landlord could say, " My trade's suffering, but you're making
the town a different place, so we can't grumble. Go on and
prosper ! " and he gave Captain Handel Boot a five-pound
note. Nearly 200 seekers followed upon the conversion of

the terror of the district, Sam Chumbley, a gaolbird and deserter. Seventeen whole families and thirty-seven married couples were included in the 1,026 converts brought in during the two years' stay of Boot and his wife. One common feature in all parts of London at this time was the regeneration of degenerates.

Nearly 400 conversions were registered at Newburn-on-Tyne during the eighteen months that the corps had been open, and nearly 100 soldiers sworn in. At Birmingham VII (Small Heath) although there was "nothing cyclonic," a steady stream of seekers after Christ began in August 1909, and by November 200 of the worst people in the district had been wonderfully changed. Orthodox people were shocked, said the *War Cry*, because they were invited to "come to the citadel and hear these saved drunkards sing and speak." Of all the ministers to whom the Commanding Officer wrote concerning the awakening, not one replied to his courteous letter ; but the Jewish rabbi, in sending a fellow-religionist to one of the Army's social homes, wrote : "I would rather see her a sober Christian than a drunken Jewess." "Evidently 'orthodox people' would rather see a drunkard damned respectably than saved at any price, which is, of course, quite orthodox !" commented the *War Cry*.

In contrast to Small Heath the ministers at Newark expressed delight in the revival that had broken out in this great brewery centre about the same time. Fashionable Scarborough, of all places, awoke during Adjutant Oliver Chalker's stay, and within seven months he could report 200 conversions, including that of "Fess" Dobson, who had had seventy-nine convictions and had spent twenty years in prison, one stretch being of ten years in Dartmoor. Tipton corps was opened in 1913 by Captain Ruth Lord and Lieutenant Edwards, and within ten weeks they saw 370 seekers at the penitent form, from which they made 100 soldiers and recruits. And so one could go on. While some corps reported their hundreds, others were delighted with their scores. During the first weeks of 1913 more " broken earthenware " was remade by the Master Potter at Notting Hill, in the time of Adjutant William Spillett, when six well-known local men whose nicknames were household words became converted : Sambo, a thirty-year-old with thirty-two convictions ; two thieving brothers, Girardot I and II ; Bogey, the gaolbird son of an Oxford Street jeweller ; Shrimpo, a member of the notorious " Forty Thieves of Seven Dials " ; and Sweepo, the ever-drunken sweep. Deputy-Songster Leader Joe Cowlin, formerly of Norland Castle, fathered them as he had done the original *Broken Earthenware* characters.[1]

But not only throughout the British Isles was the revival fire burning ; it would seem that the world itself was on fire spiritually. Commissioner Booth-Tucker, the Foreign Secretary, visited seven European countries about the time of the outbreak and witnessed 381 souls at the Cross within seventeen days ; Lieutenant-Colonel Rauch reported 170 seekers in Jamaica within a week ; Commander Eva Booth's campaigns in Boston in 1907 resulted in 280 conversions and in New York in January 1908 of 200 within nine days. Three hundred were converted within a week during Lieutenant-Colonel Cooke's campaign in Zürich, Switzerland, during the same month ; between 800 and 900 seekers were registered at Gefle, Sweden, in a campaign led by Adjutant Hjalmar Akerberg ; more than 800 within ten days at Stockholm I ; and 143 at Örebro within a fortnight in May 1909. The Adjutant was appointed an Evangelist in 1908 and saw 432 conversions at Norrköping within fourteen days ; 255 at Malmö within six days and 183 at Kristianstad within six days.

[1] p. 170

BRENGLE AND CADMAN

A new star in the international firmament made his appearance in Europe, first in Paris, following the 1904 International Congress, then in Scandinavia in 1905 and 1906 and at the latter end of that year in Holland and Switzerland : Colonel (later Commissioner) Samuel Logan Brengle,[1] of the United States of America, whose holiness books and teaching were attracting world-wide attention. The Colonel's first week in Rotterdam resulted in 108 adult and seventy-six junior seekers. The children's meetings had been so successful that they had become a regular feature of his campaigns. Later, in Switzerland, there were 298 seekers, and in February 1907 the whole of Norway was stirred by the Colonel's addresses [2] ; the editor of a leading evangelical paper and some prominent professors were among the 1,600 seekers in eight weeks. Indeed, Europe itself was in a boil, such happenings being described as similar in character to those experienced during the Welsh Revival. They began as the result of the preaching of the Rev. Albert Lunde of the State Church in Christiania.[3] It is said that 5,000 people gathered at the wharf at midnight to bid Brengle farewell from Bergen. Booksellers were unable to cope with the heavy demand for Bibles. Things were not so easy for the evangelist in Finland in the following October, but many decisions were arrived at outside the meetings ; then came a break and 240 seekers came forward to acknowledge Christ, included among them being several titled people. Brengle's fifth campaign in Europe opened in Copenhagen in March 1908, then he suffered a physical breakdown, but not before 600 seekers had been counted at the penitent forms. The year 1910 saw him

[1] p. 89   [2] p. 41   [3] p. 40

in Australia and New Zealand, where he claimed 2,600 converts in his meetings.

While revival was blazing throughout the United Kingdom, " Fiery Elijah," Commissioner Cadman, who had seen 270 seekers within a month at Cardiff, was stirring up things during a six months' campaign in New Zealand and Australia, nearly 2,000 penitents being recorded in the early part of 1907. Sometimes he created a sensation when he rode through the streets of a town on a white charger. Not always was the animal a hunter ; sometimes a heavy shire-horse sufficed. A fortnight's meetings in Ceylon, where, attired in turban and dhoti, he rode an elephant, resulted in some 1,000 converts to Christianity. On the way to Australia he was almost washed overboard during a violent storm. In Newfoundland and Canada, at the end of 1908 and the beginning of 1909, he swept through the whole length of the Dominion like a spiritual tornado ; within six weeks he saw 1,400 conversions, and delivered fifty-two lectures, " The Story of my Life," each of two and a half hours' duration. At every town he visited in Newfoundland he was greeted by the firing of guns ! In October 1909 he set off for a five months' tour of the U.S.A., during which he counted 600 seekers. The year 1912 saw him in Germany.

CONVERSIONS EXTRAORDINARY

Following the example of her stage-manager husband, who had found salvation at York Citadel on the previous Sunday, Ethel Buchanan, an actress of world-wide repute, knelt at the penitent form at the end of the week and immediately became an open-air soloist. This was in October 1904. The principal newspaper in Minneapolis, U.S.A., devoted, in the summer of 1906, a column to the life-story of two comrades whom the journalist described as having been " two of the toughest specimens of humanity that ever wandered about loose." One was an ex-prize-fighter who had fought fifteen rounds with the champions of America. About the same time Salvationists at Lyon, France, " captured " a professor of theology and an anarchist who was engaged in the secret manufacture of bombs.

No fewer than 1,046 recruits were sworn in as soldiers under the colours at Exeter Hall on Monday, 21 January 1907, among them a city police sergeant. It was a meeting without precedent, and they were all from the London Province.

Frau Hedwig Wangel, of the Deutsches Theatre, Berlin, one of the most famous of German actresses, astonished her friends by announcing her abandonment of the stage for a religious life, said the *Daily Mail* in September 1909. She stated that her desertion of the footlights was precipitated by her attendance at a Salvation Army meeting, although she did not become a Salvationist.

For several weeks during the early part of 1905 Salvationists connected with Barking and Upton Park corps held meetings in the workmen's trains which took them to the City. Passengers expressed appreciation of this spiritual innovation.

The principal newspaper in Minneapolis, U.S.A., devoted a column to the life-story of " two of the toughest specimens of humanity that ever wandered about loose." This was in the summer of 1906.

CHAPTER TWO

THE INTERNATIONAL CONGRESS OF 1914

The first of the 2,000 overseas delegates to the International Congress of 1914 arrived from Australia in May with Commissioner James Hay. Ex-President Theodore Roosevelt and Commander Eva Booth travelled with the 687 of the 720 U.S.A. delegates on board the *Olympia*. Of Indonesia's fifteen representatives, only six were more than five feet tall. This Congress, the first to be held without the inspiring presence of William Booth, and to be the last of its kind for more than fifty years, was heavily clouded by the *Empress of Ireland* disaster.[1] A week prior to the opening of the Congress a great memorial service was held on Friday, 5 June, in the Royal Albert Hall, in which 133 vacant chairs, each representing the seat of a Canadian delegate who had been drowned, were draped with a white sash on which was emblazoned a crimson cross and crown. Commissioner Whatmore, who mourned the loss of his only son, Captain Guido, spoke on behalf of the bereaved. Earl Grey, a former Governor-General of Canada, the Archdeacon of London, Prebendary Wilson Carlile, of the Church Army, and the Rev. Dr F. B. Meyer were among the congregation.

Three days later General Bramwell Booth was received by His Majesty King George V at Buckingham Palace, he being accompanied by Colonel (later Commissioner) Isaac Unsworth, who at His Majesty's special request was also received in audience.

The Congress opened in the Royal Albert Hall with an unparalleled demonstration of international unity and British

[1] p. 100

solidarity, and, to an unprecedented degree, with the good wishes of royalty and rulers, the classes and the masses, finishing fifteen days later. Messages were read from H.M. George V, H.R.H. the Duke of Connaught, Governor-General of Canada, and President Woodrow Wilson of the U.S.A. The reception by the General of the delegates to this Congress of the Nations was an event stupendous in its significance and fascinating by its manifold beauties and crowded interests. The *War Cry* reporter said :

Those from New Zealand, " finest country in the world," most progressive in social legislation and that which pertains to physical well-being, were followed by Zulus garbed in horns, wild-cat tails, rawhide and red blankets—and bearing in their hands the implements of primitive savagery. There were Parisians with white gloves, and Texan cowboys with woolly caps and buckskin breeches ; Alpine guides with alpenstock and knapsacks, and Albertan broncho busters with lariats and quirts, Hollanders, French, German and British ; Canadians, Australians and Javanese all marched by in fraternal unity and with such kaleidoscopic changes of form and colour, with alternations of the bizarre and the beautiful, that no one was left with nothing of the scene, but an inexpressible and delightful recollection, and a sense of bewildered astonishment.

Never before had such people as the eight representatives from Korea been seen on a British platform. Thousands of tiny flags, bearing a greeting, fluttered down upon the delighted audience when the Danish contingent marched in ; the South Americans had more spectacular interest and emblematic splendour to the square inch than any other contingent. A London paper thus summarized the entrance of the American delegates :

Men and women in grey and red uniforms, and red and blue uniforms ; negroes and negresses clad in red and white-striped material, star-spangled blue coats and tall white hats ; Californian miners with pick and shovel ; Chinese men and women from San Francisco ; a cowboy contingent fresh from the Western plains—they presented a picture of the Army's diversified work, the like of which will perhaps never be seen again.

The General was able to report an advance of one-third in all branches of Army activity since the last Congress ten years previously, despite the prognostications of the Jeremiah Press. At this time the Army was at work in fifty-eight countries and colonies ; ministering to people of eighty-four nationalities in thirty-four languages. There were 9,516 corps and outposts, 16,438 officers and cadets, 1,674 bands, 26,000 bandsmen, 13,000 songsters and 55,520 local officers and 1,168 institutions ; 700 persons were employed at International Headquarters and 650 at the Trade Headquarters. The eighty-one periodicals were printed in twenty-five languages. Other centres of Congressional activity were the Strand Hall, the Westminster Central Hall, Kingsway Hall, Clapton Congress Hall, the Princes Theatre, in which Commander Eva Booth presented an illustrated lecture, " My Father," and the Crystal Palace, where, it was estimated, 50,000 had passed through the gates before 8.30 a.m. and 40,000 took part in the March Past at which the General took the salute. One of the most spectacular processions London had witnessed marched from the Victoria Embankment to Hyde Park, with the General and Mrs Booth at its head, on the first Saturday, when 12,000 Salvationists took part, following which twelve simultaneous meetings were conducted in the open air. Said the *Daily Telegraph* :

Salvation Saturday is something that will live in the memory of London when many costlier spectacles have grown dim.

And the *Evening News* had this to say :

London has never seen, apart from the great State spectacles, a procession more exciting and brilliant than that of the Salvation

Army, which assembled this afternoon on the Embankment and marched to Hyde Park.

And the *Daily Sketch* :

One of the most wonderful sights ever seen in London.

On the Sunday the various contingents created minor sensations in different parts of London, and for several weeks after the events went into the provinces, where miniature congresses were held. The General and Mrs Booth visited Bristol, Manchester, Glasgow and Nottingham. The West Indian Party sang to H.R.H. Princess Henry of Battenberg at Carisbrook Castle in the Isle of Wight. The Strand Hall, an immense corrugated-iron building, holding some 5,000, erected on a site in the Strand near to where Bush House now stands, was filled to capacity on the Wednesday and Thursday for a " Two Days with God." On the Wednesday, H.M. Queen Alexandra, who was accompanied by her sister, the Empress Marie of Russia, received General and Mrs Booth in the drawing-room of Marlborough House, and Commissioner Booth-Hellberg and members of the Danish Party in the private garden. Early on the morning of the Saturday following, the General conducted a service of remembrance at the grave of William and Catherine Booth in Abney Park Cemetery.

Summing up the Congress as a whole *The Challenge*, an Anglican journal, wrote :

Nothing could be more suggestive than the way in which the International Congress of The Salvation Army and the appearance on the streets of London of so many uniformed saints have impressed the people of the metropolis—except, perhaps, the unanimous tribute of the Press of London to the success of the Army as evidenced by these important gatherings. The spirit in which the Salvos have been greeted is well illustrated in this paragraph from *The Nation* :

" So many agreeable and happy faces, such varied gaiety of garb, have hardly been witnessed before. But those who recollect the despised beginnings of The Salvation Army, over thirty years ago, will recognize it for a famous victory. ' Corybantic Christianity ' was the contemptuous term forged by the wit of Professor Huxley, and superior persons discoursed in the Press upon Tarantism and the nervous disorders associated with it."

The Congress showed that, in a sense, The Salvation Army had found itself and stood strongly upon its own feet.

CHAPTER THREE

BANDS AND BANDMASTERS

No feature of the Army's advance during the previous twenty years was more remarkable than the astonishing progress made by its bandsmen, who, in 1904, numbered 17,000. The story of their perseverance, self-sacrifice and achievements constitutes one of the most inspiring records in religious history. The *War Cry* describes the personnel of one London band :

An insurance agent, a bricklayer, a photo etcher, a civil service clerk, a compositor, a carpenter, a plumber, a milkman, a painter, a warehouseman, a poulterer, a grocer, a pointsman, a paper-hanger, a boot maker, a stereotyper, a hairdresser, a musical instrument maker, a salesman, an advertisement canvasser, an accountant, a traveller, a shorthand writer, a greengrocer, a glazier, a gardener, a booksalesman, and a packer.

At the second council for bandmasters, held in November 1904, the Chief of the Staff, Bramwell Booth, announced his intention of instituting examinations for bandmasters,

deputy bandmasters and songster leaders, and issuing certificates for proficiency. The first bandmasters' training session
was held at the Staff Lodge, Clapton, in April 1906. Chalk
Farm Band, numbering fifty-one players, toured Holland for
ten days in the summer of 1905 under Bandmaster Alfred W.
Punchard, and was given a wonderful welcome home by the
people of this North London district. The band visited
Holland again in 1907, also playing in Germany, during a
1,000 miles' tour. For the first time in the city's history a
Salvation Army band played in Utrecht's public park and
to 15,000 listeners. Chatham and New Brompton (Gillingham) Bands played on the Japanese cruiser *Tsukuba* in
Chatham Basin in the evening of 22 June 1907.

An enquiry set on foot by the Chief of the Staff in 1906
decided once and for all that Consett (Co. Durham) corps
was entitled to the honour of having been the first to possess
a properly organized band. Northwich's claim dated back
to March 1880, but Consett possessed a small band during
the latter part of 1879.[1] Its bandmaster, Edward Lennox,
passed away suddenly in February 1905. When, in 1906,
Peterborough (Canada) city council agreed to make the corps
a grant of £30, it was the first occasion upon which a
Salvation Army band had been so honoured.

Invited to comment on the playing of Salvation Army
bands, George Bernard Shaw attended a festival in the
Congress Hall, Clapton, on 7 December 1905 and wrote :

In point of discipline, alertness, and conscientiousness, all the
bands were first rate. Professional orchestras never do their
best unless they have a good conductor. I have repeatedly heard
a vapid, absent-minded, careless performance in London under
a mediocre conductor, followed in the same week by a splendid
performance of the very same work, by the very same players,
under Richter or Mottl. This tendency of professional orchestral

[1] *The History of The Salvation Army*, vol. ii, p. 114

players to earn their money with as little trouble to themselves as possible does not exist in The Salvation Army, where the men are playing, not for money, but for the glory of God. All the bands did their best eagerly and enthusiastically. But mere enthusiasm could not have produced the remarkable precision and snap in their execution. They must have worked hard and been well coached by their conductors. And there were no incompetent conductors—for instance, no gentlemen set to wield a baton because they had won a musical degree at a university. The bandmasters had evidently won their places by their aptitude and efficiency.

The first musical festival to take place in the Royal Albert Hall—on Wednesday, 30 October 1907—and presided over by the Chief of the Staff in connection with his silver wedding celebrations, was described as " the greatest demonstration of a musical character that the Army has ever held." The report further stated that " to fill this classic Temple of Harmony on the strength of Salvation Army music alone, and to make them [the enthusiastic followers and eager admirers] pay for their tickets was a stroke of genuine daring ! " In addition to a huge singing battalion, brass bands, timbrels, bagpipes, the grand organ, concertinas, the banjo, drums and fifes and handbells were given the chance of sounding forth their capabilities.

In 1907 the Chief of the Staff appointed Bandmaster Edward H. Hill, of Southall Citadel, to be the first Band Inspector for the British Territory. It had been un-expectedly announced by the Chief in 1905 that Brigadier Richard Slater was to become Secretary at National Head-quarters of the Bands and Songster Brigades, but for " several reasons " the Brigadier could not accept the conditions of his appointment, so nothing further was heard of the matter for several years. New uniform insignia for Deputy Bandmasters and Young People's Bandmasters was introduced in May 1908.

More than 1,000 bandsmen were present for the 1910 councils, and for those held in 1913 when General Bramwell Booth made the interesting announcement that he had it in mind to institute an award for bravery in life-saving, which should be bestowed by the Army in any part of the world where such instances came under its notice. There were then 25,000 bandsmen in the Army's ranks. Under Mr Winston Churchill's Prison Reform Scheme, Bedford Congress Hall Band was permitted to give a festival in the local gaol in October 1910, and thus became the first corps band to participate in the working out of this beneficial enterprise, which was arranged by the Mayor, Councillor Longhurst.

Chalk Farm Band undertook a motor campaign through the Midlands, Lancashire, Yorkshire and the Eastern Counties during the summer of 1911. The first day's journey of 103 miles greatly taxed the capacity of the cars, some of which were unable to bear the strain of so long a distance. All the bandsmen were attired in dust-coats.

Holland was revisited by the International Staff Band under Lieutenant-Colonel (later Commissioner) George Mitchell [1] at Easter 1905, it having campaigned in the country two years previously. Permission was given by the burgo-master for the band to play through the main thoroughfares of Amsterdam, this being the first time for twelve years that such a privilege had been granted. It was said that the crowds which greeted the band were larger than those that had welcomed Queen Wilhelmina and her Consort when they visited the city the previous year. Next year the band visited Switzerland, slipping into both France and Germany. These incursions were not on the original programme, but they made history, for never before had British Salvationists played in these countries. By special authority the band played within the precincts of the St Lazare Station in Paris.

[1] *The History of The Salvation Army*, vol. iv, p. 204

Again, in 1907, the band toured Switzerland, this time being accompanied by " The Father of Salvation Army Music," Richard Slater. Holland was visited yet again in 1910, when the band was the first to march through the streets of the royal city of The Hague. *En route* Prince Henry of Prussia, brother of Kaiser Wilhelm II of Germany, was a passenger on the ship and entered into conversation with Colonel Mitchell. The band's first prison visit was to Parkhurst, Isle of Wight, in September 1910, when it became the first band permitted to play to convicts in Great Britain. Captain Mary Booth, granddaughter of the General, was then the Commanding Officer of the Newport Corps. Ascension Day 1911 saw the band again in Switzerland. During its visit to Germany in the following year the band received an unexpected rebuff, being refused permission even to march, without playing, through the streets of Halle, the home of Handel.

The International Staff Songsters, formed in 1897 under Brigadier Herbert J. Jackson, travelled extensively in Great Britain ; it was composed of officers and employees of International Headquarters.

A set of instruments made at the Army's Campfield works at St Albans and exhibited at an exhibition at Christchurch, New Zealand, in the spring of 1907 was awarded a gold medal. A gold medal was also awarded for a set of instruments exhibited at the Franco-British Exhibition held at the White City, London, in 1908. Incidentally, in this same exhibition the Army's Campfield Press was awarded a gold medal for bookbinding and a diploma of honour for general printing.

Great Yarmouth Band had the distinction of purchasing the first bass drum to be manufactured at the Campfield Instrument Factory.

Another interesting musical development was announced

in March 1907, when the Chief of the Staff decided to organize a combination to be known as the London Orchestra, under the leadership of Brigadier (later Lieutenant-Colonel, O.F.) Richard Slater,[1] but apparently nothing came of it.

The Band Gratuity Scheme, for relieving the necessities of widows and orphans of bandsmen, came into operation on 5 July 1907. Each band entering the scheme had to pay 6d per week up to a membership of twenty, and an additional 1d per week for each man over that number. A widow received £20 on the death of her husband and each child £5, to a maximum of £50. The scheme remains in operation to this day.

For the first time in the history of Calton (Scotland) Prison, a Salvation Army band (Leith) provided a festival; this was on the afternoon of Coronation Day, 22 June 1911. Springburn Band was the first band to enter Barlinnie Prison, and on the same day; and in the afternoon Regent Hall Band, under its new Bandmaster, Herbert W. Twitchin, occupied the bandstand in Hyde Park, adjacent to the processional route.[2] This Band had made a gramophone recording of " Onward, Christian soldiers " in 1902, which was probably the first Salvation Army record to be produced. Six years previously, the Trade Headquarters Band had contributed to a phonograph recording, but this was not a permanent production because of the softness of the wax.

[1] *The History of The Salvation Army*, vol. ii, p. 122
[2] p. 247

CHAPTER FOUR

EVENTS

Memorial services for " Our Officers in Heaven " were instituted and conducted in October 1905 throughout the world, the General leading the principal service in the Royal Albert Hall. Said the *War Cry* :

The underlying idea is eminently Scriptural and is stimulated to faith and good works. . . . The lives of the saints are heritages of the Church. The purity of their lives, their triumphs of faith, their zeal for souls, together with their trials, afflictions, weaknesses and shortcomings, should be recalled from time to time.

The great occasion provided a mixture of sorrow and triumph, with three bands thundering forth the " Dead March in ' Saul,' " and 400 youngsters singing " I have a Home that is fairer than day." The name of the first Army officer to be promoted to Glory was Captain Jane Anderson. There were melodramatic moments when, for instance, the widowed Booth-Tucker appeared with his motherless children—his wife, The Consul, was killed in a railway accident in October 1904.[1] The General spoke of his own wife :

The memory of St Catherine, the Salvation Mother, shall linger in the hearts, anyway, of our own people, so long as the sun and the moon endure.

Another such memorial service was held in the following year. The leading London newspapers, including *The Times*, gave prominence to the occasion. And yet again, in 1907, in Birmingham Town Hall, St Andrew's Hall,

[1] *The History of The Salvation Army*, vol. iv, p. 361

Glasgow, and the Free Trade Hall, Manchester, memorial services were conducted by the Chief of the Staff and Mrs Booth.

As a vice-president of the British and Foreign Bible Society, the General took part in its annual meeting in the Royal Albert Hall in November 1905.

The Army's anniversary was not always celebrated on the grand scale, but the forty-second was " brilliantly celebrated," at the Crystal Palace on Monday, 15 July 1907, when the fourth great motor campaign was inaugurated.[1] The surprise of the night, it was stated, was the young people's band from Clapton, which had been formed two years previously. In 1908 the General was welcomed at the Crystal Palace from his fifth motor campaign, and in 1912, the forty-seventh anniversary at the Alexandra Palace was conducted by the Chief of the Staff in the absence of the General, who was too ill to attend.

For twenty-six years the Army had held many of its most important gatherings in Exeter Hall, Strand, and thousands of souls had been converted there ; but on 6 May 1907 a great farewell meeting of " war memories and thanksgiving " was conducted by the Chief of the Staff, as the building was no longer to be used for public services. The Strand Palace Hotel, now also demolished, was erected on the site.

A concentrated ten days' effort for the conversion of the Metropolis took place at the beginning of November 1912. It was known as " The Siege of London " and included in it were : Commissioners Howard (the Chief of the Staff), Railton, Cadman and Higgins (the British Commissioner) whose idea it was. He was responsible for all the evangelistic work in the Territory except that of the Training Division, over which the Principal of the Training College, Com-

[1] p. 141

missioner McKie, had complete control, including all corps now known as the East London Division. Prayer meetings were held daily in the City Temple. At the conclusion of the attack the British Commissioner swore in 450 new soldiers at Camberwell. So successful was this new venture that a second " Siege of London " took place in the same month of the following year, being described as " A great ten days' assault upon the strongholds of Hell " ; 1,000 " prisoners " were taken during the first week-end, and 3,750 altogether. Again daily prayer meetings were held in the City Temple. The British Commissioner led a midnight raid on the public houses of Penge and conducted no fewer than thirty meetings, finishing with another swearing-in ceremony of more than 400 soldiers at Camberwell.

Mother's Day in The Salvation Army throughout the United Kingdom was instituted in 1913 by the British Commissioner, Edward J. Higgins, and was held on the last Sunday in November. All young persons and children who attended the meetings were asked to give, or send, a white flower to their mother, or, if she be dead, some white flowers should, it was suggested, be placed on her grave to keep her memory green. In 1914 it was decided that Mother's Day should be held on 31 May, " when the flowers bloom."

It was announced in the *War Cry* for 29 November 1913 that

In connection with the International League for the Protection of Women and Children a General Council has been constituted, having for its aims the promotion of the objects and the development of the operations of the said League. Mrs Booth is the President of the League and Council, and Colonel Unsworth is the Secretary. The members of the Council consist of the International Secretaries of the Foreign Office—Commissioners Whatmore and Lamb, and Colonel [later Commissioner] Pearce, Commissioner Adelaide Cox and Colonel [later Commissioner] Duff.

Evidently the League did not survive for long, for nothing further is mentioned concerning it.

Field Officers' Councils conducted by the General, then eighty years of age, were inaugurated at Bristol Citadel in June 1909, and he spoke for seven hours on each of the three days, dealing in a masterly way with matters of the most far-reaching importance. Similar councils were held in Manchester, Glasgow, Leeds and Clapton successively.

"THE SALVATION NAVY"

Commissioner Ridsdel had hoped to introduce motor-boats in 1905 for use among the island populations living off the northern coast of Norway, thousands of these people within the Arctic circle never having had an opportunity to hear the Gospel preached. The Army's lifeboat *Catherine Booth* [1] had been used to visit some of these fishing villages, but the unsuitability of a sailing boat for such work had been long evident. When the Commissioner eventually acquired a steam yacht, the Queen of Norway consented to its being named *Queen Maud*. The boat operated from a centre at Oksningen. A report published in 1912 showed that since its launching in 1900 the *Catherine Booth* and her crew, under Adjutant Ovesen, had rescued more than 500 vessels and 1,800 men whose lives were in danger. In addition, upwards of 100 fishermen had been converted to Christ.

By the purchase in 1910 of an old-fashioned wooden barge at a cost of 300 guilder, Army operations in Holland were brought to bear upon a section of people living in villages not hitherto reached. It was named *Hoop voor Allen* (*Hope for All*). A meeting-room to hold a congregation of 140 was constructed on board. Work among the children who spent

[1] *The History of The Salvation Army*, vol. iv, p. 42

their lives on barges on the canals was also undertaken. Commissioner Railton spent three days on the barge and wrote glowingly of its work in the *War Cry*. Captain Wynold, the skipper, and his assistant themselves pulled the barge from one village to another with a rope slung across their shoulders, thus saving the hire of a horse. As a result of this work three halls were erected and a circle corps was established within the first two years.

The launching of another yacht for The Salvation Navy took place in June 1911, within a stone's throw of the spot in New York where Commissioner Railton and seven lasses had launched The Salvation Army thirty-one years previously.[1] This ceremony was conducted by Commander Eva Booth. Major and Mrs Erickson were in command of a crew of five. The vessel, donated by Mr Bradford Lee Gilbert, a noted architect, who died a few weeks later, was employed for conducting meetings among longshoremen and sailors at various ports along the extensive American coast. The first soul won for Christ in " our American Naval Warfare," as it was called, was a fisherman who had followed the sea for forty-five years.

THE DRINK QUESTION

Mrs Bramwell Booth, speaking at the Queen's Hall, London, at the Annual Meeting of the British Women's Temperance Association in May 1905, said, in what a London newspaper described as " the speech of the evening " :

What will it avail our children if at great national cost they learnt facts about the world around them while at the same time we are legalizing and encouraging every facility for converting them presently into a drunken, drinking and besotted people ? No

[1] *The History of The Salvation Army*, vol. ii, p. 232

system of education could succeed until the drink question has been dealt with.

As the result of Mr George R. Sims's series of articles in one of London's important newspapers in the spring of 1907, the national conscience was awakened regarding the conditions under which tens of thousands of slum children were being reared. Investigations revealed that in some districts, and especially in the daytime, public houses were filled with married women, to the exclusion even of men. These women were generally accompanied by young children, who were occasionally dosed with gin to keep them quiet. At an important conference of medical and social experts held in London under the presidency of Sir Thomas Barlow, a resolution was unanimously approved in favour of prohibiting children under fourteen years of age from admission to licensed houses other than residential hotels. Mrs Booth and Commissioner Alex. M. Nicol represented the Army, the Commissioner making a speech in support of the resolution. In May of the same year another practical step was taken, when a large and influential gathering was presided over by the Bishop of Ripon in the Royal United Services Institution, Whitehall, where Mrs Booth seconded a similar resolution to that made on the earlier occasion.

In the following year, 1908, Mr Asquith's Government brought in its Licensing Bill, which called for a reduction in the number of public houses and naturally called forth considerable opposition from " the Trade." The General was all for the Bill, although he regretted that the Prime Minister had not seen fit to go further with respect to Sunday closing ; the measure for preventing the evils associated with clubs were insufficient, but the local veto on new licences was good. He refused, although constantly urged to do so, to enter the political arena on this vexed question, but in accordance with his own firmly-laid-down regulations regarding the Army and politics, he steadfastly refused ; he would, however, "fight the evil at the root." Mrs Booth spoke also on alcoholism at the International Congress in the Imperial Institute, London, in August 1909.

The Army launched an Anti-Drink Crusade on 30 August 1913 with the special object (1) to save drunkards, (2) to warn the young and get them to become abstainers, and (3) to agitate for the closing of public houses on Sundays, which, in the main, was welcomed by the publicans ; indeed, in one case a publican offered to speak at a meeting in favour of Sunday closing.

CORPS UNUSUAL ACTIVITIES

An unusual activity and a rapidly developing feature of ordinary field work for a corps was that at Liverpool VI, where Adjutant Gwynne provided relief for many weeks during the spring of 1905, when unemployment was particularly acute. On an average 250 ablebodied men of all trades, and clerks, formed up two hours before the time of admission, 8 p.m. Following a meeting they were all given a bowl of soup and a round of bread. Passing out into the street they returned at 11 p.m., when they retired to rest in the hall, lying on the floor or on the seats, sometimes using their boots for a pillow. At 4.30 a.m. a bugle awoke them to hot coffee, then they set off to seek for work. Sixty men were converted during this period.

Renovations at Regent Hall, Oxford Street, London, caused the corps to take possession of the Holborn Empire Theatre in August 1909, after which the General reopened the hall.

★   ★   ★

The indefatigable traveller, Commissioner Railton, visited Austro-Hungary, Servia, Bulgaria, Romania and Russian-Poland in the early part of 1908, and Greece and Egypt later in the year.

VII PERSECUTION AND PROSECUTION

ONE would have thought that "The Fight for the Streets,"[1] the trouble at Torquay, the Eastbourne riots, the *cause cèlébre* which brought notoriety to Whitchurch, Hampshire, and the several prosecutions for technical obstruction which took place all over the country, and particularly the judgment given in favour of the Army in the High Court of Justice and the statements made from time to time in the Houses of Parliament during the period from 1886 to 1904, would have put an end to the sufferings of Salvationists for preaching the Gospel in the open air, which was their right. But official bigotry again raised its ugly head when, in November 1904, Bangor (Ireland) Urban Council directed proceedings against the women officers for causing an obstruction on the esplanade. It was stated that the council was opposed to street preaching. This was the first complaint of its kind the Army had received in Ireland. The defendants were fined 1s each and costs. They refused to pay on principle, and the fines were paid by one of the magistrates.

In the early part of 1905 an officer was sent to prison for refusing to pay the fine inflicted upon him by a particularly weak Justice of the Peace. A publican had objected to an open-air meeting being held in the neighbourhood of his premises. Among other indignities heaped upon him in gaol, the officer was called to an interview with the governor and

---

[1] *The History of The Salvation Army*, vol. iv, p. 264

made to stand with his face to a stone wall for nearly an hour before that august personage would deign to speak to him.

Widnes (Lancashire) Salvationists were hauled before the magistrates time and again during 1906 and fined, with costs, for " obstruction," although they had regularly conducted meetings on the same spot, Victoria Square—which was capable of accommodating 10,000 people—for twenty-five years. The absurdity of the situation was emphasized one night when a travelling show rendered one of the streets practically impassable for two or three hours without a word of remonstrance from the police. When, however, five Salvationists, four of them women, were sent to prison for twenty-one days in the case of three of them, and for fourteen days in the case of the other two, a great public indignation meeting was held in the Alexandra Theatre, under the presidency of an alderman, and 2,000 citizens unanimously passed a strongly worded resolution protesting against the ill-advised action of Superintendent Strickland in interfering with the privileges the Army had enjoyed for so long. The resolution was sent to the Home Secretary. The women officers had been awakened in their quarters, which the police had tried to enter by force, before 6 a.m., and later in the day were dragged like common felons to the prison cells. The treatment given these officers was eventually brought before the notice of Parliament. There was a brief lull in the storm following the protest meeting, but it broke out again in fury, the police—an inspector and four constables, all new to the town—renewing the attack and taking the names of thirty-five officers. Twelve of them were sentenced to fourteen days' imprisonment. The Mayor of Hyde, a neighbouring town, wrote to express his strong disapproval of the Widnes police, and offered personal support to the Army. At long last the *War Cry* for 12 January 1907 announced that free speech had been vindicated, and that the Army was to continue to hold its meetings in the square, the Mayor, Mr S. Owens, having called a private conference in his parlour to discuss the matter.

Then trouble appeared in Scotland, the home of religious liberty, where, at Motherwell, the women officers, " first blood " of subsequent prosecutions, were sent to prison. As at Widnes, and, indeed, at many places throughout the country, Salvationists at this time were being called upon to give up their open-air rights at the Cross, Merry Street, because certain hot-headed political agitators were causing considerable antipathy and creating difficulty for the police, who, generally speaking, were performing what to them was a disagreeable task in summoning Salvationists. Later, nine were sentenced to fourteen days' imprisonment after a seven hours' trial finishing at ten o'clock at night. They were removed to Barlinnie Gaol, Glasgow, by brake at four o'clock the next morning. The public was astonished and enraged, and on the following Sunday week an orderly crowd, estimated at 5,000, gathered at the Cross, but not a policeman was to be seen. After serving ten days of their sentence the nine prisoners were released by order of Captain Sinclair, Secretary of State for Scotland, and publicly welcomed home by a crowd of some 10,000 in the streets and in a capacity-packed town hall for a protest meeting. Unfortunately, certain local newspapers aggravated the trouble. In October the magistrates withdrew their unreasonable proclamation of June, but on the following Sunday the names of Salvationists were again taken. October 19 saw a second proclamation which, in spirit if not in form, was as sweeping as that for which it had been substituted, for " written permission " was demanded by the provost and magistrates before an open-air meeting could be held. Twelve Salvationists, whose names had been taken at the same time as the nine who were convicted, were now brought to trial. They were fined 7s 6d each or, alternately, sentenced to three days' imprisonment, which they served. At the request of Bailie M'Lees, a conference took place, it being attended by the bailie himself, Commissioner Cosandey, the Territorial Commander, Lieutenant-Colonel Byers, whose wife was at the time in gaol with Mrs Brigadier Garrie, and the Army's solicitor, Mr Warner. This resulted in thirteen persons who had been sent to prison for seven days under the second proclamation —which was based on an Act of Parliament dated 1605, in the reign of James VI of Scotland—being immediately released, and the offensive proclamation being publicly withdrawn on 13 November.

Dartford's (Kent) Superintendent Poole blundered in July of the following year, after the Army had held open-air meetings in the Bull Centre for twenty-two years. Suddenly and rather peremptorily the Army was ordered to quit the stand, although no complaint of obstruction had ever been received by the police. Naturally the corps refused to comply with such a demand and Ensign William Roy was convicted for " unlawful and wilful obstruction " and fined 20s. He elected to serve seven days' imprisonment. Subsequent to being summoned for the second time, Mrs Roy also went to prison, although two publicans offered to pay her fine. More prosecutions and sentences followed. On the last occasion thousands welcomed home the prisoners—who rode through the town in a florally decorated car loaned by a councillor—and protested in the Drill Hall against the high-handed action of the police. But the prosecutions and the convictions continued until the friendly urban district council called a conference, when the summonses and the sentences were withdrawn and the Army was permitted to retain its stand.

On top of this regrettable series of prosecutions came news

of a similar attempt to prohibit Salvationists at Whitstable (Kent) from holding their open-air meetings at the local Cross. A farthing fine was inflicted with 7s 6d costs. Ensign Trevorrow decided to undergo a day's imprisonment. Adjutant Kerley, of Douglas, Isle of Man, was fined 20s for a similar offence and elected to go to prison. At the end of the year prejudice against the Army's open-air work arose in Halifax again,[1] Chief Constable Alfred H. Richardson prohibiting all meetings and at any time, in consequence of which Adjutant John Andrews was sent to prison for fourteen days despite " no complaints " for obstruction in George Square. At King's Heath, Birmingham, where a battery [2] was at work, Captain Harry Greenaway was fined half a crown. He went to Wakefield Prison for seven days, and 30,000 people acclaimed his release in the streets and 2,000 passed a resolution demanding a cessation of the unwise proceedings. The case against Brigadier Batsford, of the National Headquarters Legal Department, for aiding and abetting, was ungraciously withdrawn after a month's delay. The Brigadier appeared at several courts on behalf of various " defendants."

When a bye-law was passed at Hastings in 1896 for the " preservation of order and good conduct in the town," it was specifically stated that it was not intended to apply to The Salvation Army, nevertheless Adjutant Slee's name was taken in August 1909 for infringing it by holding an open-air meeting in Denmark Place, where a stand had been established for nearly forty years. Eleven months later he was fined 10s with the alternative of fourteen days in prison and given time to " think it over," whereupon he ejaculated, " God bless The Salvation Army ! " This so infuriated the somewhat turbulent clerk to the magistrates that he cried :

[1] *The History of The Salvation Army*, vol. iv, p. 291
[2] *The History of The Salvation Army*, vol. iv, p. 186

" You ought to have known better than that, you know ! If you had been seized by the scruff of the neck and thrown out, it would only have been what you deserved." When Slee said that he preferred imprisonment, the magistrates twitted him with a desire to be a martyr. When he faced a second trial, one of the two magistrates was a local preacher. Slee was fined £1 or, in default of distress, was to serve twenty-one days in prison. It was not, however, until June 1911 that he was arrested in Guildford, where he was then stationed, and taken to Lewes Gaol to serve the sentence imposed upon him at Hastings eleven months before. An unknown person paid the fine and the Adjutant was released after six days. For a similar offence at Hastings Bandmaster Caleb Jeffery, who had been married for only six weeks, was fined 30s, but served fourteen days' imprisonment. Meetings were resumed in Denmark Place and on the beach at Whitsuntide 1911, but the new Commanding Officer, Adjutant Walter J. French, was warned of the consequences, which eventuated in a fine ; this a friend paid. For several months the local Salvationists were engaged in a painful, but determined, fight, and five of them were convicted. When the Army suggested a compromise, the town council rejected it by only one vote. It appeared that two councillors, one of whom sat on the bench, had shares in the Queen's Hotel, whence came the principal opposition. Charged a second time Adjutant French went to prison in October for fourteen days. Other Salvationists were fined, including Corps Sergeant-Major Sully, some of whose household goods were seized and sold by the police. Further convictions followed, sentences of fourteen days' imprisonment being inflicted on Captain Florence Bartlett, Recruiting Sergeant James Gilman and Band Sergeant Bean, who had already served one sentence. The *War Cry* stated that

the whole persecution is the most trumpery, paltry, pettifogging piece of superfluous interference with existing rights and usages that can be imagined.

By the end of September 1911 twenty-six summonses had been issued and seven Salvationists had suffered imprisonment. When Mrs French was charged the chairman of the bench said that " they were not influenced by the fact that she was a woman and had a baby." One of the magistrates, Councillor Pelham, made a dramatic protest and left the court after being rudely ordered to sit down by the chairman, who had no right to make such a demand of a fellow-magistrate. Brigadier Mary Murray, who was summoned while a visitor to the town, was fined, but the fine was immediately paid by an unknown outside friend. Fined a second time, the same thing happened. It was thought that she, being the daughter of General Sir John Murray, who had been engaged in the Indian Mutiny, the authorities shrank from placing a woman of her high social connections in gaol, as was the case with Brigadier Chatterton at Eastbourne.[1] Ensign William Waters, of Burgess Hill, served fourteen days in gaol in December 1911 for speaking on Hastings Beach in October, and in January 1912 Mrs Sully was arrested and taken to Lewes Gaol, while her husband was at work and her children at school. Lieutenant Charles F. Stevens, although sentenced in October 1911, was not imprisoned until the following January, while stationed in Deal. He spent fourteen days making nose-bags for horses.

When Captain Mary Booth was appointed to the command of the Hastings Corps in December 1911, the authorities had approached her in a friendly spirit as she was the granddaughter of the General, but while she was ill her Lieutenant, May Whittaker, had her name taken on two occasions. What finally happened is summed up by the *Hastings Argus* in the early part of 1913 :

[1] *The History of The Salvation Army*, vol. iv, p. 276

Miss Mary Booth found Hastings a storm centre and left it in peace. The finest tribute to her work at Hastings is that nobody ever troubles to ask whether the Army or the Corporation won in the fight. When she was laid aside by illness the heart of Hastings and St Leonards was touched. When she recovered all classes rejoiced. Out of her peacemaking was born new life for The Salvation Army in the town.

Folkestone [1] was one of the worst of places for rioting in the early days, and as a result it was considered too dangerous, even after twenty-five years, for the Army to hold open-air meetings in the Fishmarket, which was approached through some low arches. Once in, the Salvationists were unable to get out at the other end, and so were trapped and brutally attacked. But in 1911 Regent Hall Band visited the town for Easter, accompanied by its Commanding Officer, Major (later Commissioner) Frank Barrett, who decided that it was time to return to this old and historic battleground, which was once the headquarters of the local Skeleton Army.[2] Folkestone Salvationists had their misgivings about such a venture ; nevertheless, the band went bravely forward into the lion's den. Contrary to expectations the fishermen " took to " the visitors, and not only did they accept the invitation to attend the meetings in the Town Hall, but brought with them their own drum and fife band. Today the Army is received with open arms in the Fishmarket, and a portion of it is roped off on Sunday evenings during the summer to prevent car-parking on the stand.

Summoned at Walton for breaking a bye-law which protected the townspeople from " itinerant musical per- formers," Adjutant Herbert Parsons, of Felixstowe, was dis- charged with £1 11s 6d costs, owing to the extenuating

[1] Colonel Edward H. Joy gives a vivid account of the shocking happenings at Folkestone in his fascinating book, *The Old Corps*, published in 1944.
[2] *The History of The Salvation Army*, vol. ii, p. 193

circumstances surrounding the case. At Scunthorpe Adjutant Alfred F. Feltwell was sent to Lincoln Prison for seven days for obstruction in July 1912, he refusing to pay the fine of half a crown with costs. All Salvationists wore prison garb while " doing time," and most were placed in the second division, but Adjutant Feltwell was placed in the third division, which meant that he spent his days picking oakum. When he was welcomed home the *Daily News* said :

Never since the Relief of Mafeking have such scenes of enthusiasm been witnessed.

The Steelworks Silver Band led a procession of sympathizers a quarter of a mile long.

It seems paradoxical that when some of the *Broken Earthenware* characters [1] visited Hastings in July 1912, the Mayor presided, he being supported by several councillors, but the Commanding Officer, Captain Gaunt, had his name taken during that same month !

★   ★   ★

A spell of bigoted opposition was encountered by Salvationists in the city of Long Beach, California, U.S.A., during the early part of 1906, when they were arrested for preaching in the streets ; they were released on their own recognisances. Such an outcry of public opinion was roused, however, that the authorities had to climb down immediately. Every newspaper in the city condemned the opposers. That same week the Mayor signed a permit allowing Salvationists to hold meetings wherever and whenever they chose. The high-handed action of the police in arresting Salvationists at Reno, Nevada, for holding open-air meetings, in violation of the enacted ordinance of the city fathers prohibiting such

[1] p. 192

gatherings, led to unprecedented scenes of public sympathy. The Methodist minister held an open-air meeting of protest with his members, and was arrested with some of them and fined, as was the corps officer. Several thousands marched with them to prison.

VIII WILLIAM BOOTH

Chapter One

OLD AGE HAS ITS REWARD

THAT it neglected the Holy Bible, that its General had issued an "imitation Bible," and that he had presumed, as one Christian periodical put it, to invent or indite a Bible of his own, was at one time the most popular of all the calumnies associated with The Salvation Army, so that when, in May 1905, William Booth was invited to become a Vice-President of the British and Foreign Bible Society, the honour was pleasingly significant to one who had been so persistently and maliciously slandered by certain sections of the religious Press.

A much greater honour was to be accorded him five months later, on 26 October, when, in his seventy-seventh year, bareheaded and accompanied by his son Bramwell and 1,000 of his officers, he marched through the crowded streets from International Headquarters to the Guildhall to receive the Freedom of the City of London from the hands of the City Chamberlain, Sir Joseph Dimsdale, Bart., in the presence of the Lord Mayor, Sir John Pound, the Corporation, and a very distinguished representation of national life. The Common Councillors wore badges, specially made for the occasion, on which the Army crest and the City arms were emblazoned. This event put into concrete and ornamental form the phenomenal change in the public esteem for the work of the Army and its General, for there had been no

" wire-pulling," no " engineering." The illuminated parch-
ment was enclosed in an oaken casket, the wood of which
had been taken from the roof of the old Guildhall, which
had been constructed under the supervision of Sir Christopher
Wren after the Great Fire. The Corporation had suggested
a golden casket valued at 100 guineas, but William Booth
considered this a waste. But the 100 guineas were found to
be in the wooden casket ! It was a personal gift to the
General, but he immediately handed the money to the
Social Fund. In the course of a speech of singular eloquence
the City Chamberlain spoke of the " imperishable monuments " that the General had erected. These, he said,

> Speak a divine ambition and a zeal
> The boldest patriot might be proud to feel,

and continued :

We are glad to pay the highest tribute which can be rendered by
us and accepted by him, namely the regard of the City of London,
and through the City our country, expressed in our offer of the
Freedom of " no mean city " ; a city which has ever striven for
religious liberty ; and a city which has benefited incalculably by
General Booth's exertions.

To the City Chamberlain's striking oration the General made
a memorable reply. Prior to the ceremony the International
Staff Band played in the gallery between the images of the
mythical Gog and Magog.

The city of his birth, not to be outdone by London, also
honoured her most famous son—" the greatest man that
Nottingham has ever bred or seen "—with the Freedom of the
City on 6 November, the Mayor, Alderman Joseph Bright,
presenting the casket and the emblazoned roll in the Council
Chamber at the Exchange Hall. The casket had been made
from oak taken from one of the last piles of the old Trent
Bridge, dating back to the eleventh century. After the

presentation a procession marched to the Mechanics' Hall, where the function was continued. The streets were gorged with cheering people. William Booth was also a Freeman of Boston, Mass. In 1906 Nottingham Corporation placed a commemorative tablet on the front of the house in Nottintone Place, Sneinton, where William Booth was born. On the Easter Monday of that year, 16 April, he received the Freedom of the royal and ancient borough of Kirkcaldy, Scotland, from the hands of Provost H. M. Barnet, in the King's Theatre. The silver and red moroccan casket was tubular in shape.

On 26 June in the following year the University of Oxford conferred upon him the honorary degree of Doctor of Civil Law, the Prime Minister, Sir Henry Campbell-Bannerman, and Rudyard Kipling [1] and Professor Hubert von Herkomer, who had painted his portrait,[2] among other outstanding men, being honoured at the same time. William Booth already possessed other honorary degrees, including that of Doctor of Science of the University of Brussels, of which he had made no public mention, but which added to the spiritual freight of his soul. The *Morning Post* stated, in its delineation of the scene at Oxford, that " no one seemed to be a greater favourite than General Booth." The *War Cry* lamented that Professor Huxley, the man who had once described the Army as " corybantic Christianity," [3] a pun, surely, on the names of John and Richard Cory, of Cardiff, who were strong supporters of the Army in its early days—had not been alive to have seen the recognition. The ceremony took place in the Sheldonian Theatre. Speaking in Latin the Marquis of Curzon, Chancellor of the University, who had put forward the General's name for the honour, said :

[1] *The History of The Salvation Army*, vol. iv, p. 324
[2] *The History of The Salvation Army*, vol. iv, p. 327
[3] *The History of The Salvation Army*, vol. iii, p. 82

O Man, Most Venerable, Compassionate Patron of the lowest of the people, and Commander of The Army for the winning of souls, I admit you as a Doctor of Civil Law to this ancient University.

Toward the end of 1907 Lord Ashton gave a Victorian statue to Lancaster, his native town, " as a lasting memorial of the long and illustrious reign of a great and good Queen." The four panels below the bronze figure of the Queen contain the figures of a number of Victorian celebrities, the North panel including that of William Booth.

On 9 July 1910, to celebrate the forty-fifth anniversary of the birth of The Salvation Army, and in the presence of a number of Christian Missioners, Commissioner David M. Rees, Head of the Training Territory, placed a commemorative stone in position near the spot on Mile End Waste where the General first preached in East London. The simple inscription reads : " Here William Booth commenced the work of The Salvation Army, July 1865." The memorial is placed at the entrance to a public garden facing the Great Assembly Hall. The old " Vine Tavern "[1] has entirely disappeared, the Quakers' Burial Ground, on which the meeting-tent was erected, has been converted into a place of recreation. Mile End Green, or Common, was the scene of many stirring events during the centuries, dating back almost to the time of the Norman Conquest.

In a lengthy article the London *Times*, toward the end of 1910, paid a striking tribute to the General and his labours on behalf of the poor and outcast classes. Referring to the launching of the *Darkest England Scheme* [2] the writer said :

The comparative paucity of completely satisfactory results means that the *Darkest England Scheme* was, as a scheme,

[1] *The History of The Salvation Army*, vol. i, p. 20
[2] *The History of The Salvation Army*, vol. iii, p. 75

impracticable. It was too sanguine ; the task which General Booth set himself was superhuman. He probably sees that himself in looking back after the lapse of twenty-one years. But that does not make his work a failure. On the contrary, it is an amazing, one may even say, a stupendous, success. It has developed in other directions and on different lines. To have built up this world-wide Organization, which encircles the globe with a net-work of varied institutions, all engaged in active, helping, human work, holding out a hand to those who need it, men, women, and children ; and to have done this through the power and on the basis of a pure, Christian enthusiasm in these latter days of materialistic and rationalistic domination—such an achievement can only be called great. It is the work of a great man.

CHAPTER TWO

THE BEGINNING OF THE END

Although possibly the world's greatest traveller in his day, William Booth was miraculously preserved from accident, but on an evening in November 1905 he had a narrow escape when a wheel of the hansom cab in which he was riding from King's Cross to International Headquarters came off, and the body of the vehicle dropped to the roadway.

Toward the end of December 1908, and in his eightieth year, the General complained that his sight, which had caused him difficulty for some two years, was giving him considerable trouble. He was successfully operated upon for a cataract on the right eye at his home, " Rookstone," Lancaster Avenue, Hadley Wood, Hertfordshire, by the eminent oculist, Mr Charles Higgens. The Queen telegraphed the General from Sandringham :

Have felt so much for you, and hope operation successful. Trust you are getting on toward complete recovery, and that the sight you need so much will soon be completely restored.

All the while during his period of recuperation he was conferring with his top officers on matters of business, and was hoping to conduct a great Sunday campaign in The Congress Hall, a special feature of which was to have been the reception of the largest number of cadets ever to be gathered into one session ; but his recovery was too slow. On 8 February King Edward VII sent him a message of sympathy, together with a cheque for 100 guineas " towards the great work in which you and your officers are, with such success, engaged." By 10 February he was back " in the firing-line," meeting the International Headquarters staff at Clapton prior to leaving for a Continental campaign. A second operation on the eye was performed in April, and yet another immediately following the abandonment of his sixth motor campaign.[1] On 21 August, however, it was discovered by Mr Higgens that the sight had gone, and so the right eye was removed and an artificial eye substituted. Again the Queen sent a telegram of sympathy, this time from Balmoral Castle, Scotland. Other messages came from the Prince and Princess of Wales, and the Prime Minister, Mr Asquith. That the eye of the General had been removed was kept a secret from the world, but a personal letter to Commissioner Cadman, written on 13 September 1909, reveals the tragedy :

We have not thought it wise as yet to give any details to the public, or to our officers and soldiers in particular, of the extent of the injury suffered, but it seems desirable that you should have a little more exact information. . . . It happened very suddenly. I had no knowledge of it on the morning of Tuesday 17th August, while at night I found that the sight had gone from the

[1] p. 145

eye altogether. The doctors ascertained that an abscess was rapidly forming, which soon became so angry and alarming that for fear of injury to the brain it had to be cut out, which was done, destroying the power of vision. Its only utility now will be to carry an artificial mask, which they tell me will not, in a general way, be noticeable by the public.

Asked, during a Press interview, if he thought the strain and risk of his motor campaign had been justified, the General replied decisively :

I have never had a question as to what my duty was with respect to it . . . the doctors are of the most confident opinion that, while a considerable effort was no doubt involved in the undertaking, it had no direct connexion with the unfortunate occurrence which brought it to an end so suddenly. The poisonous insect to which they attributed the evil might have entered the eye in other circumstances. . . . Evidences of the good done by the campaign are not far to seek. Newark was stirred by my visit.[1] That march through the town with the Mayor I shall never forget.

On Wednesday, 27 October, after ten weeks' absence, he was welcomed back to public work with overwhelming demonstrations of affection by conducting a meeting in The Congress Hall. That he showed little trace of the trying experience he had undergone is evidenced in that he spoke for an hour and a half with vigour and humour, and without a note.

For two and a half years the old warrior fought unceasingly, then, in the *War Cry* for 18 May 1912, it was announced that he had decided to undergo the long-talked-about operation for the removal of a cataract on the left eye, to take place on Thursday the 23rd. He was dictating letters close up to the time for the operation, which was again performed by Mr Higgens, in the General's house, " Rookstone," Hadley Wood. The operation was considered to be completely satisfactory, but soon disappointing

[1] p. 144

bulletins began to make their appearance. The King was " anxious to be informed as to your condition," and other messages flowed from members of the Royal Family and the peerage. In the 8 June issue of the *War Cry* William Booth wrote a most pathetic letter :

If the unexpected blow has not actually fallen upon me, it is hovering painfully and dangerously near. Instead of the restoration of my sight, on which I had so long and ardently counted, the doctors tell me that I am on the very eve of entire darkness. In a few hours my comrades may be under the painful compulsion of announcing that the General is hopelessly blind. In that event, what a loss—what an indescribably painful loss— will be mine ! Never again to see the light of day ! Never again to behold the countenances of my friends ! Never again to look into the sympathetic eyes of my comrades ! Never again to witness that which, for sixty years gone by, has been to me the sight of sights—men and women kneeling at the Mercy Seat ! Well ! Pile up all my losses—and they are many and serious, I admit—but look, as I have been looking these last few hours, at all the mercies that are left me !

Then follow brave words and gratitude to God. The news was broken to him by the Chief of the Staff, that all hope had been abandoned, that he *was* blind, and with characteristic fortitude, after a momentary silence the indomitable veteran exclaimed : " Well, the Lord's will be done. I have done my best for my God and for the people with my eyes ; now, if it is His will, I must do my best for Him without my eyes."

Everywhere the Press was eulogistic in its sympathy. " Hopelessly blind ? " wrote the *Californian Sun*. " Nay, the good old man is one of the blind who really see ! " Yet another message came from the Queen, who had heard the news with " the greatest distress." But within a few days the General was again transacting business, signing his first letters without the aid of sight, and he was still hoping to campaign in the U.S.A. and Canada. On 27 July it was announced he would make his first public reappearance at the Alexandra Palace on the occasion of the Army's forty-seventh anniversary; but the doctors thought otherwise, despite his message to the *War Cry* that he was on the upgrade. Sleeplessness and enforced activity owing to the unfavourable weather were beginning to take their toll, however. The *War Cry* for 17 August 1912 reported that the General was " not so well." Three days later, on Tuesday the 20th at 10.13 p.m., and following a terrific thunderstorm—as had occurred just prior to the passing of the Army Mother twenty-two years before [1]—the Grand Old Man of The Salvation Army " laid down his sword."

CHAPTER THREE

THE WORLD MOURNS

In accordance with a widely felt desire, the body of the General lay pavilioned in state at The Congress Hall, Clapton, on the Friday, Saturday and Monday following his passing, when some 65,000 grief-stricken people passed the bier to gaze upon the ivory-like features of " the world's best-loved man "—the Mayor of South Shields had described him as " The Archbishop of the World." A public memorial service was arranged at Olympia [2] on the following Wednesday, when 35,000 people attended, including Queen Alexandra, who came incognito, and representatives of King George V and Queen Mary. The procession took

[1] *The History of The Salvation Army*, vol. iv, p. 303
[2] *The History of The Salvation Army*, vol. iv, p. 305

twenty minutes to pass down the long-extended central aisle. It was impossible for everyone to hear the speakers in that vast auditorium, so great boards, bearing numbers coinciding with numbers on the fifty-two-paged programme, were stood on either side of the platform to indicate what was happening during the service. Although this was announced to commence at 7.30 p.m., it was estimated that 10,000 people were waiting to enter the building at 4 p.m.

The funeral was conducted by the new General, Bramwell Booth,[1] on Thursday, 29 August, at Abney Park Cemetery, Stoke Newington. The heart of London stood still for nearly four hours as the lengthy procession of some 7,000 Salvationists, including forty bands, wended its five-mile way through densely crowded streets from the Victoria Embankment, no fewer than 580 City and 2,370 Metropolitan police being on duty. The Acting Lord Mayor, Sir John Knill, Bart., stood at the salute on the steps of the Mansion House as the cortége passed, the Maharajah of Jhalawar and other distinguished people being with him. The estranged Mrs Booth-Clibborn and Herbert Booth were among the mourners, and Ballington Booth and his wife sent a telegram of love and sympathy.[2] Bramwell Booth delivered a striking address at the graveside, in the course of which he said :

If you were to ask me, I think I could say that the happiest man I ever knew was the General. He was a glad spirit. He rose up on the crest of the stormy billows, and praised God, and laughed at the Devil's rage, and went on with his work with joy. That gladness communicated itself to others. . . . I rode the other morning on a ministering journey with Commissioner Sturgess up a little lane in Limehouse, in the East End of London, and oh, how my mind turned back to forty years ago, and to a fishmonger's shop there ! The fishmonger was friendly to us,

[1] p 273
[2] *The History of The Salvation Army*, vol. iv, p. 355

and used to take out the windows of his shop for us on Sunday mornings. I have heard the General from behind that fish counter pouring out his soul on the people.

Messages of sympathy addressed to Bramwell Booth arrived from leading men and women in all parts of the world. King George wrote :

Only in the future shall we realize the good wrought by him for his fellow creatures. Today there is universal mourning for him. I join in it.

Queen Alexandra, the Queen Mother, who also sent a wreath of flowers from the royal gardens at Sandringham, wrote :

Thank God, his work will live for ever !

The Emperor Wilhelm II of Germany explicitly commanded that a wreath should be placed on the coffin by Baron von Bülow. A wreath was also received from King George and Queen Mary. King Christian of Denmark sent a message, as did President Taft of the U.S.A. :

In the death of your good father the world loses one of its most effective practical philosophers.

The Prime Minister (Mr Asquith) and the Governors and Prime Ministers of Commonwealth countries, the Archbishop of Canterbury, and the Lord Mayor of London paid their tributes. The newspapers of the world devoted columns of space to high and affectionate tributes :

Whatever we may think of William Booth, and of the wonderful organization which he so triumphantly established, it is certain that he belonged to the company of saints. . . . We judge him to be one of the chief and most serviceable figures of the Victorian age.—*Daily Telegraph*

General Booth, who has gone to his rest full of years and honour, after a long life of inexhaustable activity, will live in history as

NOTABLE OFFICERS OF THE PERIOD

1 Commissioner Thomas McKie 2 Commissioner David M. Rees 3 Adjutant Harry
Munn 4 Major Jack Stoker 5 Commissioner Edward Higgins, senr. 6 Staff-Captain
Joseph ("Joe the Turk") Garabed 7 Lieut.-Colonel Elisabet Liljegren 8 Commissioner
Alex M. Nicol 9 Colonel Catherine Bannister 10 Colonel Othilie Tonning, and
11 Major W. Brindley Boon

FRIENDS ROYAL AND LOYAL

1 Her Majesty Queen Mary 2 His Majesty King Haakon VII of Norway 3 Her Majesty
Queen Alexandra 4 G. Bernard Shaw 5 H.R.H. Prince Louis of Battenberg
6 Björnstjerne Björnson 7 The Rt. Hon. H. H. Asquith 8 The Rt. Hon. Winston
Churchill, and 9 The Rt. Hon. David Lloyd George

one of the most remarkable figures of these times.— *Westminster Gazette*

The news of General Booth's death will be heard with emotion by all England, by all America, by almost countless communities in every quarter of the world.—*Manchester Guardian*

What defines the character and genius of General Booth better than anything else is the fact that he changed the world's mind.— *Pall Mall Gazette*

The world has lost its greatest missionary evangelist, one of the supermen of the age. . . . Not one country, but fifty, will feel today a severe personal loss.—*Daily Chronicle*

What to others was a form had become to him the one reality. In an age of business, money, fashion, politics, pleasure, of everything but the spiritual, religion was to him first and only —the rest nowhere. It was not to be hid in a corner, but shouted on the housetops, dinned into the ears of every living soul. And where it found men it expressed itself in the same way ; not in the decorous formalities which time had consecrated ; but in the words, the actions which the heart dictated. It was a living thing, and a live thing takes always its own form. This freedom of expression meant, in essence, that the emancipated soul, conscious of its own thought and feeling, is greater than all tradition.—*The Christian World*

His sympathy, as a man, his ingenious faculty as an organizer, his glowing enthusiasm and self-sacrificing devotion to the Cause opened and levelled the way for him, and nobody whether friend or foe will withhold admiration and esteem at the bier of this honourable warrior.—*Berlin Lokalanzeiger*

He offered strong meat to those who were spiritually famished, and saw that they ate it.—*New York Herald*

His undisputed greatness has long been recognized. Surely a great king is dead in Israel.—*Evening News*

As a man of quality and courage his is independent of any individual opinion on The Salvation Army.—*Daily Mail*

It may be questioned whether Wesley or Loyola, even Napoleon himself, possessed great ideas and the power to carry them out successfully to a more conspicuous extent than General Booth.
—*Evening Standard*

The Times correspondent in Toronto telegraphed that feeling in Canada was that the dead leader should be buried in Westminster Abbey.[1] The *Daily Mirror* particularly distinguished itself by producing, two days after his death, a special memorial number. The *War Cry* for 31 August was entirely devoted to the General's passing. Sir Owen Seaman, editor of *Punch*, wrote a poem, a verse of which read :

> Scorned or acclaimed, he kept his harness bright,
> Still, through the darkest hour, untaught to yield,
> And at the last, his face toward the light,
> Fell on the victor's field.

But there were Jeremiad voices. The editor of *John Bull* prophesied that " the old General's death spells the death of The Salvation Army " ; and *The Times*, in its four-column obituary notice, wondered whether " the Army had sufficient vitality to go on without the driving force of William Booth."

Memorial services were held at The Congress Hall, Clapton, and in many provincial centres on the Sunday following the funeral, and late at night Bramwell Booth went out to Linscott Road, Clapton, to address the greatly disappointed throng unable to get into the crowded building.

To the surprise of his critics, who spoke and wrote of his millions, William Booth willed to the Army his small private property, the net value of which amounted to only £487 19s. Other property, to the value of £5,295, which represented monies settled on him many years before by

---

[1] A plaque, surmounted by a bust of William Booth, was unveiled in Westminster Abbey by his grandson, Commissioner W. Wycliffe Booth, during the Army's Centenary Celebrations in 1965.

Henry Reed for his private use,[1] he left to his children, with the sole exception of Ballington, who had to be content with an inkstand ! It was this provision which enabled him throughout his life to draw no stipend or remuneration of any kind from the Army. Actually William Booth lived in a state of impecunity, as is obvious from the following, almost pathetic, extracts from letters written to Bramwell :

Bring me 20/- if you can remember—10/- in shillings and half a sovereign. Why can I not have some arrangement by which I can know whether I have a shilling to give away and be able to give it without somebody's *knowledge* or CONSENT ?

Send the enclosed off to L—— with £5 from my personal account, if it will stand it. I don't know whether I have a sovereign to give away or not. I am going to tell Kitching he must let me have a cheque book.

He was then seventy-seven years of age !

Following his appointment as General, Bramwell Booth received from the Army's solicitors a letter of between fifty and sixty pages written by William Booth in his own hand, and addressed " To my Successor." The object of the letter was to address a certain measure of counsel and advice to him upon taking up the responsibilities of the Generalship of the Army. It was divided into several sections, each dealing with a different matter. The first section was devoted to what he considered to be of supreme importance, the teaching The Army stood for before the world, the truths which he desired it should specially enforce and insist upon. In conducting his first holiness meeting as General in The Congress Hall, Bramwell Booth spoke of this letter and quoted :

I want you to impress this upon the people that they should seek after and find, and confess, a full salvation from all sin by the

[1] *The History of The Salvation Army*, vol. i, p. 260

power of the Holy Ghost—that full salvation which I and my late dear wife have striven to press upon the attention of the world.

Within days of his father's passing the new General proposed a national tribute to William Booth which should be in the nature of a memorial training college costing some £200,000. This was erected in 1930 at Denmark Hill in South-East London. Mr Francis Rickett contributed the first £5,000. Among the contributors was the Rt. Hon. Winston Churchill. *The Times* applauded the scheme :

It is evident that such an institution would become the ganglion or nerve centre of the whole system, and there is nothing visionary in the suggestion that it might exercise a powerful moral influence in binding the Empire together.

Mr Ratan Tata donated 6,000 guineas for the Indian memorial.

The first Salvation Army building in the U.S.A. erected to the memory of the Founder was opened by Commander (later General) Eva Booth at Grand Rapids in November 1913. This was a splendidly equipped rescue home. On their own initiative the minister and trustees of Wesley Chapel, Nottingham, erected a bronze tablet, framed in alabaster, to the memory of William Booth, who was converted in its Sunday school. The unveiling was performed by the Rev. F. Luke Wiseman, President of the Conference.

A memorial service for the Founder and the Army Mother was conducted by the General in the Royal Albert Hall on 29 September 1913, and a special memorial number of the *War Cry* was published on 4 October. On Tuesday, 7 July 1914, the General and civic representatives laid the foundation stones of the halls which were to be Nottingham's memorial to her famous son, in the presence of thousands of people, including numbers of Congress delegates.

IX FRIENDS

Chapter One

OF THE PALACE

WITHIN a few days of his visit to Buckingham Palace, where he was accorded an audience with King Edward VII,[1] William Booth was received by Queen Alexandra, following the International Congress of 1904. The date was 23 July. Although Her Majesty was particularly interested in the Army's work of amelioration and rescue, she had never before met the General. This interview was to be the beginning of a personal acquaintance, one might well say friendship, which was to continue until his passing, for the Queen was to attend his Memorial Service at the Olympia in person, an unusual honour to be accorded a commoner.[2] On the occasion of this 1904 visit to the Palace the General was accompanied, as on his previous visit, by Commissioner Pollard, the International Chancellor, they driving there in a hansom cab. Her Majesty congratulated the General on the success of the Congress, and spoke of the kindly feelings with which her brother, the Crown Prince of Denmark, viewed the Army's work in that country. In April 1909 the General was again received at Buckingham Palace by Queen Alexandra, who was accompanied by the Dowager Empress of Russia, both of whom asked him to sign their autograph books.

[1] *The History of The Salvation Army*, vol. iv, p. 256
[2] p. 238

William Booth washes his hands in a workman's bucket following his inspection of the newly erected International Congress Building in the Strand, London. Immediately afterwards he drove to Buckingham Palace to be received by His Majesty King Edward VII.

Lieutenant-Colonel (later Commissioner) Isaac Unsworth attended the General on this occasion.

Mrs Lieutenant-Colonel Lilian Wright tells this story:

When stationed as a Lieutenant at Snettisham, Norfolk, my Captain and I were asked to visit a sick person at Wolferton. We were taken part of the way by donkey and cart, the driver of which was a woman of hefty proportions. While we were talking to the invalid, a large white car suddenly appeared outside the house, and before the Captain and I could leave we were confronted by no less a person than Her Majesty Queen Alexandra, who stopped to speak to us about our work before going in herself to visit the lady who was sick. " Get in quickly ! " urged the woman-driver of the donkey cart. Then she drove off like a veritable Jehu, saying, as we flew down the road : " The Queen would be very angry if she saw three people sitting in a little donkey-cart ! " The Captain and I weighed about seven stone each in those days, but the female Jehu was twice our weight !

King Edward VII died on Friday, 6 May 1910, and, on the Sunday afternoon following, Regent Hall Band, under Bandmaster Herbert Twitchin, played His Majesty's favourite hymns, by special permission of Queen Alexandra, in the quadrangle of Buckingham Palace. Accompanied by the Commanding Officer, Major (later Commissioner) Frank Barrett, the band marched from its hall in Oxford Street, evoking considerable interest. *The Times* described the event as " the chief incident of the day, unique in its way, and entirely unexpected." It was estimated that some 7,000 people listened to the band behind the high, gold-tipped railings. Commemoration services were held on Sunday, the 15th, in all corps throughout the country, the General conducting that at the Clapton Congress Hall. Mr Bramwell Booth's tribute in The *War Cry* was considered in some circles as a slight upon the late King.

The suggestion [said the *War Cry* in the 11 June issue] that has been made that there is anything here which is in the nature of a " slander " upon his late Majesty is just one of those false statements reflecting upon the Army's work which are often made by unprincipled persons.

Presumably the " offending " words were these :

King Edward did not win his renown on the field of battle. He was not a great ruler ; our system of government leaves little place for the reigning monarch in the real governing of the nation. He was not a profound thinker. He was not a moralist, or a philosopher. He kindled no great religious enthusiasm ; he inspired no great social movement.

But surely what followed weighted the scales heavily in honour of the King's memory :

Yet he is, perhaps, the most sincerely mourned of all the dead monarchs of the past thousand years in Old England. The secret was this—The King who closed his eyes at Buckingham Palace on Friday night last was, perhaps, the most devoted servant of the State which the State possessed. And his service was given without stint in the highest earthly interest alike of his own and of all nations—Peace. The King was a servant. The King was a Peacemaker.

The General had an exceptionally long interview with T.R.H. the Prince and Princess of Wales (later King George V and Queen Mary) in February 1909 at Marlborough House. In reporting the event the *War Cry* recalled that, when a midshipman in the Royal Navy, the Prince had vigorously remonstrated with a Canadian tough who was hurling abuse at two Salvation Army girls who were preaching on a street corner.[1] In 1914 Queen Mary visited the Mothers' Hospital, Clapton, and LORNE House, Stoke Newington—which H.R.H. Princess Louise, Duchess of Argyll, had presented to the Women's Social Work for friendless women in 1911. Mrs Booth rode with Her Majesty in her electric brougham between the two institutions ; the royal car then being sent back by order of the Queen to pick up Commissioner Adelaide Cox and Colonel Unsworth. Later in the year Her Majesty sent a parcel of books for the Officers' Home of Rest, enclosing a note in her own hand-writing " in answer to the appeal in *All the World*."

[1] *The History of The Salvation Army*, vol. iv, p. 316

King Chulalonkorn of Siam, accompanied by his two sons, attended a Salvation Army open-air meeting at Brevik, a little village on the South coast, while travelling in Norway in the summer of 1907.

When Pokesdown (Hampshire) Band paid a visit to Swanage in October 1904, H.R.H. Prince Oscar of Sweden started the collection on the sea-front with a sovereign.

For the first time in the Army's history a prince of the Napoleonic House contributed to its funds when Prince Victor Napoleon, a nephew of Napoleon the Great, sent a donation to the Self-Denial Effort in Switzerland in 1906.

For the first time since The Army commenced a member of the British Royal Family graced one of its functions. This was on 19 November 1908, when H.R.H. Princess Louise, Duchess of Argyll, a daughter of Queen Victoria, opened a sale of work at the Doré Gallery, in Bond Street, London, in aid of the Army's work among women and children. The Duke accompanied his wife without pre-announcement, and spoke. Two years later the Duke opened an extension of the Army's elevator at Spa Road, Bermondsey, and addressed the 1,000 men present. When accompanying Princess Louise, who had laid a memorial stone in July 1912, and who opened the Mothers' Hospital at Clapton in October 1913, the Duke, speaking in the hospital grounds afterward, said, " I am glad you still have the good old uniform ! " The Duke of Argyll died in May 1914 and General and Mrs Bramwell Booth attended his State memorial service in Westminster Abbey by royal invitation, the King and Queen and many members of the Royal Family being present.

Noticing a Self-Denial collector in a toy shop at Hunstanton, Norfolk, in 1909, H.R.H. Princess Victoria contributed to the Fund. H.R.H. Princess Henry of Battenberg laid a dedicatory stone of the Portsmouth Naval and Military

Home in July 1912 ; and H.R.H. the Duchess of Albany opened the new Naval and Military Home at Harwich in July 1914. The Duchess had previously opened a new hostel " for respectable women and girls stranded in London." Vice-Admiral H.R.H. Prince Louis of Battenberg, soon after his arrival at Gibraltar in November 1908, to take charge of the Atlantic Fleet, made an unexpected visit to the Army's Naval and Military Home. The Admiral was the father of Admiral of the Fleet Earl Mountbatten.

Chapter Two

OF THE PEN AND THE BRUSH

No history of The Salvation Army could be written without adequate mention of its friends, for without them there would have been no Salvation Army. Some gave generously of their substance ; others, because of their status in Society, enhanced the Army's reputation by their mere association with its people ; and others again provided it with world-wide publicity with the aid of pen or brush.

Among those who used a facile and prolific pen in both defending and eulogizing the Army's operations were Mr (later Sir) Hall Caine, who wrote of its shelters in Reykjavik, Iceland, in his novel *The Prodigal Son*, he having himself attended a Sunday-night meeting in the Middlesex Street shelter in London ; Miss Marie Corelli, who lectured on the Army's work in Northampton Town Hall in 1905, to help its local free breakfast fund and later invited William Booth to tea in her home at Stratford on Avon ; Mr (later Sir) H. Rider Haggard, whose favourable report on the Army's colonies [1] was issued as a blue book by the Colonial Office ; Mr George R. Sims, who wrote :

Every soldier who is fighting under the General's banner in his glorious crusade of social salvation is rendering golden service to his God and the country.

Mr F. A. McKenzie, who produced the Army's annual social report in 1908 ; Sir Arthur Conan Doyle, who assisted in the opening of Crowborough's new hall in June 1908 ; and the Rev. Silas K. Hocking, the novelist, who laid a foundation stone at Crouch End Citadel in 1912.

William T. Stead, who once described himself as the Honorary Trumpeter in Ordinary of The Salvation Army, had by voice and pen for many years championed its cause, and was lost in the wreck of the *Titanic* in April 1912. During his last interview with Bramwell Booth he had declared : " Ah ! It is in God I trust—only the living God can hold up a living soul." In paying a personal tribute to his fellow-defendant of Old Bailey days,[2] Bramwell Booth wrote in *All the World :* " He stood for the soul of man as requiring something more to feed it than its own performance."

Ex-President Theodore Roosevelt, one of the editors of the New York *Outlook*, contributed a striking article upon The Salvation Army, which was actually a review of Sir H. Rider Haggard's *Regeneration*[3] in 1911, and another article in 1913 on General Bramwell Booth's scheme for a memorial to the Army's Founder and the provision of a new training college in Chicago and New York.

The *War Cry* of 4 November 1905 published the following paragraph :

[1] *The History of The Salvation Army*, vol. iii, p. 146
[2] *The History of The Salvation Army*, vol. iii, p. 25
[3] p. 170

A leading dramatist has written a new play " Major Barbara," which concerns the love affair of a Salvation Army officer, and was woven more or less around the General's slum work. The second act was laid in a Salvation " doss-house," and the dialogue was largely the expression of views on General Booth's religious campaign. " I greatly admire his rescue work," said the dramatist.

Not a mention of George Bernard Shaw !

A month later, however, although having no sympathy, apparently, with *Major Barbara*, the *War Cry* wrote, " If the newspapers are to be believed, she is quite unlike the real article." Nevertheless, it was grateful to Mr George Bernard Shaw for his spirited defence of the Salvation Army's bands, and quoted his " tomahawking " reply to a dramatic critic who had characterized them as ill-tuned :

Never was a grosser libel penned. From the early days of the Army, when I first heard a Salvation Band play, as a march, that wedding chorus from Donizetti's " Lucia di Lammermoor," which I have introduced into my play, to the great meeting at the Albert Hall two months ago, when the massed Salvation Bands played the Dead March from " Saul " as I verily believe it has never been played in the world since Handel was alive to conduct it, I have never heard a Salvation Band that deserved your critic's reproach. I have heard Handel's great march snivelled through and droned through by expensive professional bands until the thought of death became intolerable. The Salvationists, quite instinctly, and probably knowing as little of Handel as they do of Donizetti, made it a magnificent paean of victory and glory that sent me—a seasoned musical critic of many years' standing—almost out of my senses with enthusiasm.

Writing in the *Daily Citizen* in the latter part of 1912, Mr Shaw said :

When I was writing " Major Barbara," I often used to attend the Army's meetings at street corners, and I was greatly impressed by their fervour and enthusiasm.

Björnstjerne Björnson, the Norwegian poet, who died in 1910, boldly defended the Army, and those who heard the magic of his oratorical thunder were filled with wonder while he declaimed against its opponents in Norway when it was attacked in its early days. When Adjutant Rosarios visited him in his Aulestad home she spoke to him about religion. " I believe in the good," he said, and from that time purchased the Norwegian *War Cry* regularly. On one occasion when the Adjutant called at Aulested, she met a German lady who ironically asked : " Are you fighting for your ideas ? " Björnson answered for the Salvationist : " No, madam, she does not fight for her own ideas, but for what she has found to be the most beautiful in life, and she now seeks to bring this to others." During the crisis of his last illness the doctor brought the poet slowly back to life. " Why did you do this ? " he asked. " I just now met with God."

Following the great San Francisco earthquake which laid waste the city in April 1906, Mark Twain, the humorist, presiding over a meeting in New York of Californians who had met to organize relief, said, " I know of no better way of reaching the poor than through The Salvation Army. They are of the poor, and know how to get at the poor. I have seen their work in foreign countries." Mark Twain (Samuel L. Clemens), who died in April 1910, received the honour of a D.C.L. Oxon. degree at the same time as William Booth.

T. P. O'Connor, an outstanding journalist M.P., writing a character-sketch in *M.A.P.* in connection with a series on prominent personalities, had this to say about the General :

In a land and age of self-indulgence, of almost brutal over-eating and over-drinking, this man had kept white and pure and undefiled the fine temple of his body, and is thus, in his old age, the same lithe, fiery, untrammelled and restless spirit of his youth.

In a brief notice of his biography of William Booth, the author, Harold Begbie, wrote in *The Book Monthly* :

Those who read these two volumes will find that it is the story of as valiant a spirit as ever lived, perhaps the very bravest man of his time.

A. G. Gardiner, of *The Observer*, one of the foremost writers of his day, in a column-length obituary notice concluded with :

Today we feel that a great lamp has gone out.

And Dr Ronald Cambell Macfie, an Anglo-Canadian poet, lifted The Salvation Army to the level of a high crusade, in company with the Knights of King Arthur and Richard Coeur de Lion in his short ode entitled *General Booth* :

> Out of the slums
> Wild music comes,
> The pipe of flutes, the boom of drums,
> And down the street strange banners flare.
> What mean this noise ?   What means this blare ?
> This clash of song, this crash of prayer ?
> What mean these mingled tears and flame ?
> This glory on the face of shame ?
> It is the Army of the Lord,
> It is the clashing of His sword ;
> It is His axe's merry din
> Upon the brazen casque of sin.

A young American versifier, Horace Vachel Lindsay, who had had personal experience of the Army's helping hand, wrote a poem in gratitude to the organization, which immediately spread around the world.   It was entitled *General William Booth enters Heaven*, and began " Booth led boldly with his big bass drum."   Said Lindsay :

The poem is *my* monument as well as General Booth's, and I hope that my entrance in Heaven will be as certain as his.

When, in February 1908, Beatrice Webb (Lady Passfield) spent a week-end at Hadleigh Farm Colony, she was even more impressed by the officers themselves than by the work they were doing for the unemployed and the unemployable :

On the colony are some half-dozen other officers engaged in philanthropic administration, and two spiritual officers (women). . . . In respect to personal character, all these men and women constitute a *Samurai* caste, that is, they are men and women selected for the power of subordinating themselves to their cause, most assuredly a remarkable type. . . . Remarkable because there is no inequality between men and woman, because home life and married life are combined with a complete dedication of the individual to spiritual service.

Louis Wain, the famous cat artist, contributed a whole page of coloured illustrations depicting, " for our little folk and others," The Grand Motor Tour in Pussy-Cat Land for the Christmas number of the 1904 *War Cry*. Sir Hubert von Herkomer, who had painted William Booth's portrait,[1] died in the spring of 1914.

One of the striking pictures exhibited at the Royal Academy in 1907 was " Greatest of These " by Mr Sigismund Goetze. It was discribed as a fine piece of allegory in which a Salvation Army procession symbolized the life of self-sacrifice.

[1] *The History of The Salvation Army*, vol. iv, p. 327

CHAPTER THREE

OF THE LEGISLATURE

Prime Ministers and prospective Prime Ministers were almost all on the most cordial terms with the General. Sir Henry Campbell-Bannerman, who died in 1908, when Prime Minister, granted William Booth an interview at 10 Downing Street, spending an hour and a quarter with him in animated conversation. " I apologize for keeping you so long," said the General. " Not at all," replied the P.M., " the favour is entirely on your side. The talk that we have been having is like a breath of the fresh air of Heaven in the midst of all the turmoil of this world."

In his early days Mr David (later Earl) Lloyd George on more than one occasion took part in Salvation Army open-air meetings, the first being at Port Maddoc, North Wales. When President of the Board of Trade he was frequently to be seen listening to the meetings on Wandsworth Common. In May 1908 Mr J. Ramsay MacDonald, M.P., spoke strikingly at Leicester of his knowledge of the Army's work, following the General's ninety minutes' lecture :

I am bound to say this, that however large the errors of The Salvation Army may be made to appear to the most critical, the work they are doing blots all those errors out. Whatever agency comes or goes, the country cannot spare one agency—and that is The Salvation Army.

When in July 1910 Miss Violet (now Lady) Asquith presented the cadets of the International Training College with their certificates in domestic hygiene from the Royal Institute of Public Health, she brought to them a personal message from her Prime Minister father. Never before nor

WARM SUPPORTERS

1 Mr W. T. Stead   2 H.R.H. Princess Louise (Duchess of Argyll)   3 Sir Hall Caine
4 Sir Joseph C. Dimsdale, Bart.   5 Lord Haldane of Cloan   6 Mr J. Ramsay MacDonald
7 The Rev. F. B. Meyer   8 Sir H. Rider Haggard, and 9 Signor Guglielmo Marconi

1

2

3

OUTSTANDING
SALVATION
ARMY
SOLDIERS

4

5

6

7

1 Baroness Elisabeth Nordenfalk   2 Lektor Gustaf Ericsson   3 Lady Sarah Sladen
4 Poll Cott   5 The Hon. Anna Jane Peckover   6 Henry F. Milans, and 7 Frank C.
("Salvation") Smith

since has a British Prime Minister sent a personal message to cadets. Mrs (later Lady) Lloyd George also spoke on this occasion, which was presided over by the eminent brain specialist, Sir James Crichton Browne.

Among those present at the closing function of the Army's International Social Council held in London in the spring of 1911, and presided over by the Lord Mayor of London, Sir T. Vezey Strong, was the Hon. Andrew Fisher, Prime Minister of Australia, who said of the General, " He is, I believe, the one General in the world's history who has been waging war for nearly forty years with every country, and yet been in friendly relations with them all." Sir Edward White, Chairman of the London County Council, revealed that he sometimes attended the meetings at Regent Hall, especially when Mrs General Booth was announced to speak. A message was received from King Edward VII.

When Governor-General of Canada, Earl Grey, while in London, called at International Headquarters to see the General, and when back in Toronto he visited, unannounced, the Army's home for service girls. During his presidential address at the Army's South African Congress in Cape Town City Hall in February 1912, the Governor-General, Viscount Gladstone, son of the great Prime Minister, stated that while he was Home Secretary he had been guided by the advice of the Army in framing Acts of Parliament which were already bearing good fruit.

The Rt. Hon. John Burns, President of the Local Government Board, was seemingly as changeable as a barometer so far as his opinion of the Army was concerned ; sometimes he was " Fair," but in the main " Stormy " ! Writing to Bramwell Booth on 27 January 1906, W. T. Stead had this to report :

John Burns came to dinner last night and we had a stiff talk about The Salvation Army. He is quite hopelessly irreconcilable,

I fear. He pummelled me roundly for having had anything to do with promoting the success of the biggest fraud of the century. That is the way in which he described our Social scheme. He said that you had sunk £600,000 in the Labour Colony at Hadleigh without securing any return. He had been to see " Major Barbara " and entirely differed from my estimate of the piece. He said that it was the most smashing exposure of the Army that he had ever seen, and if he were a millionaire he would spend his money in having open-air performances of " Major Barbara " at all the established Salvation Army stations in the country. He further said that you kept over 200 people every night shivering in the cold before you would give them tickets, simply in order to advertise the Army. As he was going away I begged him to take a more kindly view of the Army, but he replied that he had seen the Army in America, and that was enough. What he meant by that I do not know.

Stead adds a postscript :

I think at the bottom of his prejudice is his grudge against you for sterilizing so many progressive men in the County Council Election.

What exactly Stead meant by that is incomprehensible, for the Army's leaders had and have religiously abstained from discussing politics, and particularly at election times. But what is one to make of the mind of John Burns, after reading the following extract from a letter from William Booth to Bramwell written three days later from Stockholm ?

John Burns. Sturgess [Commissioner] was telling me a few minutes since, that he saw him on Sunday, that he was very friendly and told him that he highly appreciated our religion and our temperance work and wished us to stick to it.

In his personal library the author has a copy of John Manson's *The Salvation Army and the Public*, a religious, social, and financial study, which is, nevertheless, a slashing attack on these three aspects of the movement's operations.

Certain passages are marked in thick black pencil, with critical comments. An inscription on the first blank page reads : " To The Right Hon. John Burns, M.P. With the author's compliments and homage. 22.VIII, '06," and underneath is the strong, firm signature of John Burns. There can be no doubt that Manson's onslaught had its sinister effect upon the mind of the President of the Board of Trade, for some time later he bitterly attacked the General in the House of Commons, to the amazement of his Cabinet colleagues. A supporter on this occasion was Will Crooks, Labour M.P. for Woolwich, who could say, " Even the General himself has little knowledge of the enormous sacrifice his people have made. Some of the women are refined and sensitive to a fault, as we should say, yet they have gone down into the most degraded places and made their influence felt for good." In November 1905, at a musical festival arranged by Woolwich Band on behalf of the unemployed of the town Mr Crooks said, " Often I have been under the greatest possible obligation to General Booth and his dear wife." It is passing strange that two men of such like views on labour matters could be so different in their view of one who also had the welfare of the people at heart. Dressed with a view to concealing his identity Burns was among the homeless men who were fed with soup and bread by Salvationists at 1.30 a.m. on a day in December 1906.

Lord Wolverhampton, better known as Sir Henry H. Fowler, passed away in February 1911. A Methodist peer, he succeeded in inducing Parliament to remove the obnoxious clause from the bye-law that brought stormy days for the Army in both Torquay and Eastbourne.[1] Lord Onslow, at one time Governor of New Zealand, died a few months later, in October. He was chairman of the Committee

[1] *The History of The Salvation Army*, vol. iv, pp. 243 and 277

which inquired into the affairs of the General's *Darkest England Scheme* in 1892.[1]

The Hon. Richard Seddon, Premier of New Zealand, died at sea on 11 June 1906 while returning from Australia. William Booth described him as " my unfailing friend." On the last occasion that Mr Seddon championed the Army he did a thing entirely without precedent, by turning the lobby of the Parliament practically into a Salvation Army hall, and the visit of the General into a great State occasion, 400 people of all classes being packed into the long passage. The Premier extolled the Army from an extemporized platform. To complete his disregard for mere etiquette and precedent, he went into Parliament Square and invited the corps band to enter the House and take tea with members of his Cabinet !

Marquis Ito, Governor-General of Korea, received Colonel (later Commissioner) Henry Bullard, Territorial Commander for Japan, in 1906. The Marquis requested the Army to do in Korea what it had done in Japan.

CHAPTER FOUR

OF OTHER DAYS

This period in the Army's history was a particularly sad one for the General, for one after another of his early-day benefactors passed away. On 29 October 1908 Mr Richard Cope Morgan, the Welsh head of the publishing firm of Morgan & Scott, and founder and proprietor of *The Christian*, died. His association with William Booth went back to

[1] *The History of The Salvation Army*, vol. iii, p. 92

East London Christian Mission days.[1]   At one time, when
friends were few and foes were many, he manifested the
warmest sympathy with the Mission and later with The
Salvation Army.   Although not always in full agreement with
its methods, and crossing swords more than once with the
Army Mother,[1] he never questioned its aims.

Mr Thomas Anthony Denny,[2] who died on Christmas
Day 1909 at the age of ninety-one, had stood by the Army
for nearly thirty years and had contributed heavily to its
funds during the days of its financial straitness.   Although
sometimes caustic in his utterances, even in public meetings,
at which he spoke often, he was always perfectly friendly.
He thought the General was altogether too comprehensive,
desperate and venturesome in the schemes he launched from
time to time.[2]   Greatly impressed by the preaching of the
Army Mother, Mr Denny used to conduct her meetings in
order to relieve her of all else but the address.   On one
occasion he marched up Regent Street, London, with a party
of singing Salvationists, to the amazement of his affluent and
titled associates.   Among his many gifts was his contribution
toward the purchase and fitting-up of the Congress Hall and
Training College at Clapton.   William Booth wrote a
memorial sketch of Mr Denny's life that extended into four
issues of the *War Cry*.

Another great friend and supporter of the early days who
died at this time, in January 1910, was Mr John Cory, of
Cardiff, head of a coal-shipping business which was possibly
at that time the most extensive in the world.   He often stood
side by side with Mr Denny on Salvation Army platforms,
vieing with him in generous rivalry when responding to the
General's appeals.   Two years before the commencement of
the East London Christian Mission John Cory had invited

[1] *The History of The Salvation Army*, vol. i, p. 117
[2] *The History of The Salvation Army*, vol. ii, p. 73

William and Catherine Booth to conduct revival meetings in Cardiff. So affectionately disposed was he toward them that he named one of his ships the *William Booth*, and a share of the profits it helped to make went into the Army's treasury. John Cory was one of the few men who have had a statue erected to them during their lifetime. The General also paid John Cory a splendid tribute in three issues of the *War Cry*.

A comparatively new friend, Mr George Herring, died suddenly in November 1906. Although he was very much a man of the world, he and William Booth were drawn to each other in a singular degree. George Herring founded the Westminster shelter, provided the equipment for the Middlesex Street shelter—he often dropped in to talk to the men—and made provision in his will for the fulfilment of his promise of a loan of £100,000 without interest, to enable the General to give effect to his Home Colonization ideas. William Booth wrote a eulogy in the *War Cry*, in which he said, "Two years ago, in a somewhat unusual manner, he came into my life in response to an appeal for shelters for the homeless." He left behind, said the *War Cry*, a name for genuine philanthropy, straight-dealing and unselfish enthusiasm for the welfare of the weak and outcast.

An American philanthropist and Army supporter, Mr Warner van Norden, President of the National Bank of North America, died in February 1914 in New York. His eldest daughter was an officer in the Editorial Department at International Headquarters until her sudden passing in 1905. Another daughter was also an officer.

For many years an Army friend, Miss Elizabeth Julia Emery died on 16 February 1913 at the age of eighty-five. She was the founder of the two Emery hospitals in India [1] and of Institutions in Italy and Japan. Commissioner T.

---

[1] *The History of The Salvation Army*, vol. iii, p. 167

Henry Howard, the Chief of the Staff, conducted the funeral service, the International Staff Band heading the procession to Highgate Cemetery, the Army service being in fulfilment of Miss Emery's written desire. She left in her will £20,000 for the Army's work among women and girls in missionary countries, and was known as " The Queen of Charity."

Miss Ann Fowler, of Liverpool, who died in January 1913, had a long-standing friendship with William Booth, who was often her guest, and bequeathed a considerable sum of money to him for the use of the Army in Liverpool. Certain questions, however, were raised by some of her relatives, and legal proceedings were instituted in July 1914. Mr Justice Astbury decided in the Army's favour.

Other friends of long-standing were General Wilfred Kitching's grandfather, William Kitching, who died on Christmas Eve 1906, and Mrs Josephine Butler, who died a few days later. The first-named was a minister of the Society of Friends. His song, " Who comes to Me, the Saviour said," appears in the Salvation Army songbook. Mrs Butler, widow of Canon Butler, was at one time greatly maligned because of her efforts to repeal the Contagious Diseases Act and her inauguration of a crusade on the Continent which could chronicle a thousand triumphs to its cause. She fought with William T. Stead and Bramwell Booth for the amendment of the Criminal Law.[1] Mrs Butler also spoke out fearlessly on behalf of Salvationists in Switzerland when the fight was hot against them.

Sir Joseph Dimsdale, Bart., a former Lord Mayor of London, who, in his capacity of Chamberlain of the City of London, presented to the General the casket containing the Freedom of the City, died in August 1912.[2]

[1] *The History of The Salvation Army*, vol. iii, p. 25
[2] p. 230

When, in June 1911, the General opened a new men's shelter in Birmingham, one of his platform supporters was Sir Oliver Lodge. In the course of his speech the Principal of the University stated that children were born good. The General, however, not willing for a moment to concede the point, promptly sprang from his chair with the rejoinder, " They get bad pretty quick then ! " " Well," said Sir Oliver, " they are made bad by circumstances. I am amazed at the goodness of my own children. They didn't get it from me ! " " No," exclaimed the General. " They got it from their mother ! "

Gustav Hamel, a brilliant young pioneer airman, who was the winner of the aerial race around London, and who tragically disappeared during a flight across the English Channel in May 1914 and whose death was widely mourned, frequently attended Salvation Army meetings at Hendon.

CHAPTER FIVE

OF THE PULPIT

The Rev. R. J. Campbell, of the City Temple, London, whose *New Theology* shook the religious world in 1908, was driving into the country, he said, and it was raining.

I met on my journey two Salvation Army girls. They looked road-weary, tired out with their day of hard work. As one of them passed the vehicle she raised her face and looked at us, and I remarked to my companion, " How true is the saying that you never behold a coarse face under a Salvation Army bonnet ! "

In the course of an eloquent sermon Dr J. H. Jowett, of

Carr's Lane Chapel, Birmingham, one of the outstanding preachers of his day, said :

I tell you that if my faith in the power of Jesus to redeem the beast were ever to waver and grow weak, I would go and search out some Salvation Army Captain, and would put myself under his guidance, and I would ask him to show me " the marvellous works of God," and he would take me to houses which were once mere sties, but are now clean and beautiful homes ; which were once occupied by Caliban, but are now tenanted by the purified saints of God.

Dr G. Campbell Morgan, of Westminster Chapel, who asked for the presence of the children of " The Nest " to provide items at a meeting in May 1908, the congregation being addressed by Mrs Bramwell Booth, said The Salvation Army was always welcome at his church :

I thank God for The Salavation Army's theology. The Salvation stands for the Bible in these troublous times. If any man is helped to Christ by the big drum, then God bless the big drum. If he is helped to Christ by the testimony of the uniform—and it is no easy matter to put it on—then, thank God for the uniforms, and though we don't put them on we believe in them !

In a *War Cry* interview in April 1910 Dr Wilbur Chapman, the famous American evangelist, declared that he owed a great debt of gratitude to The Salvation Army. He was very dissatisfied with the results of his ministry until he read the life of Catherine Booth, which decided him to become an evangelist. While in Korea he had laid a foundation stone of the Army's first citadel in that country—Seoul 1.

A regular reader of the *War Cry*, which he once said in public never failed to provide him with inspiration for his work, the Rev. John Watson, D.D., better known by his *nom de plume*, Ian Maclaren, died suddenly in the U.S.A. in the spring of 1907 while on a lecture tour. He was for twenty-five years one of the best-known ministers in Liverpool.

On the question of The Salvation Army joining forces with the Church of England, which had arisen more than once,[1] Dr Sinclair, Archdeacon of London, had this to say :

If The Salvation Army could be recognized as a philanthropic, revivalist, and preaching order, any further questions might, possibly, be left alone for the regular clergy. The Salvation Army would be able to keep its full identity, but it would have also the great advantage of the advocacy of the Bishops and clergy of the National Church on its platform.

But this " great advantage " has been achieved through the years without the union, which, owing to the Army's peculiar constitution, could not possibly be made to work. During the Centenary Celebrations in 1965 the Archbishop of Canterbury graced the platform at the Inaugural Meeting in the Royal Albert Hall, and many of the cathedral pulpits throughout the country were occupied by Salvation Army officers, General Frederick Coutts himself preaching in Westminster Abbey.

When Ensign Bateman, the Commanding Officer at Peterborough, called upon the Bishop, Dr Carr Glynn, in connection with the 1906 Self-Denial Appeal, his lordship not only contributed to the fund, but at the conclusion of the interview led the officer to the Palace Chapel, where, in the dim religious light of the Sanctuary, the two knelt together to pray for the Army. The Bishop then gave the officer his paternal blessing.

The Bishop of London was reported to have said in 1904 that he " was never happier than when he was on a platform surrounded by Nonconformist brethren, and listening to the eloquence of Mrs Bramwell Booth."

[1] *The History of The Salvation Army*, vol. ii, p. 146

X THE COMING ARMY

BRAMWELL BOOTH, the Chief of the Staff, continued to give considerable thought to the Army's young people, and within six years his councils [1] had won their claim to permanence as an institution among the Army's activities. They reached a climax in November 1905, when the attendance at Clapton rose to 1,000 for the day. Later they were conducted in relays of two Sundays, and the Chief decided that such councils should be held more often. The Young People's Day on Sunday, 27 October 1912, was a memorable occasion, for not only were the councils the first Bramwell Booth conducted since his succession to the Generalship, but they were associated with a fresh departure in the taking of the Hackney Empire. The attendance, more than 2,000, was larger than the combined totals of any two Young People's Sundays held at Clapton, and resulted in no fewer than 578 seekers and 170 new candidates for officership.

In December 1905 an Advisory Bureau was set up and two Young People's Counsellors—Lieutenant-Colonel Mary Tait and Staff Captain Arthur Trounce—were appointed to help those who found themselves in spiritual or personal difficulties. April of that year saw the establishment of a Board of Health, consisting of six men and six women officers whose responsibility it was to deal with the acceptance of candidates for officership. During the summer an open-air holiday camp for seventy boys was arranged on Canvey Island, Essex, and so completely fulfilled the

---

[1] *The History of The Salvation Army*, vol. iv, p. 349

expectation of the officers concerned for its management that camps for young people were later organized at Dunoon (Scotland), Herne Bay (Kent), Clacton-on-Sea (Essex), Felixstowe (Suffolk) and Fleetwood (Lancashire). A holiday home for young women was opened at Southend-on-Sea (Essex) in 1906. In this same year a new magazine came into being. It has had a chequered career so far as its title is concerned. First it was called *The Y.P.*; this was later changed to *The Warrior*, and then, when the Life-Saving Scout organization [1] was inaugurated, it became *The Warrior and Life-Saving Scout*. Then *The Life-Saving Scout and Guard* became a magazine on its own. This magazine and *The Warrior* have now become *Vanguard*.

Another important landmark was reached in July 1906 when week-end young people's staff councils were instituted by the Chief of the Staff and Mrs Booth at Clapton. It was stated that 5,600,000 young people between the ages of seven and twenty-one were untouched on Sundays by any religious influence. The Chief spoke for a total of more than twelve hours concerning the several danger-signals confronting the youth of the British Isles which today makes interesting reading. He was troubled by

their disregard of authority; their love of fierce sports and excitements, which cultivate the brutal spirit; the rising tide of immorality, fed and fostered by the lowest class of poisonous literature; the increase of gambling and lunacy among the young; the boy and girl suicides.

A big soul-saving campaign among young people was launched in November under the guidance of the National Young People's Secretary, Colonel Charles Rothwell. A notable experiment in the interest of young people was the opening by Mrs Booth in the presence of the Lord Provost, of an institute, originally a hotel, in the centre of Glasgow

[1] p. 165

where young business girls living in lodgings could profitably spend their spare hours ; sleeping accommodation was also provided for seventy girls. This was the first Salvation Army institution of its kind. Two days after Christmas the Staff Lodge at Clapton [1] received thirty-five daughters of officers for a special training session lasting a week ; this was followed by a session for twenty-three sons of officers, whose average age was sixteen. These sessions were so successful that they were continued into the following year.

The War Cry for 12 October 1907 reported that the day school at Hadleigh [2] for the children of officers and employees of the Land and Industrial Colony, and children from the village, had 138 scholars on the roll and was the only Salvation Army day school in the United Kingdom. Another departure : when the Chief of the Staff visited Rochdale for a Saturday-night gathering in May 1908, he made it a condition that he should be given a meeting with young people in the afternoon. It was the first of its kind he had led. A new training venture entirely in the interests of corps cadets, candidates and company guards was instituted by Commissioner Hay when he opened a new hall at The Grove, Hackney. The corps cadets were under the command of a training-home officer known as the Central Corps Cadet Guardian.

The League of Promise was commenced that year by the Chief of the Staff for the benefit of officers' children engaged at International Headquarters who had pledged themselves for officership. The league of seventy members was divided into two courts—one for men and the other for women. The leaguers visited corps to conduct week-end meetings, held court meetings once a month and united once every quarter, the first united court being held in December at Holloway Citadel. *The Young Soldier* Anti-Smoking

---

[1] p. 176   [2] *The History of The Salvation Army*, vol. iv, p. 349

League, which discouraged juvenile smoking, had more than 25,000 members.

Yet another experiment, described as daring and successful, was the bringing together in June 1910 of 1,000 *junior* young people ranging from twelve to sixteen for a whole day's council at Clapton, conducted by the Chief of the Staff and Mrs Booth. While, during this year, the Chief had held a gathering of young people's local officers, that held on a Sunday in 1912 for nearly 500 young people's census local officers was also something new. On this occasion it was announced that the young people's band leader would henceforth be a member of the young people's census board, and that an Intelligence Bureau and Library, with a system of education by correspondence, would be opened at National Headquarters. While the actual transfer of young people from the young people's corps would remain at fifteen years, in future the junior soldier's name would be placed upon a roll as a recruit for the senior corps at the age of fourteen, and he would at once receive the senior cartridge [1] and provisionally sign the Articles of War. Juniors' outposts were to be established in order to gather in the children of the poorest quarters of towns and cities. Directory examinations [2] were to take place quarterly instead of annually. A Home Section, divided into three branches, was to be established : (1) Cradle Roll ; (2) Home Company, composed of those children who lived at such distances from the hall that they could not often attend ; and (3) a Central Company was to be formed among those who worked on Sundays and so could not attend meetings. The Band of Love and the Young People's Legion [3] were to be amalgamated under one leadership.

[1] *The History of The Salvation Army*, vol. ii, pp. 53 and 82
[2] *The History of The Salvation Army*, vol. iv, p. 351
[3] *The History of The Salvation Army*, vol iv, p. 345

A new distinctive badge designed in June 1913 for the young people's sergeant-major—hitherto known as the juniors' sergeant major—consisted of the letters " Y.P.S.M." worked in white silk upon the shoulder straps. When 400 young people's local officers met Commissioner and Mrs Higgins in council at Blackpool in the previous month, it was stated that during the past decade, while 1,600 juniors had been transferred to the senior corps, the juniors' roll still showed an increase of 1,600 ; attendances showed an increase of 50,000 weekly, although the Churches were mourning a general decrease in membership of children. It was hoped, among other features, to form a hundred young people's singing brigades, the one formed at Blackpool within the previous few weeks having shown what could be done ; its members wore no uniform. The Soul-Winners' Legion, connected with higher grade corps cadetship, sprang into being in this same year.

The Young Life Crusade, inaugurated by General and Mrs Booth at Clapton Congress Hall on Monday, 21 July 1913, included the public presentation of the newly formed Life-Saving Scouts.

There are many things associated with the world-wide Scout movement which are not acceptable to the mind of the Salvationist [said the *War Cry*], but there are at the same time many things which are entirely admirable, and it has been felt by the General and Commissioner Higgins and those under them who are immediately responsible for organizing the young people's work, that if the best in the Scout idea can be developed on Salvation Army lines, a great deal of lasting good will be done for the boys' ripening years. The very name " Life-Saving Scouts " will mark this boys' organization out from all other. . . . The uniform is quite distinct—colonial slouch hat turned up at one side with red cockade, grey shirt and knickers with red facings, and red neckscarf.

The chief officers of the new organization were the General

(President), Commissioner Higgins, the British Commissioner (Commander-in-Chief), Colonel Philip Kyle, National Young People's Secretary (Chief Superintendent), Brigadier Thomas Lewis (Secretary of the Territorial Council), and Major (later Commissioner) Hugh Sladen (Territorial Organizer). It is interesting to note at this juncture, that when Sir Robert (later Lord) Baden-Powell was considering applying for a charter for the Boy Scout Association, he invited William Booth to become its one and only Vice-President, but the General could not see his way clear to accept the generous gesture and signal honour. Sixty Life-Saving Scout troops had been officially registered at National Headquarters by 30 May 1914 and another fifty were almost ready. The first was that at Chalk Farm, North London, and the first Scout was Robert James. The first life-saving scout bugle Band was commissioned at Pontymister, Wales, in March 1914.

XI THE BIRTH OF AN ERA

Chapter One

THE SECOND GENERAL

ON the day following William Booth's passing, all the Commissioners present in London were called together to meet the Army's solicitors at International Headquarters to hear the reading of the document the General had left appointing his successor.[1] Mr (later Sir) Washington Ranger stated that the sealed envelope had been handed to him exactly twenty-two years to the day by the General, who, as the whole Salvation Army rightly surmised, had no one else in mind than his eldest son and Chief of Staff, William Bramwell Booth. The Commissioners having pledged their loyalty to the new International Leader, the Army's second General was legally installed, and immediately he announced his appointment to the world. The body of William Booth having been laid to rest, General Bramwell met his staff the next day in the Lecture Hall of the International Training College.

In an interview with a *Daily Telegraph* reporter the General said :

He [William Booth] must be my example, my model, so far as it is possible for anyone below him in experience and ability to follow him. He was a Napoleon of our warfare of love, a Napoleon without Napoleon's great fault of selfishness. He never knew what selfishness was. That must be for ever before me.

[1] *The History of The Salvation Army*, vol. iv, p. 316

In this interview Bramwell Booth somewhat underestimated his own merits and achievements, giving all the glory, humanly speaking, to his illustrious father ; but any student of The Salvation Army must come to the inevitable conclusion that while William had been the picturesque personality, the visionary, the architect, the creator, the man who had laid its foundations, Bramwell had been the clerk of works, the builder. William had given the orders, sometimes peremptorily ; Bramwell had unfailingly carried them out. Sir Christopher Wren is the recognized architect of St Paul's Cathedral, and the glory will be his until Time shall end ; but who knows the name of the clerk of works, the man who actually built this monumental edifice stone by stone ? As the years have passed The Salvation Army has become acutely aware of its behind-the-scenes clerk of works, the actual builder, Bramwell Booth.

When the *Daily Chronicle* interviewer put these questions to him :

Will the Army still be governed upon military lines of absolute obedience under one supreme head ? Will its form of government remain an autocracy ?

the new General replied, and his answer is of considerable interest in the light of future happenings :

I have no doubt that the military system will be maintained. But those critics who talk of autocracy do not realize that it is an autocracy modified by the system being spread throughout all grades of rank from top to bottom. It is indeed true to say that the greatest victories have been obtained in reality as the result of its application on the lower rungs rather than on the highest rungs of the ladder. It is the sense of individual responsibility animating the simple Bandmaster, and the Officer with a handful of men, which has brought out so many heroic workers from the depths. This individual command rising through all stages, and this unswerving obedience to the next in command, gives a tremendous cohesion, simplicity, and power to the whole

Organization. Something of the same sort is seen in the wonderful organization of the Roman Catholic Church.

"The General," says the interviewer, "spoke one very striking sentence to me, leaning forward with solemn and shining eyes":

It is a hard thing to say, but I shall rejoice in the decline of The Salvation Army if the spirit goes out of it. I hold no brief, believe me, for keeping dead things above the ground. I want them alive, in the service of God.

It will be as well at this juncture to look back upon the activities of Bramwell Booth during the six years prior to his becoming General. As Chief of the Staff he conducted Scandinavian councils with his officers for twelve days, visiting Sweden, Norway and Denmark in the early part of 1906. In March he celebrated his fiftieth birthday. In the following year, on 12 October, he and Mrs Booth celebrated their silver wedding, and on the next day conducted meetings in The Congress Hall, Clapton, on the platform of which William Booth had joined them in holy matrimony. The celebrations went on for a whole week, and world-wide congratulations were forthcoming. In a moving letter the General, away in the U.S.A., wrote:

You, my Son, have indeed truly honoured your Father and your Mother as the Lord your God commanded you, and I cannot doubt that your Father's and Mother's blessings have followed you to this day. . . . You have indeed been a dutiful Son. Called from your early days to tread a path of peculiar difficulty and to carry a burden of particularly heavy responsibility in assisting me with the Herculean task my Heavenly Father has assigned me, you have, I believe, been loyally faithful to the trust I have reposed in you. You have shared my many sorrows, wrestled with my abounding perplexities, defended my honour from its many adversaries, and with untiring assiduity and without regard to your own position and standing before men, sought to carry out my wishes, and maintain my authority, fighting with ceaseless devotion for that which is the dearest passion of my soul, the interests of the precious Salvation Army. . . . You, my Daughter, have been a zealous and untiring helpmate to my Son. You have strengthened his hands in hours of darkness, and comforted his heart in times of trouble. You have toiled with a marvellous wisdom, courage, and perseverance in that part of the battlefield in which it has been your privilege to fight.

On Christmas Day 1909 the Chief of the Staff set on foot a new venture for " brightening the lot of those who, especially in the Metropolis, were far away from the family circle, without friends or acquaintances, or who, for other reasons, felt isolated and lonely." This was the conducting of three unique public meetings at Clapton. It was prophesied that such a great central Christmas gathering for social and spiritual intercourse and good cheer would be established as an annual event, not only in the Metropolis, but in the provinces. Next year a similar day's meetings were held in the Regent Hall : the band held an open-air meeting and then, headed by the Chief of the Staff, the procession to the hall changed to a slow march, a huge crowd following, in memory of the 340 miners entombed in the Pretoria Pit, near Bolton—one of the worst disasters in the country's history—and the three policemen shot dead in the notorious Houndsditch affair of which Winston Churchill was an observer. The funeral service of the policemen had been held in St Paul's Cathedral. It would appear that no further full-day Christmas meetings were held, either in the Metropolis or in the provinces.

Bramwell Booth was a member of a deputation consisting of representatives of almost every Christian society in Great Britain and the Dominions which, in March 1911, was received at Buckingham Palace by King George V, who was presented with a memorial volume of the Bible in commemoration of the tercentenary of the issue of the

Authorized Version. Lord Northampton made the presentation and the Archbishop of Canterbury read an address.

At the invitation of His Majesty, and by the wish of the General, Bramwell Booth was present at Westminster Abbey on 22 June 1911, as a representative of The Salvation Army, at the Coronation of King George and Queen Mary, as he had been nine years before at the Coronation of Their Majesties King Edward VII and Queen Alexandra.

In the following year, having succeeded as General and having conducted memorial services for his father in different parts of the country, the new International Leader, accompanied by Mrs Booth, held his first salvation campaign in the Empire Theatre, Sheffield, in October. Then came several All Nights of Prayer at various provincial centres, followed by his first visit to the Continent in his new capacity —for the Repentance Day meetings in Berlin. In the spring of 1913 he visited Holland with Mrs Booth and his eldest daughter, Staff-Captain Catherine Booth ; and Switzerland, to be received with as great enthusiasm and by as great congregations as had his father. Writing a dispatch from Stockholm on 7 July of that year, the General, highly elated with the success of the Danish and Swedish congresses, especially the unexampled offering of many people for missionary service, said,

I have decided at once to make up a party of 100 officers from Sweden, Norway, Denmark and Finland for the East Indies, Japan, Korea, India and, I hope, China.

This party left for the missionary field in February 1914. From the deck of his " flagship " the General reviewed a fleet of thirteen vessels crowded with Salvationists and friends bound from Stockholm to Sodertelge, where the meetings were to be held. Two meetings were conducted *en route* on each boat. Prince Bernadotte, brother of the King of Sweden, with the Princess and their family, attended the salvation gatherings and afterward greeted the General. While in Denmark, then under the command of his youngest sister, Commissioner Mrs Lucy Booth-Hellberg, the General opened the new National Training College, which had accommodation for fifty cadets.

A service in the State Church in Christiania (Oslo) was attended by several Cabinet Ministers and more than fifty Members of Parliament. " The Salvation Army is appreciated by all classes from the King to the poorest in the land," the Prime Minister of Norway assured the General. The *War Cry* reported that " a scene unparalleled, I think, in the history of Christiania was witnessed on Sunday night in the Calmeyergaten Mission Church, when the climax of a very remarkable week-end was reached, with 154 seekers for the day." Everywhere he went the General spoke of the life and work of his father. In October the General ventured on his first transatlantic campaign, travelling in the *Lusitania*, the ill-fated ship sunk by the Germans two years later. He was welcomed by his sister, Commander Eva, in New York, after a terribly rough passage in which a member of the crew was lost. The campaign had a magnificent send-off in Toronto. Thousands were turned away from his meetings in Winnipeg, which city overtopped his reception in Toronto. The Territorial Commander, Commissioner David M. Rees, was unable to participate, he lying seriously ill and not expected to recover. Chicago Salvationists declared that, " Nothing like this campaign has ever been seen in the history of this city." Colonel (later Commissioner) Theodore Kitching wrote in his *War Cry* report that a leading businessman had told him : " New York never before received a Britisher in such a fashion." The General reviewed a march past of 3,000 Salvationists, Mayor Kline officially received him at the City Hall and then led him to the steps which overlooked a plaza crowded with 10,000 singing people. Upon his return the General received a great ovation in the Central Hall, Westminster. The last Sunday in 1913 was spent by the General with 1,000 city colonists[1] —men who had graduated from the shelters to the elevators— in Bermondsey Town Hall. January 1914 saw the General and Mrs Booth in Paris, where the last-named opened a new rescue home for women in the suburb of Asnières.

CHAPTER TWO

THE BRAMWELL BOOTH FAMILY

Not for twenty-two years—since the Army Mother died in 1890—had the Army a " Mrs General " as its First Lady, although, as the wife of the Chief of the Staff, Mrs Bramwell Booth had, from its commencement, been the Head of the Women's Social Work in addition to being the mother of seven children. She had always been one of the busiest women engaged in public life. She travelled far, wrote considerably, was thoroughly acquainted with every phase of Salvation Army warfare, conducted councils, led holiness and salvation crusades, and found time to minister personally to many who were distressed, discouraged and in danger. Her new position as the wife of the General naturally added to her already weighty burdens, and she felt compelled to relinquish her much-loved task in connection with her work for women to Commissioner Adelaide Cox, her chief assistant for many years.

In April 1913, in her new capacity, she visited Paris, in which city she had served her apprenticeship as a Salvation

[1] *The History of The Salvation Army*, vol. iii, p. 101

Army officer with the Marechale.[1] She spoke part of the time in excellent French. Brigadier (later General) George L. Carpenter reported that the Finnish Congress conducted by Mrs Booth in June had been " the mightiest thing in the history of the Territory." In July she was the leader of Germany's annual congress, and Commissioner McAlonan, the Territorial Commander, stated that " it was the sweetest and most blessed he had ever known." In the month following Mrs Booth led a triumphant campaign at Marchiennes, Belgium, marching to and speaking at a night open-air meeting in the historic Rue de Mons. Back in Germany again in November, Mrs Booth conducted great meetings in the Circus Busch, Berlin, on Repentance Day, an event to which the Founder had attached so much importance. A colonel in the Imperial Army, converted during the previous year's campaign, had become a recruit and was devoting his spare time to work on the National Headquarters. After concluding a visit to Holland, Mrs Booth opened an officers' nursing home at Highbury Park, North London. Queen Wilhelmina received Mrs Booth in an unusually long audience at the Royal Palace, " Huis ten Bosch," near The Hague on 14 May 1914.

The *War Cry* for 23 June 1906 announced that the General (William Booth) had approved the engagement between his son-in-law, Commissioner Booth-Tucker, Secretary for Foreign Affairs, and Lieutenant-Colonel Mary Reid, of the Irish Province, daughter of a one-time Acting Governor of Bombay. The Commissioner's second wife, Emma Moss Booth, had been killed in a railway accident in the U.S.A. in 1903.[2] The semi-private marriage ceremony was conducted by the General a few days after the announcement, in the South Tottenham Citadel.

[1] *The History of The Salvation Army*, vol. ii, p. 261
[2] *The History of The Salvation Army*, vol. iv, p. 361

" And still there are more of the General's family to follow when age and strength permit," prophesied Commissioner Railton in his historical sketch, *Twenty-one Years Salvation Army*, published in 1886. On one page one reads the startling paragraph :

" Curse those Booths, there's no end to them ! " exclaimed a man while passing our International Headquarters the other day ; and the man was right, and will no doubt prove to be right as to his facts for many years to come.

At the time this volume of the Army's history ends, Bramwell's sister, Commander Eva Booth was in charge of the work in the U.S.A., and Lucy (Commissioner Mrs Booth-Hellberg) was the Army's leader in Denmark, to which command she had been appointed in April 1910, following her husband's death. It had been announced in the *War Cry* for 7 December 1907 that, owing to continued indisposition, Commissioner Booth-Hellberg—who had relinquished his command of Switzerland nearly four years previously owing to ill-health—would, with Mrs Booth-Hellberg, take an extended furlough in his native Sweden. But on 5 June 1909 Emanuel D. Booth-Hellberg passed away suddenly in Berlin on his way home to Sweden following a futile visit to Carlsbad in search of health. The Commissioner, a former student of Uppsala University, had suffered imprisonment for refusing to close his meetings at 8 p.m. while the Captain at Wisby. He was sentenced to forty-eight days in prison, but upon the personal intervention of the King of Sweden was released after a month. A girl-Salvationist had pleaded for the Commissioner during an interview she had had with His Majesty.

Of Bramwell's children, Staff-Captain (now Commissioner, retired) Catherine, after having served as a corps officer, was on the staff of the International Training College ; Ensign (now Colonel, retired) Mary was serving in the

Candidates' Department at National Headquarters ; Captain Miriam, who had been appointed to Germany, was seriously ill and died in December 1917 ; Captain (later Colonel, retired) Bernard was the commanding officer at Harlesden, North London ; Candidate (now Lieutenant-Colonel, retired) Olive was expecting to enter the International Training College in the August ; and Corps Treasurer (now Major, retired) Dora and Songster Leader (now Commissioner, retired) Wycliffe were serving as local officers in the corps at High Barnet. Captain (now Mrs Commissioner, retired) Motee Booth-Tucker, eldest daughter of Commissioner and the late Consul Emma Booth-Tucker, was the commanding officer at Redhill, Surrey.

In an interview given to the *War Cry* exactly twenty years after the passing of the Army Mother, William Booth revealed new facets of her remarkable personality :

But for being marked by smallpox, from which she suffered severely in her childhood, she would have been what the world calls a beautiful woman.[1] Her form and features were perfection. Her eyes, for brilliancy and expression, I have seldom seen surpassed. When lit up with the fire kindled by the passion that ever mastered her in speaking, her expression in a remarkable manner approached what might almost be said to have something in it of the Divine. . . . We were as perfectly one as few beings ever become in this world. No one seemed ever to think of one of us without thinking of the other in any important enterprise. . . . When men listened to her, all questions of sex were forgotten. That it was a woman who was speaking was seldom thought about. Her personality was lost in the message she delivered. It was a common thing in some parts for men to walk all night in order to be present at her afternoon meetings, and to walk back those long distances to their homes.

When only in her teens she fairly revelled in grappling with the deepest theological problems, and at the age of sixteen wrote an analysis of Butler's *Analogy*.

[1] *The History of The Salvation Army*, vol. iv, p. 308

XII THE BRITISH TERRITORY

CHAPTER ONE

DISASTERS

FIVE Salvationists were entombed for thirty-six hours in the pit accident at Wingate Grange, Co. Durham, in October 1906, and among the twenty-four miners killed, two were Salvationists. Nine Salvationists were engaged in rescue work below ground. When twenty-five miners were imprisoned in a burning pit at Hamstead Colliery, near Birmingham, in March 1908, Salvationists, as at Wingate Grange, took a prominent part in comforting the bereaved. The *Daily Chronicle* said, " The noble women of The Salvation Army have been angels indeed."

One of the most appalling pit disasters to be experienced in the North of England took place at West Stanley, Co. Durham, in February 1909, when 168 miners died, among them two Salvationists and the brothers of two well-known officers. Bandsman Matthew Elliott had a most miraculous escape. He was blown up the shaft by the explosion, and, burned and blackened almost beyond recognition; nevertheless he recovered, although seemingly beyond hope, and lived for many years to play his drum.

But the greatest coal-mining disaster Great Britain had ever experienced happened at Senghenydd, in South Wales, where no fewer than 435 men perished as the result of an explosion, among them ten Salvationists, during what became known as " The Black Week." This was between

11–18 October 1913, and included the burning of the *Volturno* in mid-Atlantic, which resulted in the loss of 136 lives, a railway accident in which six were killed and twenty-two injured, and the exploding of a German airship in flight, the crew of twenty-eight being killed. The latter was described at the time as " the greatest tragedy in the history of air navigation." Training College cadets were sent down to Senghenydd where they visited the homes of the bereaved and generally assisted with relief work organized by the officers of the district under their divisional commander, Brigadier Thomas Greenaway. The Army arranged a great memorial service in Cardiff, under the presidency of the Lord Mayor. The last Salvationist's body was not recovered until two months after the accident.

Following Christmas 1906 the whole country was horrified by the railway disaster which occurred near Arbroath, Scotland, during a raging snowstorm, and which resulted in the death of twenty-one passengers. Corps Secretary Allan, of Dundee was seriously injured and died later.

When the *Suevic* went ashore on the rocks off the Lizard, in March 1907, two Australian officers were rescued by lifeboat. The sinking of the supposedly unsinkable *Titanic* as the result of its collision with an iceberg on 14 April 1912 was one of the greatest disasters in the history of shipping, for of a complement of 2,340 passengers and crew, only 605 were rescued. Among the 1,635 lost was Mr W. T. Stead,[1] one of the Army's oldest and strongest defenders. Two women Salvationists among the saved, but one of them lost her two sons. Commander Eva Booth was present to meet the survivors when they arrived in New York and to arrange for many of them to be assisted and accommodated in various institutions.

[1] *The History of The Salvation Army*, vol. iii, p. 25

The General sent £1,000 to the Lord Mayor of London's Fund.

As the outcome of the Coal Dispute in the spring of 1912, no fewer than 1,200,850 workers became wholly unemployed and upward of 395,100 were put on half-time in factories and workshops. Apart from the miners themselves, fewer than a third of the people affected by the strike were able to obtain aid of any kind other than from private or public charity. In the Potteries alone 100,000 workers were out of employment for more than a month. Wherever there was distress, and it seemed to be almost everywhere, Salvation Army halls were transformed into food-distributing depots and soup kitchens, and the corps officer was usually a member of the distress committee of the town. The *Daily Mirror* instituted a system of milk distribution through the efforts of Salvation Army officers to thousands of homes in London in which there were babies ; some of the big food manufacturing firms also sent food to the Army. Hundreds of thousands of children were fed daily in all parts of the country, and Salvationists took both coal and groceries to starving families. Swansea Salvationists alone fed 100 families with soup and bread daily and every day fed 300 destitute and homeless men.

CHAPTER TWO

FAMOUS CORPS

For a long period *All the World* ran a series of articles on the work of famous corps in the British Territory, and the following information is culled from some of them :

The appointment of Major and Mrs Orsborn, in 1902, to the command of the Clapton Congress Hall was largely in the nature of a bold experiment, for they were given a complement of officers to assist them : a second-in-command, a visiting officer, a Young People's Captain and a nurse to attend to the sick ; but this idea had to be abandoned eventually as the corps was unable to support so heavy a staff. The Major and his wife stayed for more than three years, however, which was most unusual for officers in those days— sometimes they stayed for only three or six months—and during this time they saw nearly 3,000 conversions. The Major did not hesitate to employ unconventional methods, and rather shocked the saints by publicly dedicating a donkey and cart he had secured for the exclusive use of advertising his meetings, but the novel idea brought him new congregations. The corps at that time possessed a hundred local officers.

Portsmouth, the No. 12 corps of the Army, had a roll of nearly 500 soldiers and recruits in 1905, and forty-three young people's companies (classes). Opened as " The Old Durham " in September 1878, South Shields Citadel had a similar number of soldiers and recruits. In 1906 Hamilton captured one of the champion boxers of Scotland. Norwich Citadel had 650 soldiers and recruits. It was stated in 1907 that Regent Hall held premier place in the Army as the corps whence came the greatest number of candidates for officership, 400 to date. The German corps associated with Regent Hall, although inadequately housed in a former wine-shop, was a popular rendezvous for Continentals, and at the time, 1913, that Captain Elvera Werner—a Russo-German reared in Scotland—was in charge, as many as twelve different nationalities were represented in one meeting. The hall was situated in Tottenham Street, off Tottenham Court Road, and the soldiers frequently conducted their open-air

meetings in cosmopolitan Soho. A thousand Salvationists
worked in the cotton mills in Oldham. Captain (later
General) and Mrs Albert Orsborn were in command of
Ipswich Citadel corps with between 300 and 400 soldiers in
1911. During December 1910 Leith corps, under the
command of Adjutant and Mrs Boyce, provided 15,739 free
breakfasts for poor children, and also assisted starving
families. Barking, the 15th corps, once commanded by the
first woman corps officer of The Salvation Army, was again
under the leadership of a woman in 1911, and was providing
600 women and children with hot soup every day. Adjutant
Annie Devlyn was described locally as " The Lady Bishop
of Barking." In 1910, Herbert W. Twitchin, after twenty-
five years as Deputy Bandmaster, was appointed Bandmaster
of the Regent Hall Band and many years later was to be
decorated by his Sovereign with the insignia of a Member of
the British Empire solely for his activities as a Salvation
Army Bandmaster, the first to be so honoured. Major (later
Commissioner) and Mrs Frank Barrett were in command of
the Regent Hall corps for five years. Plymouth Congress
Hall had 600 soldiers and recruits in 1913. There were sixty-
four companies in the young people's corps, two Assistant
Sergeant-Majors and eighty company guards. Mrs Matthews
revealed that she was the first " bandsman", playing a
triangle, which she made herself from an ancient poker.

CHAPTER THREE

CENTRAL HOLINESS MEETINGS

In September 1905 " a blessed movement sprang up at the very heart of the Army," Clapton Congress Hall, where Commissioner T. Henry Howard, Principal of the International Training College, again took over, as an experiment, the leadership of the Thursday-night holiness meetings, which he had begun thirty years previously on the lines of those conducted at Whitechapel by Bramwell Booth. Supported by the training-home staff and the cadets, the Commissioner raised the character and dimension of the meeting to one of metropolitan importance to which the Chief of the Staff made his contribution. Originally promoted to meet local needs, the Central Holiness Meeting, as it was now called, in the most unlikely period of the year, went far beyond local significance and influence, however. Many people came from long distances and included Continentals, Jews, Catholics and Salvationists from the provinces. The average attendance for June 1906 reached 1,500. Within twelve months the great hall was so crowded each week that people were forced to sit on the window-sills around the top of the amphitheatre ! At the fifth anniversary of these gatherings, in 1910, some 4,000 people were present, says the *War Cry*. By this time Commissioner Rees, now the Training Principal, was associated with Commissioner Howard. Then, when he became Training Principal, Commissioner Thomas McKie took full responsibility. He was an unconventional and outstanding leader of meetings, realizing, perhaps more than most, the power of congregational singing. Often he would have these great gatherings singing for as long as thirty minutes on end. It was at this time that Ensign Albert Orsborn, at the Commissioner's request, began to write his new weekly song, which more often than not he himself introduced as a solo, and which undoubtedly enhanced the popularity of these Central Holiness Meetings. Many of these songs and choruses appear in the present Salvation Army songbook.

CHAPTER FOUR

THE HOME LEAGUE

The beginning of February 1907 was marked by another new departure ; " the formation of what, for the lack of a better name, Mrs Bramwell Booth describes as a Home League," said *All the World*. Actually the name proved to be inspired, for it lives today, after more than sixty years, and the League itself is one of the most powerful influences for good the Army has produced. Its object was to combat the growing tendency to neglect the fostering of true home-life and to encourage thrift and hygiene. The commencement of the Home League was one result of the General's motor campaigns. These gave him a close insight into the habits of the people, and he determined to do something to raise the standard of home-life. Mrs Colonel (later General) Higgins was appointed General Secretary, and several wives of staff officers were appointed secretaries of branches in the neighbourhoods in which they resided. On 18 February 1907, over a hundred wives and mothers listened to Mrs Booth as she addressed the first meeting of the Home League at the Tottenham Citadel Corps.

According to the *War Cry* of 25 January 1908 a branch was inaugurated at Leytonstone under the care of Mrs Higgins. Other early branches were started at Clapton, Newington Green, Homerton, Bethnal Green, Ilford and Barking. Mrs Commissioner William Eadie, wife of the Chief Secretary, was the National Secretary of Home Leagues in 1910. The first Home League Secretary for Ilford was Mrs Lieutenant-Colonel William B. Jackson, who, happily, is still living at Bournemouth at the great age of ninety-five.

CHAPTER FIVE

CHINATOWN

A Chinese population, chiefly comprising seamen, began in 1899 to congregate in Limehouse Causeway, London, keeping almost exclusively to itself. At one time the characteristic pigtail was much in evidence, but finally disappeared in 1911. For some years Christian work among these people was carried on by a retired missionary. Then came a break, and an American lady who had been working among the Chinese of Chicago, finding nothing being done for them in London, asked General Bramwell Booth if the Army would interest itself. Captain Mary Drury, the officer in charge of Limehouse corps, began to work, and the Army uniform soon began to be both recognized and welcomed, even in the opium dens. In September 1913 Adjutant Catherine Hine, of the National Headquarters, having read of the work in the *War Cry*, visited Chinatown, and at once volunteered her services. The proprietor of a Chinese boarding-house generously granted permission for the night school (*Tox-si*), which had been closed down, to be reopened in two of his rooms. Within a few months as many as thirty men were attending the classes. Presently a converted Chinese law student acted as interpreter. At this time women were in the minority, but a Home Company was formed among the half-caste children. In July 1914 seventeen Chinese converts were sworn-in as soldiers.

*   *   *

Councils for Census Board Local Officers were instituted by the Chief of the Staff in May 1908, when the London and Training Home provinces spent a day at Clapton Temple, the lecture hall adjoining The Congress Hall. The Census Board was then made up of the senior local officers of a corps : the Sergeant-Major, Treasurer, Secretary, Band-master, Recruiting Sergeant and Juniors Sergeant-Major, the Commanding Officer for the time being acting as chairman. The Census Board's only responsibility was the care of the Soldiers' Roll.

*   *   *

More than one hundred soldiers were transferred in 1909 from Hamilton, Scotland, to Canada and the U.S.A., thirty of them being bandsmen.

XIII AFTER-WORDS

SALVATION SOCIALISM

IN an interview with W. T. Stead which appeared in the *Daily Chronicle* in April 1908, William Booth gave utterance to the subject of Socialism :

I am a Socialist, a Salvation Socialist, and always have been. A Salvation Socialist differs from a Fabian Socialist, for we begin at the other end. I am working at the tunnel on one side of the mountain, your political parties or Governments with all their schemes of social reform are working at the other end. God bless them, say I ; I have nothing against them. But my way is not their way. My side of the mountain is not their side of the mountain, but if we both keep on at our own ends perhaps we may meet in the middle.

At about the same time he was interviewed by a representative of the *Belfast Telegraph* on the same subject :

There is a great deal about Socialism that is excellent, but a certain kind of people is wanted to give it effect. Socialism is a celestial system without a celestial people. . . . As someone has said, " We are all Socialists nowadays," in one form or another, and there are few who are not agreed that much must be done to improve the conditions under which so many of our fellows are obliged to live. It is not the question of the existence of evil, but the method of removing it that causes controversy. Some over-zealous exponents of political panaceas are in danger of forgetting one fundamental fact, and that is that he who is not against them is really for them, and it would be well to occasionally recall this. . . . I think that the making of good laws is assistant to the happiness of mankind, but if you have got bad people that is not enough. If you have got a dirty man and you put a clean shirt on him every morning that will not make him a clean man. It might be favourable to it, but you must change the man and his convictions first ; you must get the man himself clean. Anyway, that is our way. We think we are doing more for the happiness of mankind that way than by any other way we are conversant with.

★ ★ ★

Writing of the first crossing of the English Channel by the French aviator, M. Blériot, in July 1909, the *War Cry* says prophetically :

It is only a beginning, but it is not inconceivable that at no very great distance the flying machine will be pressed into Salvation Army service in much the same way as the motor-car is now being used by the General. An aeroplane is cheaper than a motor-car, and the development of the former has been much speedier than that of the latter . . . it is only natural that such a feat is regarded more as a nine days' wonder than anything else ; we cannot grasp all its possibilities ; it seems too remote from our perception of things.

★ ★ ★

The Salvation Army was among the pioneers of the cinematograph exhibition, for a *War Cry* report, dated 28 January 1905, reads :

The Saturday cinematograph exhibition developed into a hot prayer battle and three souls came out for salvation.

Then, in May 1907 :

The cinematograph social continues to grow in popularity, the weekly attendance now being over 3,000.

Later the *War Cry* wrote :

The Army offers a healthy evening's entertainment, not only devoid of the polluting influences of the public-house, the penny gaff, or the music-hall, but equally free from that simpering sentimentalism which is sometimes confused with religion. . . . What photography has accomplished in the way of animated pictures has been adapted to the purposes of salvation. Begun at The Congress Hall these exhibitions have become a sort of family institution.

★　　　　★　　　　★

When Mrs Booth broke the Army's tricolour from the mast-head of the specially chartered s.s. *Vancouver*, it was the first ocean-going steamer to sail under the Army's blood-and-fire flag. This was in May 1905, when 1,000 emigrants left for Canada under the Army's auspices.

★　　　　★　　　　★

Under the heading " 52,000 shoeless Little Feet," a Trade Headquarters announcement in the *War Cry* for 28 January 1905 stated that

The Salvation Army Outfit Department was successful in securing the entire order for 26,000 pairs of boots from the London *Evening News*, which paper also employed the organization and resources of this Department for the entire collection of statistics and the securing of requisitions from the thousands of teachers whose personal orders were guarantees of these children's needs as to boots. The shoeing of so many thousands of children was accomplished without a serious hitch in less than the short space of eight weeks from the date of the placing of the order to the last despatch of goods from our warehouse, an achievement to be proud of, and one which bears emphatic testimony to the capacity and enterprise of the management of the Trade Department. Contracts were entered into with manufacturers for a " particular kind of boot to be all leather and to contain no brown paper or cardboard."

★　　　　★　　　　★

A supplementary to the original Deed Poll of The Salvation Army, approved at the 1878 War Congress,[1] was executed by the General on 26 July 1904, and approved at a Staff Council assembled in London during the International Congress. It brought into existence the High Council, and gave that Council special powers for dealing with certain emergencies that might arise in connection with the office of General, or with any vacancy in that office. It was not, however, until 20 April 1906 that the " endorsement " of a document embodying the new constitution which replaced the system of control of the Christian Mission, as laid down in the 1875 Deed Poll, was " enrolled."

★ ★ ★

In 1906 the unusual honour—in those days—of being appointed a Justice of the Peace was conferred upon Staff-Captain Alfred Head, the officer in charge of the Army's Collie Estate in Western Australia.

★ ★ ★

The presentation to Commissioner John A. Carleton of a local officer's Long Service Badge in February 1913 celebrated a record unique in Army history. Said the *War Cry* :

To have risen to the highest rank but one in the Army, and at the same time to have fought as a local officer in the same corps (Penge) for the period of the quarter of a century has not been possible with any other Salvationist.

The Commissioner had served as a bandsman, songster and corps treasurer.

★ ★ ★

[1] *The History of The Salvation Army*, vol. i, p. 233 ; vol. iv, p. 318

In May 1908 Commissioner Nicol gave evidence before the Select Committee of the House of Commons in favour of the Daylight Saving Bill.

*   *   *

The Children's Employment Abroad Bill had for its object the ensuring of protection for young English girls and children who were taken abroad for dancing and performing. Following a visit to Paris, Mrs Bramwell Booth had urged William Booth to press for legislature. After a long struggle the Government had taken the matter up, and the measure had passed through its final stages in August 1913. Queen Mary was very interested in it.

*   *   *

It was announced in the *War Cry* for 18 March 1911 that the Home Secretary, Mr Winston Churchill, had granted permission to the Army to hold mission services in various convict prisons, in addition to the quarterly music services which had already had excellent results.

*   *   *

The idea of utilizing theatres for salvation purposes occurred to William Booth in the days of long ago, and that it had been carried out with conspicuous success most people agreed. The first theatre meeting addressed by the General was held in the Garrick, London, in 1861, says *All the World* for 1909.

*   *   *

In August 1910 it was announced that an Unattached Soldiers' League was to be formed at National Headquarters for Salvationists living where there were no corps in operation ; but, as with a number of other innovations, the idea apparently fell upon stony ground, for nothing further was heard of it.

*   *   *

The wireless transmission of pictures, declared Mr H. M. Airey, in a lecture in Newcastle upon Tyne, is already an accomplished fact, and the possibility of seeing by electric waves is almost certain, reported the *War Cry* for 5 February 1910. " Who can say that we may not have the General ' projected ' both in form and speech by this wonderful invention ? "

WORLD UNREST

The leading article in the November 1908 issue of *All the World* reads uncannily, almost as though it had been written only a few days ago ; certainly it correctly sums up a desperate situation that was to burst into flames :

No one could attempt to consider the operations of the Army, during the last few months, without being profoundly impressed with the forces of unrest that are at work in nearly every part of the world—forces that for the present, at least, retard the progress of the ambassadors of the Cross.

The people are awakening to a sense of their political might. New and militant methods of agitation are succeeding those of argument and orderly propaganda. Governments feel that they are less secure than they were. The Press, irresponsible and partisan, is less scrupulous in its criticism of ministers and nations. It plays to the gallery, or gives its readers an occasional fit of nerves.

If we look abroad, the unrest is the more discernible because of the contrast with the long slumber of the nations concerned. China, for example, is going almost as strong for Western methods of government, commerce, and municipal control as did Japan forty years ago. India is gradually being honeycombed with national ideals. Egypt has a growing army of discontent at foreign control. Russia is far from pacified. The Near East is like a threatening volcano consequent upon Turkey's recent political emancipation, the ambitions of her former dependencies —Bulgaria, Bosnia, and Herzegovina—and the intrigues of the great onlooking Powers. Embers of internal strife are still smouldering in Morocco.

And if we add the eternal feud of politics and the general depression of trade in America, Europe, and South Africa, we have a situation that does not tend to help the man or the organization eager to obtain the attention of the crowd and direct their minds toward far higher questions. What shall we eat ? Wherewithal shall we be clothed ? What is the outlook for trade ? How can we make two ends meet ? How can we improve our circumstances ? These are all very important matters, and our Heavenly Father knoweth our needs. But there are two great hungers in the world—the hunger of the body and the hunger of the soul. The trend of today is to ignore the latter, or answer it by giving it that which is as inappropriate as are stones in place of bread.

Six years later, on 4 August 1914, the British Prime Minister and erstwhile solicitor for The Salvation Army, the Rt. Hon. Herbert H. Asquith, was to declare his country at war with Germany. Looking from his window at the Foreign Office in Whitehall that night, Sir Edward Grey, seeing the lights of London extinguished one by one, murmured sadly :

" The lights are going out all over Europe! "

EPILOGUE

BRAMWELL BOOTH had been the Army's International Leader for two years all but two weeks when what was to become a four years' war and envelop most of the countries of the world broke out. How stood his Salvationist forces at this perilous period ? Certainly not in accordance with the predictions of the pessimistic prophets that it was a mushroom growth.

In reflecting on his short term of leadership the General was able to state that it had been marked by unity throughout the Army's world, and by encouraging evidences of progress. Losses from emigration in the British Territory, due to unemployment and other causes, had made their wide gaps ; but every division, nevertheless, showed an increase in soldiership. " Moreover," he added, " the spirit of sacrifice and of care for the lowest, which is in reality the essential spirit of the Army, is being so markedly displayed by our people, that my heart is full of gratitude to God and high hope for the future." And just prior to leaving for his first transatlantic campaign he had written :

I think, all over the world, there are signs that better times are coming for the poorest and weakest—for those who, without being spoken of as vicious, are nevertheless having a hard time of it. For them there is coming a better day, with better circumstances, better conditions of life and better education.

But it was not to be, for beneath a façade of prospective affluence smouldered a gunpowder trail, the occasional spit and splutter of which failed to rouse a happy-go-lucky world to the danger which was to finally topple it.

The General's great missionary campaign, from the results of which he hoped, within five years, to send out

1,000 British officers, chiefly to the East, and with China particularly in mind, in keeping with one of the last promises he had made to the Founder, was well under way. This scheme was to include a similar number of officers from the other Western countries in which the Army was at work, including Norway, Sweden, Denmark, Finland, Canada and the United States of America. One of the biggest batches of cadets in its history was within a fortnight of entering the International Training College at Clapton when war broke out. The public continued to give generously to the funds, each succeeding Self-Denial Effort being an increase on the previous year. The newly inaugurated Life-Saving Scout movement was being enthusiastically taken up. More than 16,000 officers were at work in fifty-eight countries. Brass bands numbered nearly 1,700 and the bandsmen totalled 23,994. Songster brigades numbered 13,699 men and women. Shelters and metropoles throughout the world totalled 268, giving accommodation to 26,795 people. The 110 homes for fallen women dealt with some 7,450 cases. Children's homes sheltered, fed, clothed and educated 2,166 neglected, deserted or criminally inclined little ones.

The most outstanding feature of this period was undoubtedly the International Congress, which consolidated the spirit of the Army's scattered regiments and so left it unshaken by the holocaust of the 1914 Armageddon. No fewer than eighty-one periodicals were being produced in twenty-five different languages, and Holbrook Jackson, editor of *T. P's Weekly*, an influential periodical, writing on " The Salvation Press," had this to say :

What impresses one most is the remarkable fact that these 81 papers are self-supporting, and their articles and news items voluntarily contributed. Here again the impossible has been achieved, and it has been achieved in a double sense : first, by getting a regular supply of voluntary contributions, and next by getting voluntary contributions which not only serve their purpose, but which have a brightness and a sincerity quite capable of holding their own with professional journalism. Perhaps most astounding of all, they are independent of the advertiser.

Warning voices in Britain on the inevitability of war with Germany had gone unheeded, and in the Fatherland the Army's operations were extending fast. The social work was healthy and important, and the spiritual side of things was bearing good fruit, it being known that the Kaiser Wilhelm II was a warm supporter of Salvationist activity. Germany's next-door neighbour, France, had by now got to understand the Army, and people wanted it to commence operations in all parts of the country. Throughout Holland it was becoming increasingly recognized that through its methods, and its officers, the Army could help the State over many an awkward stile, putting inspiration into the hopeless, backbone into the waster, and even sense into the foolish. The Salvation Army stood high in the general estimation of the American nation, as it did in Canada, Australia and New Zealand.

Advance in every direction was reported from India. The ordinary spiritual work was going forward and was in a prosperous condition, while many new, interesting and successful branches of work had recently been established. Young people's activities were also on the upgrade. Doors of opportunity were being opened in Italy, the tide of sympathy at last flowing in the Army's direction. Japan, too, was alive with opportunity and the Army was advancing, particularly in its medical work. In Indonesia, after a period of quiet, well-doing labour, the Army had suddenly spread its wings, seeking a bigger field for its operations among lepers, children, beggars and servicemen. Things were moving steadily in the West Indies. The President of Peru was exceedingly anxious for the Army to take up social work in his country, and promised moral and financial support. The people were ready for the Army and its activities, as they were also in Chile. Sierra Leone was crying out for officers. Pressing appeals were coming from other colonies on the East and West Coasts of Africa, and also from Bulgaria, Brazil and the Falkland Islands.

So far from perishing, the Army had developed, as these pages show, as rapidly as at any time within its less than half-century of existence. It still possessed the virgin enthusiasm with which, under the inspiration of William Booth, " it came out of the East End with drums beating and flags flying, to encounter the ridicule of the world, and wrestle with the sons of men," said the editor of the *Daily News and Leader*, in 1914.

Its disciples still went out like preaching friars or knights-templar to carry their message to every land, from Korea to Peru, bronzed, hardy men, simple of speech, simple of faith, working for the wage of an under-clerk. . . . And its adherents, too, still keep their primitive fervour, crowd to the mercy seat, shout " Hallelujah ! " and observe that rigid self-denying ordinance in regard to alcohol, tobacco and similar indulgences, which the Army imposes on its members, much to its disadvantage so far as its numbers are concerned. In short, the Movement is that most unprecedented achievement, a revivalist crusade organized into a system. That it has maintained this character so long is evidence of the vision and power of the Founder.

W. T. STEAD'S INTERVIEW WITH M. STOLYPIN REGARDING THE ARMY OPENING UP ITS WORK IN RUSSIA, AS RECORDED IN *THE TIMES*

After elucidating that Russia means to achieve her political emancipation, not by revolution but by evolution, and detailing a conversation upon various questions relating to the present condition of things in the Tsar's dominions, Mr Stead proceeded to introduce The Army.

"I then touched upon another subject of great interest to many people in England," remarked Mr Stead. "I said that on my way out to Russia I had met Mr Bramwell Booth, son of General Booth, of The Salvation Army, who asked me to make inquiries whether there was any possibility of the admission of The Salvation Army to Russia.

"M. Stolypin asked, 'Whether The Salvation Army really did good work?'

"I replied, 'The Salvation Army does excellent work, apart altogether from its distinctive religious teachings, and is one of the most useful philanthropic organizations in the world.'

"M. Stolypin inquired if it meddled in politics.

"I replied, 'Absolutely not. Even in England it abstains entirely from political action, and in other countries no complaint has ever been made of any Salvationist either meddling in politics or conducting any religious propaganda hostile to the religious creed, ritual, or prejudices of any other Christian Church.'

"M. Stolypin asked, 'Whether they could be relied upon not to inflame popular sentiment against the non-Christians?'

"I replied, 'The Salvation Army work is too Christian to be hostile to anybody. For instance, in every country people of all religions and of none, Free-thinkers and Roman Catholics, recognize the solid philanthropic secular value of the work of The Army and support it with subscriptions. General Booth is on terms of personal friendship with Lord Rothschild, who has repeatly subscribed to the Social work of The Army.'

" M. Stolypin remarked that he saw no political reason why there should be any obstacle placed in the way of the coming of The Army into Russia.

" I replied that I was very glad indeed to hear this. That I was certain that the Salvationists would prove in Russia, as they had proved in countries as far apart as Germany and Japan, that they rendered valuable service to the State. In Germany twelve years ago they were under the surveillance of the police. Today German cities like Hamburg and Elberfeld make them annual subsidies. In Berlin they have about forty Halls and centres of activity. In Japan the Emperor in person thanked General Booth for the great good he had done to his people. The King and Queen of England, the Presidents of France and the United States have testified to the value of the Salvationists' work.

" M. Stolypin said that he thought The Salvation Army might come to Russia. It would at any rate interest the people and might be useful. ' But what about meetings in the open air, which are quite contrary to Russian law ? '

" I replied that ' The Salvation Army was ready to meet the views of the Russian authorities as to whether it was or was not expedient to hold meetings in the open air, and to make processions through the streets.' At the same time I reminded his Excellency that in Russia the meetings of the Mir were always held in the open air. That was, however, an unessential detail. I had for twenty-five years been in close personal relations with General Booth and the work of The Army, and could with the utmost confidence assure his Excellency that the Salvationists are good people, who do good work, making bad citizens into good citizens, without doing any mischief to the State.

" M. Stolypin said, ' I think they might be useful. I see no reason why they should not come. But let me have a copy of their statutes, so that I can examine them before I give my final decisions.' "

MINOR BIOGRAPHIES

Amongst the " Rank and File " or soldiery of the Army during the period covered by this volume, the following somewhat unusual personalities may be noted :

MRS KITTY ASCROFT, a Salvationist at Lower Ince, Manchester, England, who died in 1911, in her 92nd year, was stated to have been the last woman to work underground in an English coal-mine, this kind of employment for women being forbidden by an Act of Parliament in 1843.

ROSIE BANNISTER, an Envoy [1] of Burnley, Lancashire, U.K., was reported, in the *War Cry* of 7 March 1914, to have appeared seventy-four times before the magistrates, and to have squandered £2,000 in eighteen months. She was about to commit suicide when she came into contact with the Army and was converted.

ENVOY TOM BELLAMY, known as " Tom o' the Fens," had been a Lincolnshire poacher whose name was a household word throughout the county. During fifteen years in prison, his back had been scored by frequent lashes of the " cat o' nine tails." He had lived, before his conversion, in a hut in a corner of a field, sleeping on a bed of straw, with his only furniture a nine-gallon cask of beer. After twenty-five years as a Salvationist he died suddenly in May 1907.

WILLIAM BOTTOMLEY, reported in 1907 to be an influential mill-owner at Mossley, Lancashire, U.K., had been converted some twenty-two years earlier at Huddersfield, Yorkshire. He had been notorious for drinking, gambling, racing, pigeon-flying and cock-fighting, before conversion.

An unusual character, SIR GENILE CAVE–BROWNE–CAVE, styled " the cowboy baronet," sought Christ at an Army penitent form in

[1] A rank which gives a Salvationist laity opportunities similar to those of a Methodist local preacher.

New York, becoming an Envoy (*War Cry*, 30 September 1911). He remained a Salvationist for three years, prior to undertaking study to enter the Congregational ministry.

POLL COTT was the most notorious woman ever to be won for God by The Salvation Army in Australia. She had been convicted by the police 257 times. She remained a uniformed Salvationist for twenty years and died in 1905.

PROFESSOR MILO DEYO, one of the outstanding musical personalities in the U.S.A., signed the Articles of War [1] at the National Headquarters in New York.

GUSTAF ERICSSON, of Uppsala University, Sweden, a doctor of philosophy, was an an orchestral bandsman.

"MOTHER FLORENCE," a Salvationist very widely known in America, was a simple, uneducated woman, who would pray just as freely in the Office of the State Governor, as in a drinking saloon. She was thrown from her buggy and killed in Topeka, Kansas, in 1905. At her funeral, attended by some 3,000 people, the Governor paid a wonderful tribute to her character and influence.

GEORGE GLADSTONE, of Hove, who had The Salvation Army flag draped over his bed for twelve years, and died in 1909, was an uncle of the Rev. F. B. Meyer, the well-known Baptist minister, and of Mrs J. Ramsay MacDonald, whose husband was Prime Minister of the British Labour Government from 1929–31 and of the National Government from 1931–5.

MRS HILLYER, widow of a British Admiral, was a Salvationist for nineteen years, first at Plympton, Devon, U.K., and then at Wellington, Somerset, where she died in 1906.

BILLY MARTIN, a Company Guard [2], of Bridgwater, was unique as the smallest Salvationist in the world; he was only three feet, nine inches in height. A Salvationist for thirty-seven years, he received, on his fifty-seventh birthday, 287 greetings cards from all over the world, says the *War Cry* of 5 April 1913.

MAJOR–GENERAL J. S. MARTYR was a soldier for twenty years at Upper Norwood Corps, London, U.K. He was also an Envoy,

---

[1] *The History of The Salvation Army*, vol. ii, p. 53
[2] The equivalent of a Sunday-school teacher

and used to accompany his own solo-singing by playing a machette, or Portuguese guitar. He died in 1912.

BARONESS ELIZABETH NORDENFALK (*nee* D'Albedyhl) was described as " the richest lady in all Sweden in point of ancestry."

THE HON. ANNA JANE PECKOVER, Corps Treasurer of Wisbech, U.K., was the daughter of Lord Peckover, created a peer in the King's Birthday Honours in 1907. Lord Peckover was a descendant of one of Cromwell's " Ironsides."

NINA, DOWAGER COUNTESS OF SEAFIELD, a soldier of the corps at Otago, New Zealand, wore the Army bonnet. Later she and her daughter associated themselves with the Chelsea Corps, London, U.K.

LADY SARAH SLADEN, the daughter of the eighth Earl of Cavan, was enrolled as a soldier at the same time as her son, Hugh, who was to become a Commissioner. Lady Sladen was not only the Young People's Sergeant-Major at Ringwould, but also regularly sold the *War Cry* in public-houses. She died in 1914.

FRANK CLEMENT SMITH, known as " Salvation Smith," was a well-known member of the London Stock Exchange, and a soldier of the Clapton Congress Hall. Said the *Financial Times* in December 1911 :

Mr Smith is probably one of the most enterprising and successful charitable workers in London, and is certainly one of the most enthusiastic.

He collected hundreds of pounds by dancing and playing a tambourine in the Stock Exchange building during Self-Denial week !

MRS DE NOE WALKER, granddaughter of the Dowager Lady Buxton, dated her connection with the Army from 1866. Mrs Catherine Booth told her that the General had based The Salvation Army on *The Autobiography of Professor Finney*.

BIBLIOGRAPHY

The works listed below are additional to those in the bibliographies of previous volumes, and, unless otherwise stated, are published by Salvationist Publishing and Supplies, Ltd, Judd Street, King's Cross, London, w.c.1. Some are out of print, but may be seen at the National Reference Libraries. If information in the *History* should differ from that to be found in the books and papers listed below, it is because further research has proved earlier publications incorrect. Unfortunately, several authors have omitted to give dates, and thus valuable and interesting information has possibly been withheld in this volume.

OFFICIAL PUBLICATIONS

The War Cry, from 30 July 1904 to 8 August 1914
All the World, from July 1904 to September 1914
The Salvation Army Year Book, 1907–8, 1910–12, 1919, 1950, 1952, 1955–9, 1964–5
The Musical Salvationist (Words and music), from 1904 to 1914
The Bandsman and Songster, from 6 April 1907 to 8 August 1914
The War Cry, Chicago, U.S.A., 21 January 1950
Golden Jubilee Programme of Eastern Territorial Staff Band, 19 December 1941
The Life-Saving Scout and Guard, Volume 1931
The Local Officer, November 1904

BIOGRAPHIES

Great was the Company, by Madge Unsworth, 1963
Jan Christian Smuts, by J. C. Smuts (Cassell & Co. Ltd, 1952)
Catherine Hine—" Teacher " of Chinatown, by Matilda Hatcher, 1943
" *I can't—but I must !* "—Kate Lee, by Kathleen Kendrick, 1945
Two Men in the Snow, by Reginald Woods, 1964
Kate Lee—The Angel Adjutant, by Minnie Lindsay Carpenter, 1944

The General next to God, by Richard Collier (Collins, 1965)
Booth the Beloved, by J. Evan Smith (Oxford University Press, Melbourne, 1949)
Viking Warrior—The Story of Karl Larsson, O.F., by Flora Larsson, 1959
A Zulu Apostle—Joel Mbambo Matunjwa, by J. Allister Smith, 1953
Catherine Bannister—Given for India, 1930
A. W. P., 1894–1938—Bandmaster Punchard, of Chalk Farm
Triumph of Faith—George Marshall, O.F., by Arch R. Wiggins, 1958
Once upon a Time—S. Carvosso Gauntlett
All the Days—General George L. Carpenter, by Alfred J. Gilliard
Always in Step—Herbert Twitchin, by John Atkinson, 1956

HISTORY

Born to Battle—The Salvation Army in America, by Sallie Chesham (Rand McNally & Company, 1965)
Dear Mr. Booth—Some early chapters of the History of The Salvation Army in New Zealand, by John C. Waite (Salvation Army Territorial Headquarters, Wellington)
In Memoriam—Programme of William Booth's Memorial and Funeral Services, 1912
The Story of a Mid-Victorian Family, by Alfred G. Hamilton
A Hundred Years' War, by Bernard Watson (Hodder & Stoughton, 1964)
The Story of Chalk Farm Band, 1882–1932
Play the Music, Play! by Brindley Boon (Salvationist Publishing and Supplies Ltd, 1966)

OTHER BOOKS

Pear's Cyclopaedia: 1966
Stuff that Makes an Army, by William G. Harris (The Salvation Army Supplies, Printing & Publishing Department, New York, 1962)
The Old Corps, by Edward H. Joy
The Romance of a Motor Mission, by W. P. Ryan, 1906

Broken Earthenware, by Harold Begbie (Hodder & Stoughton, 1909)

Half-way Round the World with General Booth, by Alex. M. Nicol, 1892

Harvest of the Years—An anthology of Salvation Army Year Book articles selected and edited by Reginald Woods, 1960

PERIODICALS

Punch, 10 January 1951

REPORTS

Social Salvation, Rockefeller Survey, 1924

EMENDATIONS (1ST EDITIONS)

Volume Three (additional) :
   page 117, l. 7 : from foot of page : for " 1912 " *read* " 1907 "

Volume Four :
   page 90, last line : for " totem worship " *read* " tribal feasts "
   page 91, l. 2 : for " rancher " *read* " man "
   page 101, para. 1, l. 7 : for ' a group ' *read* " a second group "
   page 107, l. 5 : after " Lieutenant " *read* " David Smith "
   page 112, l. 3 : for " 1905 " *read* " 1903 "
   page 130, para. 1, l. 19 : for " succeeded " *read* " assisted"
   page 254, para. 1, l. 7 : for " Prince and Princess of Wales " and " Edward " *read* " Duke and Duchess of York " and " George V " ; l. 8 : for "Alexandra " *read* " Mary " ; l. 11 : for " Governor " *read* " Governor-General "
   page 289, para. 1, l. 8 : for " Micheldever " read " Laverstoke "

INDEX

Seaman, Sir Owen, 242
Seddon, The Hon. Richard, 153, 260
Shaw, George Bernard, 207, 252
Sicotte, Judge, 98
Siege of London, The, 213f.
Sierra Leone, 72
Sims, George R., 251
Sinclair, Captain, 222
Sinclair, Dr, 266
Singapore, 79
Sladen, Hugh, 272
Slater, Richard, 108, 179, 208, 210, 211
slum officers, 117, 120, 121
Smith, J. Allister, 122, 125, 127
Snettisham, 246
social work, Holland, 26 ; Denmark, 29 ; Norway, 42 ; Finland, 47 ; Belgium, 49 ; Argentina, 52 ; Japan, 68 ; U.S.A., 82, 83, 87 ; Canada, 98, 100 ; India, 115 ; Sweden, 117, 121 ; New Zealand, 129 ; books, 170 ; International Social Council, 161 ; W.S.W. Headquarters, 188 ; hostel for missionary officers' children, 188 ; Head of W.S.W., 279
socialism, 292f.
Sone, Viscount, 6
Sophia, Queen of Sweden, 148
South Africa, 122f.
South Sea Islands, 12
South Shields, 188, 286
Southampton, 188
Sowton, Charles, 29, 178
Spain, 79
Springburn, 211
Stahn, Pastor Walter Nithak, 19
Stead, W. T., 72, 73, 251, 284, 292
Stenhousemuir, 195
Stevens, William, 116
Stolypin, M., 72, 73
Strickland, Sir George, 152
Strong, Sir T. Vezey, 257

Swansea, 285
Sweden, 117f.
" Swedish Salvation Army, The," 117
Switzerland, 107f.

Taft, President, 87, 163
Talbot, Sir Reginald, 153
temperance, 216–18
Times, The, 212, 233, 242, 244, 247
Tipton, 197
Tonga, 12
Tottenham, 289
Trade Headquarters, 190, 294
training, officers, Korea, 3 ; Germany, 17 ; Rhodesia, 60 ; Japan, 68 ; Australia, 96 ; Canada, 99 ; Switzerland, 108 ; India, 113 ; Sweden, 118, 120 ; South Africa, 122, 125 ; New Zealand, 131 ; 176ff. ; officers' children, 269
Trinidad, 35f.
Tunbridge Wells, 196
Turkey, 7f.
Twain, Mark, 253
Twitchin, Bandmaster Herbert W., 211, 287

Unsworth, Isaac, Fiji, 12 ; Indonesia, 61 ; 125, 166, 182, 202, 214, 246
United States of America, 22f., 80f., 228
Uruguay, 51f.

Vanguard, 165, 268
van Norden, Warner, 262
Verestchagin, 73
Victor Emmanuel, King of Italy, 24, 150
Victor Napoleon, Prince, 249
Victoria, Princess, 249
villages, India, 113f.
Viquez, Don Cleto Gonzalez, 39
von Herkomer, Professor Hubert, 232, 255